China's Evolving Approach to Peacekeeping

China has become an enthusiastic supporter of and contributor to UN peacekeeping. Is China's participation in peacekeeping likely to strengthen the current international peacekeeping regime by China's adopting of the international norms of peacekeeping? Or, on the contrary, is it likely to alter the peacekeeping norms in a way that aligns with its own worldview? And, as China's international confidence grows, will it begin to consider peacekeeping a smaller and lesser part of its international security activity, and thus not care so much about it?

This book aims to address these questions by examining how the PRC has developed its peacekeeping policy and practices in relation to its international status. It does so by bringing in both historical and conceptual analyses and specific case-oriented discussions of China's peacekeeping over the past twenty years. The book identifies the various challenges that China has faced at political, conceptual and operational levels and the ways in which the country has dealt with those challenges, and considers the implication of such challenges with regards to the future of international peacekeeping.

This book was originally published as a special issue of *International Peacekeeping*.

Marc Lanteigne is a senior lecturer at the Department of Political Science and International Relations and Director of Research at the New Zealand Contemporary China Research Centre, Victoria University of Wellington. He is the author of *China and International Institutions: Alternate Paths to Global Power* (London: Routledge, 2005) and *Chinese Foreign Policy: An Introduction* (London: Routledge, 2009) as well as several articles on Chinese and Asian foreign relations and strategic policies, including engagement of regional organisations and norms. He is also a former researcher at the Asia Pacific Foundation of Canada in Vancouver and the Norwegian Institute of International Affairs in Oslo.

Miwa Hirono is a Research Councils United Kingdom (RCUK) Research Fellow at the School of Politics and International Relations and China Policy Institute, University of Nottingham, UK.

China's Evolving Approach to Peacekeeping

Edited by
Marc Lanteigne and Miwa Hirono

Routledge
Taylor & Francis Group

LONDON AND NEW YORK

First published 2012
by Routledge
2 Park Square, Milton Park, Abingdon, Oxfordshire OX14 4RN

Simultaneously published in the USA and Canada
by Routledge
711 Third Avenue, New York, NY 10017

First issued in paperback 2014

Routledge is an imprint of the Taylor and Francis Group, an informa business

British Library Cataloguing in Publication Data
A catalogue record for this book is available from the British Library

ISBN13: 978-0-415-50852-0 (hbk)
ISBN13: 978-0-415-75485-9 (pbk)

Typeset in Bembo
by Saxon Graphics Ltd, Derby

Publisher's Note
The publisher would like to make readers aware that the chapters in this
book may be referred to as articles as they are identical to the articles
published in the special issue. The publisher accepts responsibility for any
inconsistencies that may have arisen in the course of preparing this volume
for print.

Contents

Notes on Contributors   vii

1   Introduction: China and UN Peacekeeping   1
    Miwa Hirono and *Marc Lanteigne*

2   Principles and Praxis of China's Peacekeeping   15
    Chin-Hao Huang

3   Why Does China Participate in Intrusive Peacekeeping?
    Understanding Paternalistic Chinese Discourses on
    Development and Intervention   29
    Shogo Suzuki

4   A Responsible Power? China and the UN Peacekeeping
    Regime   44
    Courtney J. Richardson

5   The Responsibility to Protect and China's Peacekeeping Policy   56
    Sarah Teitt

6   A Change in Perspective: China's Engagement in the
    East Timor UN Peacekeeping Operations   71
    Marc Lanteigne

7   China's Charm Offensive and Peacekeeping:
    The Lessons of Cambodia – What Now for Sudan?   86
    Miwa Hirono

8   Two Pillars of China's Global Peace Engagement Strategy:
    UN Peacekeeping and International Peacebuilding   102
    Zhao Lei

Bibliography   121
Index   136

Notes on Contributors

Miwa Hirono (广野美和) is a Research Councils United Kingdom Research Fellow, School of Politics and International Relations and China Policy Institute, University of Nottingham, and a Visiting Fellow at the Department of International Relations at the Australian National University (ANU). Her publications include *Civilizing Missions: International Christian Agencies in China* (New York: Palgrave Macmillan, 2008). She has taught at the University of Cambridge, the ANU and the University of Canterbury, New Zealand.

Marc Lanteigne (兰马克) is a senior lecturer at the Department of Political Science and International Relations and Director of Research at the New Zealand Contemporary China Research Centre, Victoria University of Wellington. He is the author of *China and International Institutions: Alternate Paths to Global Power* (London: Routledge, 2005) and *Chinese Foreign Policy: An Introduction* (London: Routledge, 2009) as well as several articles on Chinese and Asian foreign relations and strategic policies, including engagement of regional organisations and norms. He is also a former researcher at the Asia Pacific Foundation of Canada in Vancouver and the Norwegian Institute of International Affairs in Oslo.

Chin-Hao Huang (黄劲豪) is a PhD candidate in the Political Science and International Relations Program, University of Southern California, and concomitantly a non-resident research fellow with the China and Global Security Programme, Stockholm International Peace Research Institute (SIPRI). Previously, he was a researcher at SIPRI, where he led research projects on China's role in UN peacekeeping and on China–Africa security relations and at the Center for Strategic and International Studies, Washington, DC. His recent publications include: *China's Expanding Role in Peacekeeping: Prospects and Policy Implications* (Stockholm: SIPRI, 2009) (with Bates Gill); 'China's Renewed Partnership with Africa: Implications for the United States', in Robert Rotberg (ed.), *China into Africa: Aid, Trade, and Influence* (Washington, DC: Brookings Institution Press, 2008); and 'U.S.–China Relations and Darfur', *Fordham International Law Journal*, Vol. 31, No. 4, 2008.

Shogo Suzuki (铃木章悟) is lecturer, Department of Politics, University of Manchester. He is the author of *Civilization and Empire: China and Japan's Encounter with European International Society* (London: Routledge, 2009) and of articles in *European Journal of International Relations, Pacific Review* and *Third World Quarterly*. He has held appointments at the University of Auckland, New Zealand, and the University of Cambridge.

Courtney J. Richardson (李康云) holds a joint appointment as a research fellow with the International Security Program at the Belfer Center for Science and International Affairs, Harvard University and as a pre-doctoral fellow with the Global Peace Operations Program at the Center on International Cooperation, New York University. She is writing her Ph.D. dissertation at the Fletcher School of Law and Diplomacy, Tufts University, exploring Chinese participation in peacekeeping as a means to understand broader trends in Chinese foreign and security policy. Courtney has completed fieldwork in New York, Beijing, and Shanghai, including an internship with the policy planning team at the United Nations Department of Peacekeeping Operations.

Sarah Teitt (田靚) is Outreach Director and China Programme Coordinator, Asia Pacific Centre for the Responsibility to Protect (R2P), University of Queensland, Brisbane, Australia. She works to promote awareness and dialogue on R2P among individuals and organizations in the Asia-Pacific, while completing a PhD on China's policy on UN responses to humanitarian crises.

Zhao Lei (赵磊) is Associate Professor and Deputy Director of International Relations, Institute for International Strategic Studies (IISS) of the Party School of the Central Committee of the Communist Party of China (CCPS). As a programme director of the National Social Science Fund of China, he is in charge of the project 'Practice of Constructing a Harmonious World: China's Participation in Peacekeeping Operations'. His area of research and expertise cover China's foreign policy, crisis management, and collective security and international organizations, especially Sino–UN relations.

Introduction: China and UN Peacekeeping

MIWA HIRONO and MARC LANTEIGNE

The People's Republic of China (PRC), after many decades of wariness and at times outright hostility towards the institution of UN peacekeeping missions (*lianheguo weihe xingdong* 联合国维和行动) has in the past two decades greatly reversed these policies.[1] China is now an enthusiastic supporter of UN Peacekeeping Operations (UNPKOs) and is seeking to deepen and widen its engagement with that institution. These changes have been in keeping with the country's larger foreign policy strategy, during the past two decades, of supporting multilateral solutions rather than unilateral actions to address strategic threats. The Chinese government has sought to illustrate its growing support for UNPKOs by committing personnel to overseas deployment. China now supplies the largest number of UN peace forces out of all of the permanent five (P-5) Security Council members. The overall ranking of China's personnel contributions has ranged from the 12th to 15th largest since May 2004, and China has been the seventh largest supplier of peacekeeping funding since 2009[2] and has promised that it would endeavour 'to enhance language, psychology and technical training for the peacekeepers and strengthen legislation work, in a bid to meet the diversified trend of UN peacekeeping functions'.[3]

The literature on China's UN peacekeeping has been growing steadily. Many studies have discussed gradual shifts in China's peacekeeping policy since that country's first deployment of civilian observers to Namibia in 1989, followed closely by the sending of military observers to the Middle East a year later as part of the UN Truce Supervision Organization.[4] As Yongjin Zhang argues, Chinese policy shifted in the 1990s from condemning UN peacekeeping activities to participating in them. In the 2000s, China's engagement in UN peacekeeping went beyond mere participation in traditional peacekeeping. It has become more flexible in dealing with the issue of sovereignty and more supportive of non-traditional peacekeeping, in which the use of 'all necessary means' is authorized under Chapter VII of the UN Charter.[5] Several studies of China's peacekeeping explain why the country's policies have shifted. For example, an International Crisis Group report claims that China's peacekeeping behaviour is motivated by five considerations: the idea of multilateralism; China's desire to be seen as a responsible power; its perception of operational benefit; the protection of Chinese interests abroad; and the One China policy.[6]

What the literature does not address, however, is the broader question of how the PRC's policymakers locate its peacekeeping engagement within China's

1

broader foreign policy. For example, China's government claims that multilateralism is one of the pillars of its foreign policy and the state's international relations literature has discussed the extent to which China has integrated itself into multilateral institutions and accepted the rules and norms of such institutions.[7] The most contentious debate, however, is not only about the extent to which China has adopted the norms, but also about the extent to which it has been reshaping the international order, and the rules and norms of the multilateral institutions it has integrated itself into.[8] In other words, the question now is whether China is a 'norm taker' or 'norm maker'.[9] One of the representative debates in this regard can be seen in relation to the Beijing Consensus discussion. The Beijing Consensus addresses the question of whether China is reshaping the global development approach away from the Washington Consensus, which prescribes economic reform based on market fundamentalism, to a more state-interventionist approach, in which China seems to prioritize economic development over political considerations such as human rights and democracy.[10]

The question of whether China is a norm-taker or norm-maker is also highly relevant to the issue of Chinese peacekeeping. Is its participation in peacekeeping likely to strengthen the current international peacekeeping regime as a result of China's adoption of the international norms of peacekeeping? Or, on the contrary, is China likely to alter the peacekeeping norms in a way that aligns with its own worldview? Or, as China's international confidence grows, will it begin to consider peacekeeping a smaller and lesser part of its international security activity, and thus not care so much about it? Lacking in the existing peacekeeping debate is engagement with these kinds of broader discussion of China's international relations.

This book acts as a first step towards addressing these questions. It aims to explore how the PRC has formed its peacekeeping policy and practices in relation to its international status, and the implications of the nature of China's peacekeeping policy and practices with regard to the future of international peacekeeping. It brings together historical and conceptual analyses and specific case-oriented discussions of China's peacekeeping over the past twenty years. It identifies the various challenges that China has faced at political, conceptual, diplomatic and operational levels, and examines ways in which China has dealt with those challenges. This introduction proposes a conceptual framework that the papers in this issue will address in varying ways. The framework consists of three overlapping and contradicting perspectives on China's international position – that of a great power, that of a middle power and that of a developing, non-Western country (or a leader thereof) – from which to analyse the nature of China's peacekeeping. Discussing the ways in which these perspectives overlap with, and contradict, one another allows one to understand the nature of China's peacekeeping policy and practices *vis-à-vis* its international position.

The following section discusses development in China's contributions to UN peacekeeping over the last two years, followed by an exploration of a conceptual framework for analysing why China has contributed to UN peacekeeping in the ways it has. We then discuss why and how China's peacekeeping matters for contemporary international peacekeeping. The final section of this chapter sets out the structure of this book.

Growing Commitment to UN Peacekeeping

Chinese views of UN peacekeeping have been increasingly positive over the past two decades. As Pang Zhongying noted, this approving attitude has been a result of growing Chinese confidence in the country's foreign policymaking skills, concerns beginning in the 1990s about American unipolarity and China's resulting need to bolster 'traditional' peacekeeping practices based on consent and respect for sovereignty, and growing enthusiasm for multilateral activity as a result of the country's political and economic growth.[11] From April 1990 to July 2010, China deployed over 15,600 personnel under the UN flag to 18 separate missions. The development of Chinese operations can be examined not only in the number of troops contributed and missions participated in but also in the methods of contribution. Although Chinese peacekeeping contributions so far have been civilian police, 'force enablers' such as logistic, medical and transport companies, and military observers, the possibility of a Chinese 'combat' force contribution has been discussed since December 2008, when Premier Wen Jiabao officially announced that China intended to contribute up to a thousand soldiers to the United Nations Interim Force in Lebanon (UNIFIL) II operation.[12] However, given that the UN did not find any vacancy for soldiers, China's contribution was limited to logistical support at that time.[13] Nevertheless, discussions continued, and in July 2010, a debate re-emerged within the Chinese government with respect to whether it would honour a future request by the UN to send soldiers abroad on peacekeeping missions.[14] An outcome of this discussion is still being awaited as of early 2012, but analysts speculate that China is likely to send soldiers in the near future (see the chapter by Courtney Richardson).

Domestically, China's interest in peacekeeping burgeoned in January 2010. Its contributions to UN peacekeeping were not well known among the Chinese population until the 'sacrifice' China made in the wake of the January 2010 Haiti earthquake. Four civilian police were killed by the quake along with four visiting officials from the Chinese Ministry of Public Security, which widely publicized the contribution China had been making to international peace for the last two decades.[15] Since China's UNPKO activities began two decades ago, the country has lost 17 people in the line of duty.[16] The eight casualties in Haiti were widely hailed as 'martyrs' (*lieshi* 烈士) in the Chinese press.[17]

In fact, the Haiti operations, especially, not only represent China's continuing support for UN peacekeeping, but also demonstrate that its approach to the activity has become more sophisticated than that in the 1990s.[18] The Caribbean state does not formally recognize the PRC, instead maintaining ties with the government of Taiwan. In the past, China had been resistant to supporting UN operations in states that did not recognize the PRC, as exemplified by the vetoing of UN peace missions in Guatemala in 1997 and Macedonia in 1999 (both states recognized Taiwan). By sending peacekeepers to a nation with which China does not maintain diplomatic relations, China 'appeared to recognise the benefits of a less punitive and more incentive-based strategy' of engagement in keeping with its ongoing policies of promoting stronger partnerships with developing regions.[19] In this way, the political obstacles, which had previously limited the scope of China's peacekeeping activities, began to give way.

The country's growing commitment to peacekeeping under UN auspices was further exemplified by the opening of the China Peacekeeping CIVPOL (Civilian Police) Training Centre in Langfang City, south of the capital, in August 2000, followed by that of the Ministry of National Defense (MND) Peacekeeping Center in Beijing's Huairou District in June 2009. Both training centres have been visited and used not only by Chinese peacekeepers but also by overseas peacekeeping personnel, scholars of international training and military personnel on exchange, and have been used for public relations purposes. In November 2009 the MND held an international peacekeeping conference in Beijing, and demonstrated China's willingness to contribute more to UN peacekeeping.[20] Furthermore, it pledged additional funding and logistical support for current and future UN missions.[21]

Coincident with this increased level of participation, an epistemic community constructed around the study of peacekeeping has evolved both inside and outside China. In addition to a corpus of literature, there have been some landmark conferences on Chinese peacekeeping, such as the above-mentioned MND conference in Beijing in 2009 and the international conference on China in peace support operations organized jointly by the Stockholm International Peace Research Institute and Norwegian Institute for Defence Studies in March 2010. As noted below, the subject is important for the future of international peacekeeping, and it is hoped that the epistemic community will develop further interest. It is the editors' hope that this book will make a further contribution to the evolving discussion of China's peacekeeping.

Why Peacekeeping: China as a Great Power, a Developing Country or a Middle Power?

China's growing contribution to peacekeeping is closely related to how the Chinese government regards its international standing in contemporary international relations. In analysing the nature of China's peacekeeping policy and practices, and its future direction, it is useful to explore how policy and practices can be understood in relation to broader discussions of China's international positions, which as noted above relate to the key debate in the study of Chinese international relations. A conceptual framework is offered here, comprising three international positions − China as a great power, as a developing, non-Western country (or a leader of such countries) and as a middle power. These positions represent different aspects of Chinese peacekeeping policy and practices. 'A great power' refers to China's attitude as a norm-maker − including attempts both to advance new norms and to reject Western-developed norms. 'A developing, non-Western country' refers to the PRC's longstanding and frequent emphasis on solidarity with other developing countries, based on historical memories of the 'colonized past'. 'A middle power' refers to China's attitude as a norm-taker, meaning that China simply goes with the flow of international peacekeeping policy development and seeks to avoid direct confrontation with major powers.

FIGURE I.1
CONCEPTUAL FRAMEWORK

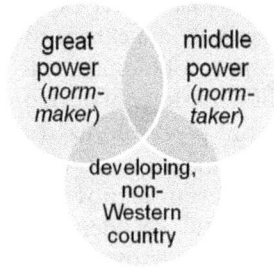

As revealed throughout this book, each position is complex, and the borders between the positions are porous rather than clear-cut. As Figure I.1 indicates, the positions are overlapping and contradictory, signifying the complex nature of China's peacekeeping. These positions will be used to distinguish different features of peacekeeping policy and practices, and to determine how the Chinese government views its peacekeeping activity in relation to its transforming international position.

There are many features by which China's peacekeeping could be understood as that of 'a great power' and there has been much debate both within and beyond China as to how the country could play a 'great-power' role in seeking to maintain international peace and stability. Although many of the missions to which China has sent forces do not have a significant impact on the country's immediate security concerns, the political stability of resource-rich regions is the basis of the PRC's economic development. There is also the argument that China benefits both from the acquisition of further knowledge of security issues well beyond its borders and from the demonstration of its 'peaceful rise' or 'peaceful development' (*heping jueqi* 和平崛起 / *heping fazhan* 和平发展) foreign policy doctrine.[22] Since Hu Jintao became president in 2003, China has sought to demonstrate that, while its power is rising in the international system, it generally seeks international stability in a cooperative fashion using methods that respect global norms. Jiang Zemin, Hu's predecessor as Chinese leader, focused primarily on improving relations among the country's immediate neighbours in East and Southeast Asia through peripheral diplomacy (*zhoubian waijiao* 周边外交).[23] Hu has built on these successes and is seeking to raise China's diplomatic visibility beyond the Asia–Pacific region. China's peacekeeping policy can be located within this broader foreign policy trajectory.

Even though China respects global norms when playing a 'great-power' role to maintain international peace and stability, at times it seeks to prioritize selected norms that suit its international strategy. The PRC's foreign policy towards the contested region of Darfur in 2008 may exemplify this. The Chinese government sent a diplomatic envoy to Sudan to persuade President Omar al-Bashir to accept UN peacekeeping forces in Darfur. China endeavoured to establish stability in Sudan while adhering to the principle of host state consent, despite other states wishing to take a more activist policy that went beyond such a principle.[24] Furthermore, the PRC reportedly prioritizes 'development' over 'imposed democracy and good governance' in international peace operations, as Zhao Lei explains in this book. This can be interpreted as China's 'great-power' trajectory to become a norm-maker.

On the other hand, other aspects of China's peacekeeping policy and practices can be interpreted as consistent with those of developing, non-Western countries. These are often less democratic, post-colonized countries still struggling with economic reform. Although it may appear odd to call China a developing country, for since 2010 it has been acknowledged to be the second-largest economy in the world, the PRC still considers itself of developing status because of its still high poverty levels, especially in the country's interior.

There are at least three reasons why China's peacekeeping policy and practices can be interpreted as consistent with those of developing countries. First, China's UN diplomatic discourse in relation to peacekeeping is based on a neo-Westphalian understanding of state sovereignty, which has been officially focused on since the establishment of the Five Principles of Peaceful Co-existence, adopted at the Bandung Conference in 1955.[25] Maintaining the principle of sovereignty is intricately related to China's 'semi-colonized' identity. The Chinese government often emphasizes that China and other developing countries share historical experience as colonized countries, as suggested in 'China's African Policy' of January 2006, for example.[26] The principle of sovereignty still forms one of the pillars of China's foreign policy and features in its peacekeeping discourse, although the PRC has become somewhat more flexible in its understanding of sovereignty, as will be discussed later.

Second, China's peacekeeping operations have been undertaken in developing countries, and peacekeeping can be interpreted as one of the components of what is called 'south–south cooperation' (*nannan hezuo* 南南合作).[27] For example, Chinese discourse on China–Africa relations often carries with it a nuance that China is a leader of the developing world, and that other developing countries can learn from China's successful experience of economic modernization. At the same time, a stress on mutual partnerships coupled with the lack of an imperialist legacy in Africa has made its approach distinct, although debate in many quarters continues about China's long-term political and economic goals for the continent.[28] Interestingly, Chinese peacekeepers, consisting mainly of engineering forces, often contribute to building or fixing basic infrastructure in the host country, such as roads and bridges, which the host country can use for economic development in the future. Irrespective of whether the Chinese government intends to do so, China's peacekeeping contribution facilitates the host country's economic development and a modernization trajectories that the Chinese government and investment corporations have tended to support.

Third, there is a tendency for developing countries, notably regional powers, to commit large numbers of troops to UN peacekeeping. In the troop contribution ranking, the top 15 countries (including China as 15th) are all developing countries.[29] Income generation is not China's rationale for providing a relatively large number of troops, as soldiers are well paid by the government;

the rationale lies more in military training opportunities, as clearly stated in China's National Defence White Paper in 2008.[30] In this document, UN peacekeeping, and other non-traditional security activities are discussed in relation to the People's Liberation Army (PLA) role in undertaking multiple military tasks (*duoyanghua junshi renwu* 多样化军事任务). Nonetheless, China and other developing countries are similar in attempting to gain some immediate benefit out of peacekeeping operations, and this can be interpreted as a representative of developing countries in general.

Although much has been written concerning whether China's status should be understood as a current or at least imminent great power or as the leader of the developing world, what also distinguishes China's current policies towards UN peacekeeping is that they are arguably very much in keeping with 'middle-power', not great-power, diplomacy. The country's immersion in cross-regional strategic issues (beyond the Asia–Pacific region), is quite new and China still lacks military power-projection capabilities, notably in the navy and air force, consistent with that of a great power. At the same time, however, China wishes to play a more visible role in regions beyond its periphery to reflect its expanding global political and economic interests. A more comprehensive engagement with UNPKOs is one solution to this conundrum, very much in keeping with strategies used by middle-level powers (Australia and Canada in the 1990s being oft-cited examples). It has been argued that due to a limited reach beyond their immediate regions, middle powers tend to play activist roles in addressing strategic issues that do not immediately affect them. They also focus on conflict reduction, often linking with like-minded states to form a consensus. While they may disagree with great powers on occasion they hesitate to challenge them directly, and they prefer to concentrate on stabilization rather than promoting abrupt change.[31] This usefully illustrates China's post-1990s policies towards UN peacekeeping operations, namely that it is adapting peacekeeping engagement policies in keeping with a mid-range power seeking to improve its international status.

Despite its growing military power and a diplomatic presence well beyond its borders, China's approach to modern peacekeeping is consistent with that of a middle power in its policy development, which has been defined as professing a multilateral approach to building peace, a willingness to compromise, an understanding of middle-power limitations, a tendency to take a targeted approach to international problems through what has been called 'niche diplomacy' or a 'helpful fixer' role.[32] There is an added concern to reduce the perception that China seeks to challenge international order through more coercive policies, the so-called 'China Threat' theory. The government's willingness in the past decade to expand the number of peacekeeping missions in which it was willing to participate is a sign that it wishes to develop a strategic presence further afield, especially in the developing world, through 'military operations other than war' (MOOTW; *fei zhanzheng junshi xingdong* 非战争军事行动). The MOOTW concept is found in the PLA's 'New Historic Missions' (*xin de lishi shiming* 新的历史使命), a term that President Hu introduced in 2004.[33] In these missions, the PLA engages with multiple military tasks, one of which is to expand the PLA's capability by participating in such operations.[34]

The concept was included for the first time in China's National Defence White Paper in 2008, which also mentioned China's deployment of civilian personnel in UN missions in Africa, the Middle East and Southeast Asia.[35] The concept includes a variety of non-traditional security activities, such as UN peacekeeping, humanitarian assistance, anti-piracy and anti-terrorism operations. They provide a useful mechanism through which China may not only strengthen its military capability but also engages in military-to-military cooperation and military diplomacy. More cooperation in these activities will enhance the image that China is liberalizing its military, making an effort towards military transparency and ensuring that China's increasing military presence abroad should not refuel the 'China Threat' theory.

Peacekeeping is arguably one area of foreign strategic policy where the government has successfully adapted the image of a middle-power, conservative and multilateralist state with positive results. China has altered its views on military intervention on humanitarian grounds since the 1990s, maintaining a current stance that such actions may be justified if the UN takes the lead in authorizing and implementing said missions. By contrast, China was unsupportive of intervention missions by other means, including NATO's air war in Kosovo in 1999 and the post-2003 US-led 'coalition of the willing' military operations in Iraq. Both events heightened China's sensitivity to unilateral uses of force in the name of humanitarianism or democratization, while at the same time China was bolstering the idea of multilateral problem-solving commensurate with middle powers seeking to expand their policy reach beyond their immediate region.

Even in cases where the UN was the primary actor in an intervention mission, China had been taking a somewhat conservative and critical view in the 1990s of what it saw as improper use of Chapter VII of the UN Charter, which authorizes force under conditions of international threat. In the case of Yugoslavia, China supported the creation of the UN Protection Force (UNPROFOR) but was critical of force being authorized under Chapter VII. According to one report, it was China's frustration at the UN being bypassed when NATO intervened in Kosovo that prompted the decision to deepen its peacekeeping policies.[36] Similar concerns were raised with the alteration of UN mandates in the 1990s – the Somalia and Rwanda missions – and China was also critical of the UN acquiescing to the use of force in 1994 to restore exiled Haitian President Jean-Bertrand Aristide to power, arguing that a negotiated settlement would be more effective.[37] In all these cases China expressed its preference for state sovereignty to be fully observed and for avoiding the use of Chapter VII as a tool by which states can push unilateral strategic initiatives.

In contrast to the previous decade, China's peacekeeping diplomacy in the 2000s reveals a stance towards the use of Chapter VII that has become more flexible and less conservative.[38] When the UN Security Council votes on authorizing a Chapter VII operation, China no longer offers a particular reason why it supports operations authorized under Chapter VII, implying that its policymakers regard these politically sensitive operations as a normal part of UN peacekeeping.[39] As Stefan Stähle argues, this change can be regarded as China's international socialization into the UN peacekeeping regime.[40] Nevertheless,

China is still regarded as 'conservative', particularly in relation to the principle of the host state's consent to a UN mission. This is clearly indicated in, among other announcements, China's Position Paper on UN reform released in 2005.[41]

The perceptions of China as a middle power and as a great power overlap and contradict when one examines its increasingly activist roles in UN peacekeeping. While the 'activist role' is part of the definition of middle power, China is seeking a greater understanding of cross-regional strategic affairs as a precursor to developing its 'soft power', and possibly 'hard power', in key regions of interest, including Africa, where China has been active in peacekeeping missions in the Liberia, Democratic Republic of Congo, Western Sahara and Sudan.[42] The last has been controversial given China's previous diplomatic and economic support for the government in Khartoum. China's contributions to operations in Southeast Asia and the Middle East have also greatly enhanced its diplomatic stature.

Nevertheless, the important question about this overlap is that, if China behaves as a middle power and uses UN peacekeeping as a means of extending its global military reach, does the PRC regard such behaviour as a permanent position or as a step to become a greater power? If the latter is the case, China's middle-power behaviour is instrumental and thus different in its long-term intention from that of 'true' middle powers.[43] If China diverges from the 'true' middle powers in terms of peacekeeping behaviour and projects itself as a great power by making alternative international norms, the area of overlap between the two power perspectives will gradually minimize, and the middle-power status will become meaningless.

There remains the question of what direction China's peacekeeping policies will take in the future. As the country continues to develop its global strengths and takes a 'great-power' trajectory, will it decide to alter its peacekeeping strategies to become a norm-maker? Or will it decide to exert some influence in a conflict area as a middle power, by maintaining the status quo of self-controlled capability, to remain largely a norm-taker? Or will it decide to develop its policy to be more aligned with other major 'developing' countries, favouring background logistical support rather than front line deployments? The current position lies in the combination of these different trajectories. Arguably, China's peacekeeping policy and practices lie in the centre of the three overlapping circles, as shown in Figure I.1. It is possible that the current deep engagement in UNPKOs represents a transitional period, but at present the trend towards expanded peacekeeping support is not showing signs of short-term abatement.

Why does China Matter to International Peacekeeping?

Gaining a better understanding of the nature of Chinese peacekeeping policy and practices is vital to UN peacekeeping for several reasons. This is first and foremost because China is one of the P-5 members in the UN Security Council, and its cooperation towards UN peacekeeping is a key to the success and legitimacy of UN peacekeeping, especially in missions with a Chapter VII component. As some studies on UN peacekeeping point out, the current low levels of US and British troop contributions to UN peacekeeping are alarming from the viewpoint of legitimacy, even though these countries make greater financial contributions to peacekeeping endeavours.[44]

Second, China has a particular advantage as a peacekeeping nation because it is not perceived by those in the areas of operations as having an 'imperialist' or 'neo-colonialist' past, placing China in a similar position as middle-power contributors to past UN missions such as Australia, Canada and Egypt, themselves former colonies. This advantage is prominent given that the US, the UK and France were often regarded as imperialist powers, a point further underscored by the policies of the three states towards the 'Arab Spring' uprisings of 2011. In regions with a colonial past, intervention by actors that do not carry the image of a colonial power is often perceived from local perspectives to carry greater legitimacy. Moreover, China's 'commercial diplomacy' (*shangwu waijiao* 商务外交), which seeks to channel the country's economic power into other forms of persuasive power throughout many conflict-prone regions in Africa and the Middle East, has further laid a framework for distinguishing its strategic engagement policies from those of the US and other western powers.[45] While it is important to be mindful of China's own 'paternalism' in peacekeeping operations, as Shogo Suzuki argues in this volume, the fact that China does not carry the taint of Western imperialism and projects itself as 'a friend of developing countries' is very important to some of the African nations in which UNPKOs are conducted. In short, peacekeeping is proving to be an increasingly valuable and visible component of China's oft-discussed 'charm offensive'[46] (*meili gongshi* 魅力攻势) in the developing world, as Miwa Hirono demonstrates in this book. Furthermore, peacekeeping gives a signal that China's military development does not pose a threat to international peace and security. Thus, in a July 2010 statement by the Chinese Ministry of Defence the country's peacekeeping record along with humanitarian relief and the protection of maritime convoys was cited as evidence that the Chinese military was seeking to become a 'positive force' (*zheng shili* 正势力) for international peace.[47]

Third, understanding China's peacekeeping is important to those who actually undertake peace operations. Although its contribution to UN peacekeeping is relatively limited in the number of overall troops, its engineering and logistical contributions are increasingly vital to the success of peace operations, and policymakers in the UN expect China to continue its contribution in this regard.[48] Understanding the sort of contributions China makes and can make, and how it operates in the field, is very important for the UN, other troop-contributing countries, NGOs and local populations.

Fourth, understanding China's peacekeeping is essential when policymakers of the UN and of Western governments, as well as civil activist groups, attempt to encourage or push China to take a more active role in international peacekeeping. A better understanding of policy and practices will lead to more effective communication between the Chinese government and those policymakers in the West. Ineffective communication, including 'shaming' China's policy towards the developing world, especially in the case of Darfur in Sudan in early 2008, exacerbates mistrust between the Chinese and others.

Mistrust may lead to resentment and doubt, and will adversely affect collaboration. But international peacekeeping policy can no longer afford to neglect China and its contributions. Understanding the nature of China's peacekeeping policy is an important starting point for many policymakers to overcome mistrust and misunderstanding, and to work effectively with a giant player on the world's stage.

Structure of This Book

In this book, we examine the current policies and practices of Chinese peacekeeping, with the aim of analysing the nature of Chinese peacekeeping in terms of a great power, developing country and middle power. In other words, to what extent does China take a great power, developing power, or middle power stance in the making and implementation of its peacekeeping policy? More specifically, we ask how China has altered its thinking about UN-sponsored peacekeeping operations, as well as how the concepts and policymaking structures of peacekeeping are being re-examined by Chinese policymakers as a result of increased engagement.

Chin-Hao Huang begins with an overview and examination of China's peacekeeping activities and how they evolved into the policies seen today. A great deal of rethinking was required within the Chinese government before the changes in policy towards UNPKOs could be undertaken, and it can be argued that the process is far from complete. Shogo Suzuki steps further back and examines the peacekeeping policies within the larger questions of the country's history of paternalism in its foreign relations. The next two chapters focus on peacekeeping concepts and how China has sought to interpret them. Courtney Richardson examines the idea of China as a 'responsible power', a concept that has since developed as an 'authoritative statement' (*tifa* 提法) in Beijing. The questions explored are how 'responsible power' has gained greater legitimacy in Chinese peacekeeping policy-making and how it has illuminated China's still developing UN engagement in UNPKOs. Sarah Teitt writes on the issue of the 'responsibility to protect' or R2P (*baohu de zeren* 保护的责任) in international relations, a longstanding issue in intervention and human security debates, and examines whether China is following or seeking to reinterpret these guidelines.

The next chapters focus on specific cases of groundbreaking Chinese participation in peacekeeping missions. Marc Lanteigne examines the politics and strategic rationales for China's watershed decision to support the 1999 UN Transitional Administration in East Timor (UNTAET), an operation that paved the way for the independence of Timor Leste from Indonesia in May 2002. Despite China's concerns about the importance of state borders and sovereignty, it nonetheless not only supported this operation but also agreed to send forces to assist with the multilateral mission in what proved to be a watershed set of decisions. Miwa Hirono examines the cases of peacekeeping operations in Cambodia from 1992 to 1993 and considers the implications in relation to Sudan from 2008 to late 2010. The Cambodian case shows that China's peacekeeping helped to change the local negative perception towards China, despite that country's historical support for the Khmer Rouge dictatorship. She argues that to overcome the challenge of negative local perception, China needs to maintain political neutrality in operational areas. Finally, Lei Zhao using empirical survey data to track the development of Chinese views – from peacekeeping issues to peacebuilding – examines possible Chinese policy directions towards future global engagement strategy.

Although much has been written about China's expanded role in international relations and its increasing interest in comprehensive security, its engagement in UNPKOs remains a policy under development and an area worthy of further research. These chapters survey the progress that China has made in engaging in UNPKOs in the last two decades, and suggest ways that the country could fit into future peacekeeping studies.

Acknowledgements

We thank Devon Curtis, Stefan Wolff and Yongjin Zhang for their comments on earlier versions of this chapter. Special thanks also go to Rosemary Foot, who not only read an earlier version of this introduction, but also served as the paper discussant for the panel 'China's Peacekeeping' at the 51st Annual Convention of the International Studies Association, New Orleans in February 2010, at which draft versions of some of the chapters in this book were presented.

NOTES

1. In this chapter, 'peacekeeping' includes not only traditional peacekeeping, but also transition management, wider peacekeeping, peace enforcement and peace support operations. In the Chinese language, the term *weihe* is usually used to refer to all of these kinds of operation, unless one is intentionally making a distinction between them. For example, transition management in the UN Transitional Authority in Cambodia (UNTAC) and the UN Transitional Administration in East Timor (UNTAET), wider peacekeeping in the UN Mission in Haiti (UNMIH), peace enforcement in the UN Operation in Somalia (UNOSOM), and the UN Protection Force (UNPROFOR) and peace support operation in the UN Organization Mission in the DRC (MONUC) are all called *weihe* in Chinese policy and media discourse. On taxonomy of peacekeeping in the English language, see Alex J. Bellamy, Paul Williams and Stuart Griffin *Understanding Peacekeeping*, 2nd edn, Cambridge: Polity, 2010.
2. 'China Donates 700,000 US Dollars to UN Peacekeeping Missions', *Xinhua News Agency*, 2 December 2009 [trans. by BBC Monitoring Service, International Reports].
3. 'China Actively Participates in UN Peacekeeping Operations', *Xinhua News Agency*, 20 January 2009 [trans. by BBC Monitoring Service, International Reports].
4. Philippe D. Rogers (2007) 'China and United Nations Peacekeeping Operations in Africa', (US) *Naval War College Review*, 60(2): 75.
5. Allen Carlson (2004) 'Helping to Keep the Peace (Albeit Reluctantly): China's Recent Stance on Sovereignty and Multilateral Intervention', *Pacific Affairs*, 77(1): 9–27; Bates Gill and James Reilly (2000) 'Sovereignty, Intervention and Peacekeeping: The View from Beijing', *Survival*, 42(3): 41–59; Bates Gill and Chin-hao Huang (2009) 'China's Expanding Role in Peacekeeping: Prospects and Policy Implications', policy paper 25, Stockholm International Peace Research Institute, November 2009 (at: books.sipri.org/files/PP/SIPRIPP25.pdf); Pang Zhongying (2005) 'China's Changing Attitude to UN Peacekeeping', *International Peacekeeping*, 12(1): 87–104; Stefan Stähle (2008) 'China's Shifting Attitude towards United Nations Peacekeeping Operations', *The China Quarterly*, 195: 631–55; Yin He (2007) 'China's Changing Policy on UN Peacekeeping Operations', Asia Paper, Institute for Security and Development Policy, July (at: www.silkroadstudies.org/new/docs/Silkroadpapers/2007/YinHe 0409073.pdf); International Crisis Group (ICG) (2009) 'China's Growing Role in UN Peacekeeping'. Asia Report 166, 17 April (at: www.crisisgroup.org/home/index.cfm?id=6062): 12–14.

6. ICG (see n.5).

7. For example, see Marc Lanteigne (2005) *China and International Institutions: Alternate Paths to Global Power*, London: Routledge; Alastair Iain Johnston (2008) *Social States: China in International Institutions, 1980–2000*, Princeton, NJ: Princeton University Press.

8. See Ann Kent (2007) *Beyond Compliance: China, International Organizations and Global Security*, Stanford, CA: Stanford University Press.

9. On norm maker and norm taker, see Amitav Acharya (2004) 'How Ideas Spread: Whose Norms Matter? Norm Localization and Institutional Change in Asian Regionalism', *International Organization*, 58(2): 239–75; Jeffrey T. Checkel (1999) 'Norms, Institutions and National Identity in Contemporary Europe', *International Studies Quarterly*, 43(1): 83–114.

10. Joshua Cooper Ramo (2004) 'The Beijing Consensus', *Foreign Policy Centre*; Stefan Halper (2010) *The Beijing Consensus: How China's Authoritarian Model will Dominate the Twenty-First Century*, New York: Basic Books.

11. Pang Zhongying (see n.5): 88–89.

12. ICG (see n.5): 29; 'China Ups Lebanon Force to 1,000', *BBC News* (at: http://news.bbc.co.uk/2/hi/asia-pacific/5355128.stm).

13. Interview by Hirono with UN staff, New York, 18 January 2009.

14. 'Chinese Combat Troops "Can be Part of UN Peacekeeping"', *People's Daily* (Beijing), 7 July 2010 (at: english.peopledaily.com.cn/90001/90776/90883/7055042.html).

15. Shai Oster (2010) 'China Replaces Haiti Peacekeepers, *Wall Street Journal Asia*, 25 January: 8.

16. The 17 were in Iraq, two (1991 and 2003), Cambodia, three (1992 and 1993), the DRC one (2003), Liberia one (2005), the Lebanon one (2006), Haiti eight (2010), Sudan one (2010). The Central People's Government of the People's Republic of China, '*Texie: musong haidi dizhen yunan zhongguo weihe jingcha huijia*' [特写：目送海地地震遇难中国维和警察回家] (feature article: The sending home of the Chinese policemen who died in the Haiti Earthquake), 18 January 2010 (at: www.gov.cn/jrzg/2010-01/19/content_1514397.htm); '*Zhongguo weihe zhanshi guodu laolei zai sudan xisheng: bei Pizhun wei lieshi*' [中国维和战士过度劳累在苏丹牺牲：被批准为烈士] (China's peacekeeping soldier sacrificed his life through excessive fatigue: being canonised as a martyr), 26 September 2010 (at: www1.china.com.cn/military/txt/2010-09/26/content_21004939.htm).

17. '15,000 Chinese Soldiers Join UN Peacekeeping Missions in Two Decades', *Xinhua*, 30 July 2010 (at: www.chinadaily.com.cn/china/2010-07/30/content_11072464.htm); Shai Oster (2010) 'China Replaces Haiti Peacekeepers, *Wall Street Journal Asia*, 25 January: 8.

18. We are grateful to Stephanie Kleine-Ahlbrandt for her comments on this point.

19. ICG (see n.5): 18.

20. Linda Mottram (2009) 'Praise for China's Expanding Peacekeeping Role', *ABC Radio*, Sydney, 23 November (at: www.radioaustralia.net.au/asiapac/stories/200911/s2751288.htm).

21. Hu Yumin (2009) 'China Plays its Peacekeeping Role', *China Daily*, 29 June (at: www.chinadaily.com.cn/cndy/2009-06/29/content_8331296.htm).

22. Bonnie S. Glaser and Evan S. Medeiros (2007) 'The Changing Ecology of Foreign Policy-Making in China: The Ascension and Demise of the Theory of "Peaceful Rise"', *The China Quarterly*, 190: 291–310.

23. Shaun Breslin (2009) 'Understanding China's Regional Rise: Interpretations, Identities and Implications', *International Affairs*, 85(4): 819.

24. Bates Gill, Chin-hao Huang and Stephen Morrison (2007) 'Assessing China's Growing Role in Africa', *China Security*, 3(3): 3–21.

25. Ren Xiao (2009) 'The International Relations Theoretical Discourse in China: One World, Different Explanations', *Journal of Chinese Political Science*, 15: 110–13.

26. The Chinese Government, 'China's African Policy', 20 September 2006 (at: www.gov.cn/misc/2006-01/12/content_156490.htm). On China's identity as a developing country see, Nick Knight (2007) 'Thinking about Globalisation, Thinking about Japan: Dichotomies in China's Construction of the Modern World', in Michael Heazle and Nick Knight (eds), *China–Japan Relations in the Twenty-first Century: Creating a Future Past?*, Cheltenham: Edward Elgar: 54–73.

27. The diplomatic 'package' includes aid, loans and grants, debt relief, personnel training, student scholarship grants for the military, assistance and training in energy development, infrastructure, agriculture and manufacturing and arms sales. See Joshua Eisenman (2007) 'China's Post-Cold War Strategy in Africa: Examining Beijing's Methods and Objectives', in Joshua Eisenman, Eric Heginbotham and Derek Mitchell (eds), *China and the Developing World: Beijing's Strategy for the Twenty-First Century*, Armonk, NY: M.E. Sharpe: 37.

28. See Deborah Brautigam (2009) *The Dragon's Gift: The Real Story of China in Africa*, Oxford: Oxford University Press; Ian Taylor (2009) *China's New Role in Africa*, Boulder, CO: Lynne Rienner: 1–33.

29. They are, in descending order, Pakistan, Bangladesh, India, Nigeria, Egypt, Nepal, Ghana, Rwanda, Jordan, Uruguay, Ethiopia, Brazil, Senegal, South Africa, and China. *United Nations*, 'Ranking of Military and Police Contributions to UN Operations', 30 June 2010 (at: www.un.org/en/peacekeeping/contributors/2010/june10_2.pdf).

30. Information Office of the State Council of the People's Republic of China, 'China's National Defence in 2008', 20 January 2009 (at: www.china.org.cn/government/whitepaper/node_7060059.htm).

31. Eduard Jordaan (2003) 'The Concept of a Middle Power in International Relations: Distinguishing between Emerging and Traditional Middle Powers', *Politikon*, 30(2): 167.

32. See Adam Chapnick (1999) 'The Middle Power', *Canadian Foreign Policy*, 7(2): 73–82; 'Middle Power', David Capie and Paul Evans (2007) *The Asia-Pacific Security Lexicon* (2nd edn), Singapore: Institute of Southeast Asian Studies: 155–8.

33. James Mulvenon, 'Chairman Hu and the PLA's "New Historic Missions"', *China Leadership Monitor* [Stanford, CA] 27: 1–11.

34. Michael S. Chase and Kristen Gunness (2010) 'The PLA's Multiple Military Tasks: Prioritizing Combat Operations and Developing MOOTW Capabilities', *China Brief*, 10(2): 5–7.

35. Information Office of the State Council of the People's Republic, 'China's National Defence in 2008' (at: www.china.org.cn/government/whitepaper/node_7060059.htm).

36. Andrew Higgins (2009) 'China Showcasing its Softer Side: Growing Role in U.N. Peacekeeping Signals Desire to Project Image of Benign Power', *Washington Post*, 2 December (at: www.washingtonpost.com/wp-dyn/content/article/2009/12/01/AR2009120104060.html).

37. M. Taylor Fravel (1996) 'China's Attitude towards UN Peacekeeping Operations since 1989', *Asian Survey*, 36(11): 1110–15.

38. Stähle (see n.5).

39. Examples include the UN Mission in Liberia (UNMIL) (UN doc., S/RES/1509, 19 September 2003), the UN Stabilization Mission in Haiti (MINUSTAH) (UN Doc., S/RES/1542, 30 April 2004), and the UN Mission in Sudan (UNMIS) (UN Doc., S/RES/1590, 24 March 2005). For more details, see Table 1 in Stähle (see n.5): 640–42.

40. Stähle (see n.5).

41. 'China's Position Paper on UN Reforms', *China Daily*, 8 June 2005 (at: www.chinadaily.com.cn/china/2005-06/08/content_536124.htm).

42. Zhang Yan (2010) 'Military Ties to Help China Develop', *China Daily*, 22 May: 1.

43. We are grateful to Stefan Wolff for his comments on this point.

44. For example, see Alex J. Bellamy and Paul D. Williams (2009) 'The West and Contemporary Peace Operations', *Journal of Peace Research*, 46(1): 39–57.

45. See Ellen L. Frost (2007) 'China's Commercial Diplomacy in Asia: Promise or Threat?', in William W. Keller and Thomas G. Rawski (eds), *China's Rise and the Balance of Influence in Asia*, Pittsburgh, IL: University of Pittsburgh Press: 96–7.

46. On the 'charm offensive', see Joshua Kurlanzick (2007) *Charm Offensive: How China's Soft Power is Transforming the World*, New Haven, CT: Yale University Press.

47. 'China's Military Will Not Pose Threat to Other Nations – Ministry', *Zhongguo Xinwenshe* (Beijing), 31 July 2010 [trans. by BBC Monitoring Service, International Reports].

48. Interview by Hirono with UN staff (see n.13).

Principles and Praxis of China's Peacekeeping

CHIN-HAO HUANG

China's expanding role in peacekeeping opens up a new avenue for China to strengthen global peace operations and contribute to stability and security in Africa and other developing regions, raising the prospects for China to become even more integrated into the international community. Its evolving role in peacekeeping is underpinned by a combination of factors. Through increasing socialization and interaction with the international community, China has become more willing to accept global norms and to contribute to peace and stability. At the same time, participation in peacekeeping allows China to professionalize its armed forces, to test its power projection capabilities and to pursue its aspirations to become a major global power. Whether such cooperative behaviour will be reversed or sustained is still uncertain. As such, its definitive role in peacekeeping remains largely indeterminate and thus merits continued and more nuanced observation.

In the wake of the 1989 Tiananmen Square crisis, and especially since the mid-1990s, China's foreign policy has evolved to become more pragmatic and in some respects more convergent with global norms of cooperation than previously.[1] That the Chinese People's Liberation Army (PLA) is increasingly exposed to, and upholding the principles of, UN peacekeeping is an encouraging trend and an important indicator of this shift in Chinese foreign and security policy. The active deployment of Chinese troops – in the form of engineers, military observers, transport and logistical support units, civilian police and medical staff – to UN peacekeeping operations has seen a twenty-fold increase since 2000.[2] With more than 2,100 Chinese peacekeepers abroad in mid-2010, China had more troops under UN command than any other permanent member of the Security Council.[3] China's increasing involvement in international peacekeeping activities adds a layer of perceived legitimacy, particularly among developing countries, to help contribute to peace and stability in some of the most unstable conflict regions in the world, and its important material assets and contributions come at a particularly critical time when multilateral peacekeeping is overstretched.[4] China's expanding role in peacekeeping is therefore opening up a new avenue for it to strengthen global peace operations, contribute to stability and security in Africa and other developing regions and expand its multilateral military cooperation, all of which raise the prospects for China to become even more integrated into the international community and a responsible major power.

In spite of these high stakes, there has been limited analysis to help systematically explain why China has become more involved in UN peacekeeping.[5]

To what extent is China's more cooperative behaviour on peacekeeping attributable to its social interaction with the international community, and how and where has this socialization process happened? Does material power interest factor into policy considerations? Or is it a complex amalgam of both? A more in-depth study needs to be done to better understand China's evolving approach towards international peacekeeping. This article seeks to contribute to the literature by illuminating the key factors that underpin China's expanding interest in UN peacekeeping, assessing some of the emerging challenges and limitations China faces in putting these principles into practice, and considering what future purposes will be served by a rising China in exerting its influence through an expanding role in peacekeeping activities.

China's evolving role in peacekeeping activities demonstrates just how far its foreign policy in this regard has shifted and changed in a relatively short period of time. Throughout the 1970s and much of the 1980s, the first two decades after it joined the UN in 1971, China viewed UN peacekeeping missions with a degree of scepticism, maintained a low profile and refrained from taking any substantive actions in Security Council debates on peacekeeping.[6] This cautious approach reflects a traditional understanding and interpretation of positive international law, an important norm that has underpinned the development of the modern international system. Inter-state relations were primarily governed by the view that each sovereign government has the right and authority to rule within its own territory as it deems fit and without interference from external actors. The normative sanctity of state sovereignty is also enshrined in the UN Charter, which prohibits the use of military force except in self-defence or when authorized by the Security Council to address certain threats to international peace and security. China upheld the inviolable principle of state sovereignty and often questioned the necessity of external intervention in areas of conflict, even if a particular operation was approved by the Security Council and was operating under the auspices of international peacekeeping forces. China's caution has in no small part been coloured by its earlier experiences and encounters, particularly during the 1950–53 Korean War, where the PLA fought 'UN forces' under US-led command. China thus harbours concerns about the nature and legitimacy of such interventionist operations, particularly those that are Western-led.

Towards the late 1980s, however, China's position on peacekeeping began to shift towards one of greater interest and participation. In 1988, it became a member of the UN Special Committee on Peacekeeping Operations, paving the way for increased engagement in multilateral peacekeeping activities. As one senior Chinese official put it at the time, all states should lend 'powerful support' to peacekeeping, setting a new tone for Chinese pronouncements in support of the UN peacekeeping regime.[7] A year later, it deployed 20 military observers to the UN Transition Assistance Group (UNTAG) to help monitor elections in Namibia. This was followed by the deployment of five military observers to the UN Truce Supervision Organization (UNTSO) in the Middle East. The most significant break with past practices came with the decision to deploy 400 engineering troops and 49 military observers to the UN Transitional Authority in Cambodia (UNTAC) in 1992.

From the mid-1990s, China's interest in peacekeeping activities began to steadily expand, and this can be attributed in large part to its increasing engagement and socialization in international institutions.[8] More active participation in the UN came when there were growing debates on how the international community should reconcile the imperatives of global stability and justice and strike the right balance between state sovereignty and human rights concerns.[9] A normative consensus emerged from the debates that there is political and moral (albeit not legal) currency for the 'international community' to take exceptional measures at times of need in addressing human rights concerns, especially when the state does not fulfil its responsibility to protect its citizens.[10] Although China was a relative latecomer to these debates, the issue gained much traction within China as well, a number of international law scholars and foreign policy elites pointing to the changing nature of peacekeeping and to circumstances that warranted a more flexible interpretation and understanding of the normative principle of sovereignty.[11] In October 1998, at a conference commemorating the 50th anniversary of the Universal Declaration of Human Rights, the Chinese Foreign Minister Qian Qichen said that there was a global recognition of the 'universality of human rights' and that all nations 'observe the same international norms on human rights'. Qian added, 'We all recognise that no country's human rights situation is perfect, and that all countries are confronted with a weighty task of further promoting and protecting human rights'.[12] This important acknowledgement underlines the emergence and growing relevance of human rights values in the Chinese foreign policy lexicon.

The *Zhongguo Faxue* (中国法学, Chinese Legal Studies) journal has featured an increasing number of articles discussing state obligations to its citizens and conveying that a failure to uphold these responsibilities warrants the 'international community' to intervene to protect individuals.[13] Others have also argued that human rights are moral issues increasingly shaped by the 'international community' and that all states have a right to monitor these concerns.[14] Allen Carlson's research has led him to conclude that an increasing number of Chinese researchers, scholars, experts and policymakers have adopted more flexible views of sovereignty and intervention. Moreover, Carlson finds that some of these policy elites have also gained important access to key policymakers and top leaders within the Chinese foreign and security policy apparatus and that they were shaping and influencing the foreign policy discourse on peacekeeping.[15] In 2005, for example, President Hu Jintao announced that China would endorse a 'comprehensive strategy featuring prevention, peace restoration, peacekeeping and post-conflict reconstruction'.[16] Understanding the increasing complexity and evolving nature of peacekeeping, Hu further noted, '[i]n areas emerging from conflict, ensuring the rule of law and justice should become an integral part of the overall effort to achieve peace and stability, protecting the fundamental interests of local populations and serving the overall interests of social stability'.[17] It is too early to gauge the degree to which China has internalized and accepted these global norms, but with the atrocious human rights violations in Rwanda in 1994 in the background of these debates, and a growing number of states adhering to and upholding this declaratory norm, Chinese official policy and rhetoric with regard to sovereignty, intervention and peacekeeping have reflected this trend and become more flexible. China increasingly understands the value and importance of aligning its national interests with these emerging global conventions because active participation in peacekeeping also helps to burnish China's image, standing and reputation. More importantly, China does not want to be seen as a global outlier and wants to be recognized as a contributor to, or at least not an inhibitor of, global peace and stability.

Correspondingly, China's expanding participation and evolving role in UN peacekeeping activities in the last two decades have also helped to project a positive and constructive side to its rising prominence and power on the global stage. The Chinese leadership is acutely aware that several countries are still uncertain about the PLA's military capabilities and intentions and whether a rising China would pursue a more assertive, aggressive and potentially disruptive foreign policy. Hence, concerned with China's image and global reputation, leaders in Beijing understand that China needs to be more responsive to international expectations, to minimize tensions and conflict and to make tangible contributions to international peace and security. Peacekeeping has thus become an important priority, and helps to put into action the call from senior Chinese officials for the country to demonstrate its 'peaceful development' and commitment to a 'harmonious world'.[18] China's increased peacekeeping activity provides an opportunity to display a more positive side of the PLA's military capabilities, reassuring neighbours about its peaceful intentions, and at the same time signalling that China is further integrating into the international community and acting as a responsible power.[19] Thus China also hopes that over time it can contribute more actively to the peacekeeping debate, steering it towards greater moderation and tempering calls for excessive interventionism, and helping to shape and influence the future direction of peace operations.

As China becomes increasingly engaged and socialized within the international peacekeeping regime, a widening array of voices within the Chinese academic and policymaking realms also call for Chinese foreign and security policy to be defined beyond material power interests. An editorial in the widely read Chinese Communist Party domestic and foreign affairs journal, *Liaowang*, pointed out:

> Compared with past practices, China's diplomacy has indeed displayed a new face. If China's diplomacy before the 1980s stressed safeguarding of national security and its emphasis from the 1980s to early this century is on the creation of excellent environment for economic development, then the focus at present is to take a more active part in international affairs and play a role that a responsible power should on the basis of satisfying the security and development interests [sic].[20]

Zhang Yesui, Ambassador to the United States and former vice foreign minister, remarked at a 2007 Munich Conference on Security Policy that China's increasing involvement in UN peacekeeping missions 'reflected China's commitment to global security given the country's important role within the international system and the fact that its security and development are closely linked to that of the rest of the world'.[21] There is a growing recognition that, as China's international role evolves and expands, its interests will likewise become more global in nature. Its national security is thus becoming intrinsically linked to a stable and peaceful international environment, and this in turn is an important factor in China taking a more cooperative stance and supportive role in UN peacekeeping.

Moreover, peacekeeping, anti-piracy missions, rescue-and-relief operations, counterterrorism exercises, post-conflict reconstruction, energy security and climate change dialogues have all become major components of China's increasingly complex and dynamic international strategy.[22] These activities are broadly defined as non-traditional security issues, and their growing importance parallel the PLA's interest in mobilizing its resources and preparing for military operations other than war (MOOTW) both at home and abroad. This reflects President Hu Jintao's call for the security forces to more adequately perform and engage in MOOTW as part of the PLA's 'new historic mission'.[23] Doing so will help safeguard national interests, as well as contribute to regional and global peace, security and development. In May 2009, the PLA General Staff Department announced that it would strengthen the PLA's emergency response system and rapid deployment capacity to respond to the various MOOTW, including peacekeeping activities.[24] In June 2009 the Central Military Commission, the PLA and five of the seven military area commands met in Beijing to strengthen and improve the PLA's peacekeeping role, discussing ways to streamline the selection, organization, training and rotation of Chinese peacekeepers.[25]

To be sure, deploying Chinese troops abroad to take part in international peacekeeping missions carries inherent practical benefits for the Chinese security forces. Training and operating alongside other troop-contributing countries' forces provide invaluable experience that will allow Chinese troops to improve their responsiveness, riot control capabilities, coordination of emergency command systems and ability to carry out MOOTW more effectively. Over time, participation in peacekeeping missions abroad will also help to modernize and professionalize the security forces. For example, a sustained effort to deploy troops in Africa has meant that PLA forces are gaining greater operational knowledge of different operating environments, an advantage that few counterparts in other countries have. It also provides them with 'more knowledge about logistics, ports of debarkation, lines of communication, lines of operation, operational intelligence, local "atmospherics" and *modus operandi* and means of sustaining forces in Africa over prolonged periods'.[26] All these measures allow the Chinese security forces to display their professionalism and operational competence, on the one hand, while also demonstrating their growing deterrent capability, on the other.[27]

China's evolving approach towards UN peacekeeping is thus supported by a combination of factors. Through increasing socialization and interaction with the international community, China has become more willing to accept global norms and to contribute to peace and stability. At the same time, participation in peacekeeping also allows China to professionalize its armed forces, to test its power projection capabilities and to help attain its aspirations in becoming a major global power. In the light of these important principles, where is this evolving Chinese approach towards peacekeeping activities seen in action, and where is more needed? The next section assesses the activities, contributions and limitations of Chinese peacekeeping behaviour in praxis.

Bilateral and Multilateral Peacekeeping Training and Exchanges

According to a senior Chinese PLA official, there is general acknowledgement of the continued shortage of well-trained peacekeepers and a significant gap in the PLA's peacekeeping capabilities.[28] China has been working to professionalize and improve the calibre of its peacekeeping troops, getting them better prepared with the standard operating procedures maintained by the UN Department of Peacekeeping Operations (DPKO). Chinese troops' English and French language proficiency is generally weak, limiting their levels of interaction with other contingents and local populations. Chinese officials appear to have recognized this shortcoming and are placing increased emphasis on preparation for peacekeeping. On the home front, China has sought to improve and expand its peacekeeping training facilities. In June 2009, China unveiled a new peacekeeping training centre in Huairou in suburban Beijing.[29] The new facility is used for pre-deployment training and also serves as the main venue for international exchanges on peacekeeping. The facilities include simulation rooms, shooting and driving ranges and simulated UN peacekeeping camps and demining training grounds. In Langfang, a city in suburban Beijing, the Ministry of Public Security has also established the Civilian Peacekeeping Police Training Centre to train police officers and formed police units (FPUs).

On the international front, China has supported interfaces with foreign counterparts to help expand its peacekeeping capacity. Chinese security personnel have participated in joint peacekeeping training and exchanges with other countries, including Australia, Bangladesh, Canada, France, Germany, India, Indonesia, Mongolia, New Zealand, South Africa, Sweden, Switzerland, Thailand and the UK.[30] Through these joint training exercises, the PLA has requested foreign military counterparts to provide more in-depth and rigorous pre-deployment simulation drills to better prepare Chinese peacekeepers.[31]

Beijing has also hosted a number of international seminars on peacekeeping, bringing in foreign experts, scholars and practitioners to exchange views and share lessons learned from previous peacekeeping experiences. International seminars with the UK, as well as with Norway and Sweden, for example, have opened avenues for joint collaboration in peacekeeping. The International Committee of the Red Cross has also been tasked by the security forces to provide pre-deployment briefings for peacekeepers to help train and better prepare personnel on issues related to international humanitarian law.[32]

Within its region, China is stepping up coordination for multilateral peacekeeping activities, sponsoring and taking part in such events as the China-Association of Southeast Asian Nations (ASEAN) peacekeeping seminar in 2007.[33] China has also engaged in a series of drills and simulation exercises with Russia and Central Asian countries. 'Peace Mission 2005' was one of the largest joint military exercises China has ever carried out on a bilateral basis.[34]

The exercise involved nearly 10,000 army, air force and naval personnel and included headquarters and command-post exercises in Vladivostok, coordination of battleship movements around the Shandong Peninsula, as well as amphibious landings. While bilateral training with Russia may not be directly related to UN peacekeeping *per se*, it helps the PLA to improve its mobilization capabilities and to conduct a range of operation types that could be applicable to multilateral peacekeeping missions, encouraging China to provide more contributions to peace operations, particularly troops, as the PLA's capabilities and the calibre of its troops improve. Some observers also indicate that such military exercises are contingency plans for managing a possible humanitarian crisis in neighbour-ing North Korea.[35]

These bilateral and multilateral exchanges provide an opportunity for China to explore future prospects for international cooperation in peacekeeping, opening the door to dialogue that will help assuage concerns among China's neighbours about its strategic intentions and help China be accepted as a positive international actor. Uncertain, however, is whether political cadres in Beijing will sustain these efforts and see peacekeeping as an important policy priority. On the one hand, this would mean devoting greater financial and human resources to the PLA General Staff Department, the Ministries of Defence, Public Security and Foreign Affairs, the National Defence University and the peacekeeping training establishments. On the other hand, it would also require the political leadership to encourage and facilitate greater exchanges, dialogues, joint exercises and simu-lations with other international, regional and national actors aimed at strengthen-ing Chinese peacekeeping capacities as well as building up greater expertise within the peacekeeping epistemic community in China.

Personnel, Financial and Logistical Contributions to UN Peacekeeping

China's interest in contributing to the management of peacekeeping was marked in 2002 by an agreement to join the UN Standby Arrangement System – whereby the Ministry of Defence has a 525-strong engineering battalion, a 25-strong medical unit and two 160-strong transport companies on standby and ready for deployment with other UN forces within 90 days.[36] Moreover, Chinese peace-keepers are commended for their discipline and professionalism: by mid-2010 no allegation of misconduct had been lodged. This is important for DPKO, as reports of misconduct by peacekeepers, including corruption, sexual abuse and exploita-tion have tainted and even jeopardized UN missions.[37] In August 2007, DPKO approved China's Maj. Gen. Zhao Jingmin as force commander for the Mission in Western Sahara (MINURSO), the first time a Chinese national held such a senior position.[38] Elsewhere, PLA colonels are increasingly solicited as senior level staff officers in DPKO as well as in missions.[39]

Notwithstanding these positive acknowledgements and contributions, Chinese officials stress that the ratio of Chinese appointments to senior ranking posts in DPKO remains lower than that of other major powers. This is a legiti-mate concern, as the burden of troop contributions has increasingly fallen on developing countries, while Western countries tend to deploy fewer troops but occupy key decision-making and support posts in DPKO and in UN missions.[40]

UN officials are likely to continue working closely with Chinese counterparts to see that China's interest in increasing its contributions is sustained. Chinese officials could play increasingly active roles in policy-planning, force generation, coordination and other leadership roles. As former under secretary-general for peacekeeping operations Jean-Marie Guéhenno, argued, such appointments would mark an important recognition of China's positive role and growing importance in peacekeeping,[41] not least because China is the largest troop contributor among the permanent members of the UN Security Council.

On the whole, however, China needs to engage more substantively in UN peacekeeping operations. In terms of financial contribution, China provides about 3 per cent of the peacekeeping budget, significantly less than most other Security Council members. According to the UN Multi-Donor Trust Fund Office, China has also contributed a total of US$3 million to the UN Peacebuilding Fund from 2007 to 2009, but has yet to provide financial support for other aid programmes or trust funds that are critically needed.[42] Consequently, China will need to increase its financial contributions if it wishes to play a role commensurate with its Security Council and global status.

Moreover, China's increasing social interactions in the UN peacekeeping regime means that there will be expectations of China to expand its troop commitments in areas where there are critical needs. China initially offered to deploy troops to the Lebanon in 2006,[43] and officials are on record as saying that China remains open to the idea of deploying troops if DPKO requested them,[44] though it remains to be seen whether China would respond favourably. Likewise, some UN officials have called for China to contribute such force enablers as light tactical and transport helicopters and more ground transport units to help sustain and facilitate operations. In short, as China seeks to play a more active role in shaping and influencing UN peacekeeping affairs, it could consider increasing personnel, financial and logistical contributions.

Contributions to Peace and Stability in Africa

Approximately three-quarters of China's peacekeeping contributions are currently based on the African continent, providing critical support for 'peace enforcement' and post-conflict reconstruction in Liberia, the Democratic Republic of Congo (DRC), southern Sudan and Côte d'Ivoire. Moreover, the 2009 Forum on China and Africa Cooperation (FOCAC) declaration stated that China had agreed to step up coordination with the UN, the African Union (AU) and regional African institutions to address security issues on the continent.[45] The action plan identified ways that China would provide assistance and enhance cooperation with multilateral partners in the prevention, management and resolution of regional conflicts.

China and the AU have also facilitated interaction by establishing the Strategic Dialogue Mechanism as a regularized and institutionalized measure to exchange views on relations and security issues. This effort further complements the multilateral process at the UN where Chinese and African foreign ministers jointly decided to launch a political consultation mechanism at the UN headquarters in September 2007 to ensure a more calibrated approach in addressing regional security issues.[46] Such mechanisms have increased regular exchanges, opening the door to greater consultation on areas of convergence and divergence.

As the China–Africa relationship matures, China's expanding military, political and economic ties in Africa will need to be managed to complement China's contributions to peacekeeping in Africa. UN officials report some frustration at their lack of access to details of extensive bilateral military ties between China and African countries where Chinese peacekeepers are also deployed (such as the DRC, Liberia and Sudan).[47] It is therefore unclear whether those arrangements complement China's peacekeeping activities and UN efforts to provide greater security and stability in Africa. Since 2008 UN officials have been exploring with the Chinese mission ways of supporting security sector reform and issues related to disarmament, demobilization and reintegration of ex-combatants in African states. The Chinese delegation has reportedly not been obstructive; but nor has it taken any major initiatives in this regard.[48]

Likewise, as China's diplomatic and business interests deepen in Africa, crafting appropriate policies to balance them is likely to become more complicated. The goodwill earned by Chinese peacekeeping contingents repairing roads, improving state infrastructure and offering medical assistance could be undermined by other bilateral activities of the Chinese government, state-owned companies, entrepreneurs and émigrés across the continent. As African states emerge from protracted internal conflicts, China wants to be recognized as a partner in African development. The challenge then will be to improve oversight and coordination to ensure that bilateral military engagements and a widening array of commercial links in the continent not only complement the Chinese peacekeeping presence but also contribute to development and stability in Africa.

Fundamental Concerns about Respecting State Sovereignty

Although rhetoric and government policies seem to have supported UN peacekeeping, traditional ideas about state sovereignty persist. It appears that China continues to review calls for international intervention on a case-by-case basis. There are times when China has supported intervention on humanitarian grounds, including in East Timor in 1999, though a non-UN force led by Australia. China also contributed a civilian police contingent to support the subsequent UN mission (see Marc Lanteigne's article, this issue). In 2003, in response to growing instability in the DRC and Liberia, the Ambassador to the UN, Zhang Yishan, argued that the UN should intervene in such conflict areas 'earlier, faster and more forcefully'.[49] A similar view was expressed by some observers reflecting on the tragedy that unfolded in Rwanda.[50]

Traditionally, China has objected to authorizing or extending the mandates of UN peacekeeping missions in countries that recognized Taiwan. In January 1997, China vetoed a proposed mission to Guatemala until the Guatemalan government gave assurances that it would no longer support a General Assembly vote on admitting Taiwan to the UN. The Verification Mission in Guatemala (MINUGUA) could then proceed.[51] In 1999, China vetoed the continuation of the UN Preventive Deployment in Macedonia (UNPREDEP) two weeks after suspending diplomatic ties with the country over its recognition of Taiwan, bringing an end to that experiment in conflict prevention.[52] Some Chinese peacekeeping specialists later acknowledged that this was a 'difficult lesson for China' and that the government should have 'considered Macedonia's interests more than its own national interests'.[53] In the case of Haiti, in spite of the lack of full diplomatic ties with Beijing, China supported the UN from 2004 to 2010 with FPU deployments. However, China apparently used the threat of curtailing the mission to warn Haiti against any high-profile diplomatic exchanges in support of Taiwan. Some observers contend that Haiti's continued recognition of Taiwan was a reason for the withdrawal in 2010, while others have indicated that China was 'uncomfortable' with the overwhelming US civilian and military presence following the earthquake.[54] The Haiti case may indicate that there are limitations to China's commitment to peacekeeping.

While China's withdrawal from Haiti may be a disappointment, Darfur provides a prominent example of engagement. Responding in part to mounting criticism of its relations with the Sudanese government, in 2006 China began exerting pressure on Sudan to allow UN and AU peacekeepers into Darfur.[55] In November 2006, with the humanitarian situation worsening, the Ambassador to the UN, Wang Guangya, was widely credited with gaining Sudanese acceptance of the UN/AU hybrid peacekeeping force of 20,000 troops in Darfur. Subsequently, China also became the first permanent member of the UN Security Council to commit and deploy (315) troops there.[56] In February 2007, President Hu Jintao visited Sudan and met President Omar al-Bashir. The visit drew widespread criticism internationally, particularly from the United States, since China was seen as abetting alleged genocidal acts committed in Darfur. However, Hu reportedly intervened to press al-Bashir to abide by international commitments, and he delivered a rare public statement that outlined the basis for China's approach towards resolving the Darfur crisis, stating that '[i]t is imperative to improve the situation in Darfur and living conditions of local people'.[57] While this could be interpreted as mere rhetoric, that is about as close as a Chinese leader has come to publicly warning and chiding a foreign leader. What the senior-level leadership says on these sensitive issues is important because it reflects in a large part their changing behaviour and understanding of peacekeeping and non-interventionism.

Following a broad survey of Chinese peacekeeping principles and praxis, an important question remains as to whether China will expand its engagement in international peacekeeping. To be sure, there are uncertainties that will constrain China in this respect. China will most likely be cautious and selective, and continued cost−benefit calculus will ensure that policy will follow a far from linear, predetermined path. If the UN turns to China more often, it should temper its expectations to seeing a cautious − and at times perhaps even reluctant − response on China's part. Practical matters of political, military and bureaucratic will and capacity are sure to slow China's responsiveness. With about 2,100 troops deployed abroad, an equal number of troops are currently undergoing training to prepare for troop rotation. This figure is not insignificant, given such constraints as the shortage of well-trained personnel with English or French language skills. Likewise, China's limited air-lift and sea-lift capacities further restrict the PLA's ability to rapidly deploy troops over long distances. Chinese officials also acknowledge that the PLA and the police force need to improve their understanding of peacekeeping standard operational procedures, international humanitarian law, and military regulations and manuals.

There are ways to address gaps in China's peacekeeping capabilities and to help enlarge China's role and commitment to international peacekeeping. Providing greater leadership opportunities for Chinese peacekeepers in field missions and in DPKO would engage China more closely in decision-making processes. There are also prospects of inviting Chinese delegations to participate more actively in (or at least observe) training and simulation exercises organized by other countries. Such constructive engagement could help China become more cognizant of peacekeeping norms.

In the last two decades, China's engagement in international institutions has exposed it to normative values concerning human rights and conflict resolution which are gaining traction and being factored into its foreign policy discourse. It is still early days to determine how far China has accepted these norms; more importantly, however, China's options will be increasingly shaped and influenced by measures taken by other actors, particularly Western states. When there has been broad international consensus regarding a specific intervention, as in Afghanistan, China has tended to lend its support, rather than be viewed as obstructionist. These measures thus alter China's cost–benefit calculus so that, for example, concerns about preserving state sovereignty have been moderated in certain instances, and this is evidenced in changes to China's definitions of interest or by China's linking its interests to image, reputation and status.

However, the epistemic community currently addressing peacekeeping remains small in China. There are few practitioners and scholars who have relevant expertise. There is growing awareness, however, that peacekeeping is emerging as an important topic, and more is likely to be done at the semi- and nongovernmental levels to help build and expand this epistemic community.[58] Regularized international delegation visits and exchanges could foster this process. There are precedents in other areas such as arms control and non-proliferation, HIV/AIDS and public health, and international trade.[59] Such an interactive process would forge debates and discussions among Chinese policy elites about China's future role and contributions in international peacekeeping. A socialization process is underway because China has realized that peacekeeping is going to be an important function in which its image as a global actor will be forged. Increasing Chinese involvement in peacekeeping thus provides an important and widening opportunity for other countries to build a more effective and inclusive international peacekeeping regime.

NOTES

1. See Bates Gill, *Rising Star: China's New Security Diplomacy*, Washington, DC: Brookings Institution Press, 2007; Robert Sutter, *Chinese Foreign Relations: Power and Policy Since the Cold*

War, Lanham, MD: Rowman & Littlefield, 2008; Alastair Iain Johnston and Robert Ross (eds), *New Directions in the Study of China's Foreign Policy*, Stanford, CA: Stanford University Press, 2006; Evan Medeiros and M. Taylor Fravel, 'China's New Diplomacy', *Foreign Affairs*, Vol.82, No.6, 2003, pp.22–35.

2. UN Department of Peacekeeping Operations, 'UN Missions Summary Detailed by Country', 1 Oct. 2010 (at: www.un.org/Depts/dpko/dpko/contributors/).

3. Ibid.

4. Bruce Jones, Richard Gowan and Jake Sherman, 'Building on Brahimi: Peacekeeping in an Era of Strategic Uncertainty', New York University Center on International Cooperation, 2009 (at: www.peacekeepingbestpractices.unlb.org/PBPS/Library/CIC%20New%20Horizon%20Think% 20Piece.pdf).

5. See Bates Gill and Chin-Hao Huang, *China's Expanding Role in Peacekeeping: Prospects and Policy Implications*, Stockholm: Stockholm International Peace Research Institute, 2009; International Crisis Group, 'China's Growing Role in UN Peacekeeping', Brussels, 2009; Stefan Staehle, 'China's Shifting Attitude towards UN Peacekeeping Operations', *China Quarterly*, No.195, 2008, pp.631–55.

6. See Samuel Kim, 'China's International Organization Behavior', in Thomas Robinson and David Shambaugh (eds), *Chinese Foreign Policy: Theory and Practice*, Oxford: Oxford University Press, 1995, pp.420–2; Yin He, *China's Changing Policy on UN Peacekeeping Operations*, Stockholm: Institute for Security and Development Policy, 2007.

7. See Kim (see n.6 above).

8. See Alastair Iain Johnston, *Social States: China in International Institutions 1980–2000*, Princeton, NJ: Princeton University Press, 2008; G. John Ikenberry and Charles Kupchan, 'Socialization and Hegemonic Power', *International Organization*, Vol.44, No.3, pp.283–315; Ronald Jepperson, Alexander Wendt and Peter Katzenstein, 'Norms, Identity and Culture in National Security', Peter Katzenstein (ed.), *The Culture of National Security*, New York: Columbia University Press, 1996, pp.33–75.

9. Hedley Bull, *The Anarchical Society: A Study of Order in World Politics*, London: Macmillan, 1995.

10. Taylor Seybolt, *Humanitarian Military Intervention: The Conditions for Success and Failure*, Oxford: Oxford University Press, 2007.

11. Allen Carlson, 'China's Approach to Sovereignty and Intervention', in Alastair Iain Johnston and Robert Ross (eds), *New Directions in the Study of China's Foreign Policy*, Stanford, CA: Stanford University Press, 2006, pp.217–41.

12. 'Qian Qichen Urges Further Promotion of International Human Rights', *Xinhua News* (Beijing), 20 Oct. 2008 [trans. BBC Monitoring Service, International Reports].

13. See Zeng Lingliang [曾令良], 'Lun lengzhan hou shidai de guojia zhuquan' [论冷战后时代的国家主权] (A discussion of state sovereignty in the post-Cold-War era), *Zhongguo faxue* [中国法学] (Chinese Legal Studies), No.1, 1998, pp.109–20; Xu Guojin [徐构进], 'Guojia lüxing guoji renquan yiwu de xiandu' [国家履行国际人权义务的限度] (The limits on state performance of human rights obligations), *Zhongguo faxue* [中国法学] (Chinese Legal Studies of Law), No.2, 1992, pp.13–20.

14. See Allen Carlson, *Unifying China, Integrating with the World: Securing Chinese Sovereignty in the Reform Era*, Stanford, CA: Stanford University Press, 2005; Li Buyun [李步云], 'Renquan de liangge lilun wenti' [人权的两个理论问题] (Two theoretical human rights issues), *Zhongguo faxue* [中国法学] (Chinese Legal Studies), No.3, 1999, pp.38–42; Cheng Shuaihua [成帅华], 'Guojia zhuquan yu guoji renquan de ruogan wenti' [国家主权与国际人权的若干问题] (Issues involving international human rights and state sovereignty), *Ouzhou* [欧洲] (Europe), No.1, 2000, pp.32–5; Shi Yinhong [时殷弘], 'Lun ershi shiji guoji guifan tixi' [论二十世纪国际规范体系] (A discussion of the system of international norms in the twentieth century), *Guoji luntan* [国际论坛] (International Forum), No.6, 2000, pp.8–10.

15. Carlson (see n.11 above).

16. UN doc., S/PV.5261, 14 Sept. 2005.

17. UN doc., S/PV.5225, 12 July 2005.

18. 'Hu Jintao Says China Pursues Peaceful Development', *People's Daily* (Beijing), 3 Sept. 2005 [trans. BBC Monitoring Service, International Reports].

19. See Wang Yizhou [王逸舟] (ed.), *Mohe zhong de jiangou: zhongguo yu guoji zuji guanxi de duoshijiao toushi* [磨合中的建构：中国与国际组织关系的多视角透视] (Construction in Contradiction: A Multiple Insight into Relationships between China and International Organizations), Beijing: China Development Press, 2003; Jing-Dong Yuan, 'Multilateral Intervention and State Sovereignty: Chinese Views on UN Peacekeeping Operations', *Political Science*, Vol.49, No.2, 1998, pp.275–95.

20. 'PRC's "New Diplomacy" Stress On More Active International Role', *Liaowang* (Beijing), 11 July 2005 [trans. World News Connection.]
21. Nicholas Fiorenza, 'China Bolsters Peacekeeping Commitment', *Jane's Defence Weekly*, 14 Feb. 2007.
22. See Zhongying Pang, 'China's Changing Attitude to UN Peacekeeping', *International Peacekeeping*, Vol.12, No.1, 2005, pp.87–104; 'Wang Jisi Discusses Issues in PRC Foreign Policy Strategy', *Guoji Zhengzhi Yanjiu*, 25 Nov. 2007 [trans. Open Source Center]; 'Chinese Expert Views Army Counteracting Non-traditional Security Threats', *Zhongguo Xinwen She* (Beijing), 20 June 2007 [trans. BBC Monitoring Service, International Reports].
23. James Mulvenon, 'Chairman Hu and the PLA's "New Historic Missions"', *China Leadership Monitor*, No.27, 2009, pp.1–11; Cynthia Watson, 'The Chinese Armed Forces and Non-traditional Missions: A Growing Tool of Statecraft', *China Brief*, Vol.9, No.4, 2009, pp.9–12.
24. 'PLA Constructs MOOTW Arms Force System', *People's Liberation Army Daily* (Beijing), 14 May 2009 [trans. BBC Monitoring Service, International Reports].
25. 'PLA Peacekeeping Work Conference Held in Beijing', *People's Liberation Army Daily*, 26 June 2009 [trans. BBC Monitoring Service, International Reports].
26. Philip Rogers, 'China and UN Peacekeeping Operations in Africa', (US) *Naval War College Review*, Vol.60, No.2, 2007, p.89.
27. 'The Deterrence Function of Launching Military Training Exercises', *Jiefangjun Bao* (Beijing), 29 Apr. 2008 [trans. Open Source Center].
28. 'Chinese Deputy Military Chief on Raising Army's Peacekeeping Role', *Zhongguo Xinwen She*, 22 June 2007 [trans. BBC Monitoring Service, International Reports].
29. 'China Opens First Peacekeeping Training Center', *China Daily*, 25 June 2009 [trans. BBC Monitoring Service, International Reports].
30. Ping Zhang, 'Remarks on the People's Liberation Army's Participation in UN Peacekeeping Operations', speech at conference on 'Multi-dimensional and Integrated Peace Operations: Trends and Challenges', Beijing, 26–7 Mar. 2007.
31. Ibid.
32. International Committee of the Red Cross, *Annual Report 2009*, Geneva, 2010, pp.3–4.
33. 'Defence Ministry Touts Deepened China–ASEAN Security Cooperation', *Xinhua News*, 30 Mar. 2009 [trans. BBC Monitoring Service, International Reports].
34. Alyson J.K. Bailes, *The Shanghai Cooperation Organization*, Stockholm: Stockholm International Peace Research Institute, 2007; Marc Lanteigne, 'Security, Strategy and the Former USSR: China and the Shanghai Cooperation Organization', in Shaun Breslin (ed.), *A Handbook of Chinese International Relations*, London: Routledge, 2010, pp.166–76.
35. Stephen Blank, 'Peace Mission 2009: A Military Scenario beyond Central Asia', *China Brief*, 20 Aug. 2009, pp.7–9.
36. 'Chinese Peacekeepers in Action', *People's Liberation Army Daily*, 15 Jan. 2003 [trans. BBC Monitoring Service, International Reports].
37. Sharon Wiharta, 'The Legitimacy of Peace Operations', in Bates Gill (ed.), *SIPRI Yearbook 2009: Armaments, Disarmament and International Security*, Oxford: Oxford University Press, 2009, pp.95–116.
38. 'UN Secretary-General Appoints Major General Zhao Jingmin of China as Force Commander for Western Sahara Mission', press release, UN Department of Public Information, 28 Aug. 2007 (at: www.un.org/News/Press/docs//2007/sga1089.doc.htm).
39. Gill and Huang (see n.5 above).
40. For troop-contributing countries and appointments, see 'UN Missions Summary Detailed by Country', 1 Oct. 2010 (at: www.un.org/en/peacekeeping/contributors).
41. 'UN Official Commends China's Role in Peacekeeping', *Xinhua News*, 16 Jan. 2007 [trans. BBC Monitoring Service, International Reports].
42. 'Contributor/Partner Fact Sheet', United Nations Development Group, 1 Oct. 2010 (at: http://mdtf.undp.org/factsheet/donor/00089).
43. 'China Considers Deploying Combat Troops to UN Mission in Lebanon', *People's Daily*, 28 Sept. 2006 [trans. BBC Monitoring Service, International Reports].
44. 'Chinese Combat Troops "Can Be Part of UN Peacekeeping" ', *China Daily*, 7 July 2010 [trans. BBC Monitoring Service, International Reports].
45. 'FOCAC Sharm el Sheikh Action Plan 2010–2012', Forum on China–Africa Cooperation, 12 Nov. 2009 (at: www.focac.org/eng/dsjbzjhy/hywj/t626387.htm).
46. Ibid.
47. Interviews with UN officials, Kinshasa, March–April 2008.
48. Ibid.

49. 'China Takes on Major Peacekeeping Role', *Jane's Intelligence Review*, 1 Nov. 2003.
50. Remarks at a conference on 'China and Multilateral Peace Operations', Oslo, 18–19 Mar. 2010.
51. 'Security Council Authorizes Deployment of UN Military Observers to Verify Implementation of Cease-Fire Agreement in Guatemala', press release, UN Department of Public Information, 20 Jan. 1997 (at: www.un.org/News/Press/docs/1997/19970120.sc6314.html); International Security and Institutions Research Group, *Vetoed Draft Resolutions in the UN Security Council 1946–2009*, London: Foreign and Commonwealth Office, 2009.
52. 'Taiwan Criticizes China UN Veto', *BBC News*, 26 Feb. 1999 (at: http://news.bbc.co.uk/2/hi/285835.stm).
53. Pang (see n.22 above).
54. Interviews with Chinese scholars and officials, Beijing, June 2010; 'Analysis: UN Refocuses Haiti Mission', *United Press International*, 16 Feb. 2007.
55. Chin-Hao Huang, 'US–China Relations and Darfur', *Fordham International Law Journal*, Vol.31, No.4, 2008, pp.827–42.
56. Edward Cody, 'China Given Credit for Darfur Role', *Washington Post*, 13 Jan. 2007 (at: www.washingtonpost.com/wp-dyn/content/article/2007/01/12/AR2007011201924.html).
57. 'Hu Puts Forward Principle on Darfur Issue', *Xinhua News*, 5 Feb. 2007 [trans. BBC Monitoring Service, International Reports].
58. Interviews (see n.54 above); remarks (see n.50 above).
59. Quansheng Zhao, 'Policymaking Processes of Chinese Foreign Policy: The Role of Policy Communities and Think Tanks', in Shaun Breslin (ed.), *A Handbook of Chinese International Relations*, London: Routledge, 2010, pp.22–34.

Why Does China Participate in Intrusive Peacekeeping? Understanding Paternalistic Chinese Discourses on Development and Intervention

SHOGO SUZUKI

Why does China continue to participate in highly intrusive peacekeeping operations which, it can be argued, suspend the sovereignty of the host state and attempt to transform it into a liberal democratic, market capitalist state? This article highlights the significant role of Chinese paternalism in providing the ideological justification for intervening in states' domestic affairs. Focusing on the quasi-official annual publication, the *China Modernization Report*, and its discourses on development, this article contends that some Chinese discourses interpret modernization as a linear and universal process, and interpret different stages of development in distinctly hierarchical terms. This places China as superior *vis-à-vis* many underdeveloped states. Such notions of 'superiority', in turn, lead to paternalistic thinking that justifies China (and other relatively 'developed' states) intervening in underdeveloped states and societies in order to 'guide' them to the path of 'development'.

The People's Republic of China (PRC) has been an important contributor to UN peacekeeping operations (PKOs) since the 1990s. As of 30 June 2010, it was the 15th largest contributor of military and police personnel, ahead of any other permanent member of the Security Council.[1] This was not always the case: China had previously viewed PKOs with the utmost suspicion, frequently denouncing them as tools of US or Soviet imperialism, and refusing to make any financial or human contributions.[2]

China's transformation from a strident critic to a strong supporter results from several factors. First, as noted by Miwa Hirono and Marc Lanteigne (introduction to this special issue), the PRC considers that international multilateral institutions can play an important role in furthering international stability, a positive factor deserving China's support. Thus, 'active participation is a demonstration of China's commitment to the UN and its security functions as mandated by the UN Charter'.[3] Second, participation in PKOs gives the Chinese military valuable experience of deployment overseas, providing 'some of the technical skills and knowledge necessary for force modernization'.[4] Third, participating in PKOs can bring about political and economic benefits, protecting Chinese interests in the host state, while helping to establish a pro-China government in the host state once the peacekeeping mission has concluded.[5] Finally, participation is seen as an important means to acquire the image of a 'responsible great power (*fuzeren de daguo*, 负责任的大国)'.[6] China's rise to power has often been viewed with suspicion, and participation in PKOs is regarded as a useful means to allay fears of a 'China threat' by demonstrating that the PRC is prepared to uphold international norms.[7]

Nevertheless, China's seemingly new-found enthusiasm poses several puzzles. China's increasing internalization of global norms and evolving identity as a 'status quo' power that upholds these social structures has already been documented (see Hirono and Lanteigne this issue) and one need not be overly sceptical of China's desire to fulfil this role through PKO participation. Since 1990 PKO mandates have increasingly moved away from the prevention of *inter*-state war to the reconstruction of states ravaged by *civil* war. To this end, the operations have sought to transform war-torn states into market capitalist, liberal democratic states, supported by the (sometimes tenuous) belief that such modes of governance provide the most stable and peaceful forms of government.[8] This rationalization, which I term 'international paternalism', assumes one party (in the context of this article, the UN) possesses superior knowledge of how states ought to develop, and that it possesses the unique moral duty to guide others along this 'correct' pathway to progress. Accordingly, such 'international paternalists' restrict the freedom of those who lack this 'knowledge' to choose their own mode of governance or economic development. This concept has historically manifested itself in colonialism in the nineteenth century (as epitomized by the famous term 'the white man's burden') as well as institutions such as international trusteeships. In today's context, 'international paternalism' can be seen as a by-product of the 'liberal triumphalism' that emerged after the collapse of the communist bloc in 1989. It also reflects the renewed Western dominance of the post-Cold-War 'international community', where 'legitimate statehood' is defined restrictively along Western liberal democratic models.[9]

On the surface, we would expect the PRC to be a reluctant participant in these PKOs. It has long been seen as a champion of sovereignty and non-intervention, owing to its experience of imperialist encroachment in the nineteenth and twentieth centuries (known as the 'hundred years of humiliation') and its self-perception as a member of the developing world. Its 'Five Principles of Peaceful Coexistence' include non-intervention in the domestic affairs of other states, and this is one of the core norms of Chinese foreign policy that exert considerable influence on decision-making.[10] Support for intrusive PKOs would not only defy long-held beliefs that guide China's international relations, but also make the PRC vulnerable to charges of neo-colonialism.[11] How, then, does China square its allegedly firm beliefs in international equality with its participation in these missions? Do the PRC's words match its deeds? If not, why not? Are there any alternative intellectual strands in the PRC which justify international paternalism?

This article contends that the relatively under-explored factor of Chinese paternalism may provide some of the ideological motivations for China's continued commitment to PKOs. It examines Chinese works on economic development, with particular focus on the *Zhongguo xiandaihua baogao* (*China Modernization Report*, 中国现代化报告), an annual report that represents quasi-official academic discourse on development. I argue that the PRC's understanding of development is deeply hierarchical and envisages a universal trajectory of development. It shares some common features with the 'civilizing mission' discourse that coloured nineteenth-century imperialism, modernization theory and more recent calls for the propagation of liberal democracy.[12] This, in turn, challenges the long-held view of a strong ideological aversion to international intervention in other states' internal affairs, and suggests that continued Chinese support for and participation in intrusive forms of PKOs can be anticipated.

It is extremely difficult to identify a direct and concrete causal link between a particular discourse and political decision-making. The conclusions of this article are therefore necessarily of a tentative nature, and further research must be carried out to establish the exact degree of influence of such academic discourses on the PRC's PKO policy. The intention here is to shed light on why China's participation in intrusive PKOs is perhaps not as contradictory to the minds of the Beijing policy elite as official rhetoric suggests. The academic discourses are important for several reasons. First, the increasing openness of Chinese foreign-policy-making means that '[a]nalysts with policy expertise, national reputations or personal connections with policy makers can exercise policy influence... Some policy makers actively solicit analysis that addresses current policy issues or supports their views'.[13] The *Zhongguo xiandaihua baogao* is written and edited by scholars based at the highly prestigious national academic institution, the Chinese Academy of Sciences, and it would seem plausible to assume that its findings are read by, and have some impact on, the formulation of Chinese foreign, economic and developmental policy.

Second, much has been made of China's 'charm offensive' in the developing world (such as its hosting of the Forum on China–Africa Cooperation or the hosting of the 2004 Shanghai Conference for Scaling up Poverty Reduction and Global Learning Process), whereby China is seen as increasing its political power by gathering support in the developing world by calling for a more 'democratic' international community that is less dominated by the West.[14] What much of these analyses miss, however, is China's desire to be seen as both a member of the developing world and as a 'responsible great power' that seeks to uphold the military and normative status quo of the international order, and how this may be reflected in Chinese foreign policy. The two identities can lead to very different and contradictory policy discourses in the PRC, and it is imperative that these are analysed in greater detail to get a fuller picture of how China formulates its foreign policy.

Sovereign Equality and PKOs: Rhetoric and Reality

If China's statements on its commitment to international equality and non-intervention were to be taken at face value, one would expect the PRC to display several traits with regard to assisting underdeveloped, war-torn states. First, one would expect the PRC to adhere to its PKOs policy, namely that 'the host state's consent must be sought and given in peacekeeping activities, and its sovereign independence and territorial integrity must be strictly respected'.[15] Second, the Chinese would view their relations with states hosting PKOs on equal terms, without any notion of 'superior' knowledge of economic and social development. Finally, and consequently, the PRC could be expected to avoid the propagation of a 'model' of economic and political development for other states to follow, as well as involvement in any activities promoting such 'universal' models. Instead, each state should be allowed to choose its own path of development. Indeed, Chinese analysts point out that attempts to transplant liberal democracies and market capitalism to non-Western states such as Iraq are unlikely to be unsuccessful,[16] and that 'the imposition of an essentially Western ideology ... is a form of neoimperialism'.[17]

China's decision to get involved in various PKOs since the end of the Cold War contradicts these self-professed principles in several ways. First, the new types of PKOs that have emerged since the 1990s entail a considerable erosion of the host state's sovereignty. The shift towards promoting liberal democracy and market capitalism as the sole 'legitimate' form of statehood has also made inroads into these peacekeeping roles, and many operations now aim to reconstruct war-torn states along these lines. As Eva Bertram notes, they 'are nothing short of attempts at nation building, they seek to remake a state's political institutions, security forces, and economic arrangements'.[18] For instance, the *United Nations Peacekeeping Operations: Principles and Guidelines* lists '[e]lectoral assistance' as one of its key activities. 'The holding of free and fair elections', the document states, 'is often written into the peace agreement underlying a multidimensional United Nations peacekeeping operation and represents a major milestone towards the establishment of a legitimate state'.[19] This goal is visible in the mandates for several PKOs that China participates in: the UN Organization Stabilization Mission in the Democratic Republic of Congo (MONUSCO), the UN Mission in Liberia (UNMIL), UN Mission in Sudan (UNMIS), UN Operation in Côte d'Ivoire (UNOCI) and UN Integrated Mission in Timor-Leste (UNMIT). All are charged with the responsibility to undertake and assist in legal and judicial reform, assist in the organization of local and national elections and facilitate economic development.[20]

These goals, which entail a substantial degree of top-down social engineering, are problematic in that they may constitute a violation of the sovereignty of the host state. While it is true that all PKOs are required to obtain the consent of the host state,[21] given that many post-Cold-War PKOs have frequently taken place in states ravaged by civil war and lacking a functioning government, it is doubtful 'whether [the host state] can consent to outside intervention as it may no longer represent the governed'.[22] Furthermore, the extensive mandates given to these operations often result in 'mission creep', whereby the operation ends up (at times inadvertently, given the lack of capacity for the host state to govern its own territory effectively) overshadowing the authority of the host state.[23]

Even more troubling is the paternalistic nature of these PKOs, in that they effectively treat the peoples of the host state as politically immature and incapable of making 'correct' decisions pertaining to their own future. As Philip Darby notes with regard to this new type of PKO:

[b]ringing development and security together in a single fold opened the doors to attempts to re-engineer the state, to remake whole societies and to recast the identities of ordinary people, all in the interests of 'best practice' as laid down by external experts. This is interventionism on a scale beyond the imaginings of the former rulers of empire.[24]

The *Principles and Guidelines* document makes little attempt to hide this, stating that 'experience has shown that, in the short-term, a United Nations peacekeeping operation may have little choice but to initiate longer-term institution and capacity-building efforts, due to the inability of other actors to take the lead'.[25]

Guiding Children to Enlightenment: China and Global Development

Why, then, does the PRC persist in sending personnel to such highly intrusive missions with a 'social engineering' agenda? Certainly China's own security concerns are one factor. China shares borders with states that are arguably 'failed' states or characterized by weak, ineffectual government, such as Afghanistan or Pakistan.[26] State failure in these areas could result in China's border regions becoming havens for radical Islamic groups that could potentially link up with secession movements in Xinjiang, as well as bring about economic and refugee problems.[27] Beyond the PRC's borders, as China's key national goal of economic development requires secure markets to procure resources and sell Chinese goods, the stabilization of 'failed states' through paternalistic, intrusive means is acceptable to Beijing, provided it is done through multilateral institutions such as PKOs, the World Bank or regional organizations.[28] The Chinese are therefore unlikely to oppose such efforts, even though they may be slightly uncomfortable with the dilution of the sovereignty norm that they entail.[29]

Chinese Discourses on 'Modernization': A Universalist Vision?

Yet, pragmatic reasons alone do not explain the lack of concerted Chinese opposition to 'social engineering' attempts in recent PKOs. While the West has been regularly criticized for its universalistic conceptualization of development, it is highly questionable whether or not the Chinese really do reject a 'universal' trajectory of development. While remaining wary of historical essentialism, it is possible to argue that such universalistic thinking stems from China's traumatic encounter with the expanding European international order in the late nineteenth century.[30] Where technological attainment was believed by the Europeans to provide an 'objective' marker for 'civilizational progress',[31] the Chinese gradually internalized Western notions of a unitary and teleological 'civilization' 'with emphasis on Western culture and technology'.[32]

Chinese scholars have been critical of the implied notion in these theories that non-European polities need to import Western institutions if they are to achieve 'modernity', a view widely shared by other scholars throughout the world.[33] Yet, the pathway of development as depicted in the *Zhongguo xiandaihua baogao* – which is proposed as a distinctively Chinese 'Second Modernization

Theory' – has a distinctively teleological flavour.[34] The modernization process is divided into stages of 'agricultural revolution' (*nongye geming*, 农业革命) leading to the higher stage of 'industrial revolution' (*gongye geming*, 工业革命), which is followed by an 'intelligence revolution' (*zhishi geming*, 知识革命). While conventional modernization theories tended to end at the stage of industrialization, the Chinese version goes one step further, envisaging the emergence of a high-technology, high-skilled industry- and service-sector-dominated 'intelligence civilization', which appears to be in reaction to developed states' gradual move away from traditional heavy industry. However, this almost linear depiction of development bears a close resemblance to modernization theories in Western literature (as well as lingering influences of teleological interpretations of history seen in Marxism) and effectively 'sees Western theories on the development process as the only legitimate body of knowledge on which to base the Chinese theory'.[35]

Furthermore, to measure the degree to which 'modernization' has taken place, the Chinese appear to rely heavily on seemingly 'scientific' and 'neutral' statistics such as gross national product per capita, the ratio of the population engaged in agriculture or the service industry, urbanization and literacy, and explicitly rank states in accordance with these data.[36] In this sense, modernization is 'a series of transitions from primitive, subsistence economies to technology-intensive, industrialized economies' with strong influences 'of nineteenth-century evolutionary theory'.[37] This contrasts with the more recent 'discourse of international development', which has 'veered away from the previous, strongly criticized, *unilateral emphasis on economic indicators and structural models originating in the West*' and begun emphasizing 'a socially and culturally "sensitive" framework'.[38] Contrary to Chinese claims that the PRC does not attempt to propagate a 'single model' of development, such discourses on modernization are doing exactly what many developed states of the West are accused of doing, albeit indirectly. Given that the 'idea of a "civilizing mission" has been used to describe the *hierarchical* nature' of civilizations,[39] the very notion that there are inferior and superior states in terms of attaining 'modernity' creates opportunity for paternalistic intervention in these 'backward' polities. The narrow scope given to the path of 'modernization' and its indicators also offers little leeway for alternative pathways of development, effectively transmitting the message that the goal of 'modernization' and 'development' and the means needed to achieve this are pre-defined.[40]

To explore the implications of this in the more specific context of the PRC's participation in PKOs, one should keep in mind the aforementioned overlap between the oft-criticized one-size-fits-all approaches to development epitomized by recent PKOs and Chinese definition of development. This is not to imply the Chinese do not express some misgivings about the paternalism such approaches may engender. Stressing the importance of the non-interference norm in defining the parameters of Chinese foreign policy, Sophie Richardson states that China had 'mixed feelings' about the UN Transitional Authority in Cambodia (UNTAC) because of 'UNTAC's involvement in drafting laws, organizing campaign rallies, and helping determine whether political parties had met eligibility requirements to run in the elections', fearing that this would encroach upon

Cambodia's sovereign authority.[41] Yet, it is crucial to note here that the PRC's primary concerns appear to have been 'about the extent to which foreigners were becoming involved in Cambodia', rather than the peacebuilding model upon which UNTAC was based. The PRC's shared view of 'what is good for the host' means that it is ultimately likely to go ahead with the PKO programmes aimed at reproducing market capitalist, liberal democratic states. As one Chinese analyst noted, even if the PRC had no intention of engaging in paternalistic behaviour, 'if China agrees to send PKO, it means that it thinks that PKO would help them. It is not interference [*ganshe*, 干涉] if the outcome [*xiaoguo*, 效果] is good for the Chinese military, the PKO force, and the host country, even if the host state doesn't agree'.[42]

What is visible here is the notion that the 'international community' *and* China know what is best for the 'failed' state, and that the latter is too immature to decide how to govern its country for itself. If the host does not know what is beneficial for itself, it is better if the 'international community' – China included – advises what is good for it, showing the road towards future 'happiness' and 'political maturity'.

Where Does Chinese Paternalism Come from?

This paternalistic thinking can be considered as a product of three factors. The first concerns China's own image as a 'great power' and its desire to be accepted as such. As evidenced by the three-tier conceptual framework (great power, developing country and middle power) adopted by this issue of *International Peacekeeping*, the existence of this paternalism in China (which seems odd coming from a state that claims to share with the developing world a history of suffering under imperialism and Western domination) stems partly from its longstanding self-perception as both a member of the postcolonial/developing world and a great power that deserves some form of parity with the Western powers that have long dominated the international community.[43] China's rise is now accepted as an almost inevitable fact, its political and economic clout at both the regional and international level generally providing it with special constitutional privileges pertaining to world governance. Yet, the PRC's growing political, military and economic power has often been greeted with disquiet, ranging from 'China threat' theories to more recent fears of China's rise somehow leading to the weakening of global norms based on democratic governance and respect for human rights.[44] In order to combat this negative image, the PRC has embraced the concept of a 'responsible great power' that enforces the core norms of legitimate behaviour and membership within the 'international community'.[45] To the extent that great powers have historically played the role of a paternal 'civilizer' to fulfil this duty, it is perhaps inevitable that the PRC will engage in some paternalistic activities. Its participation in intrusive PKOs that aim to rebuild war-torn states into market capitalist, liberal democratic states is partially motivated by a desire to construct an image as a 'good', 'responsible great power'.[46]

The Factors of Chinese Ethnocentrism and Racism

However, there are other factors worth noting, although barely acknowledged by the Chinese themselves. One is ethnocentrism, which sees China as exceptional and inherently superior. The other is racism, which actively labels certain racial groups as inherently inferior. As Peter Van Ness has observed, while PRC leaders often state China's common bond with and membership of the so-called 'Third World', this can be interpreted as a rhetorical device that serves to evoke domestic memories of China's 'humiliation' at the hands of the imperialist powers and 'keep alive the option of a renewed effort to build coalitions among the countries of the Third World if necessary'.[47] In fact, 'virtually all Chinese leaders manifest ... a national pride in being Chinese ... these traits point to a sense of China's uniqueness rather than of shared Third World characteristics'.[48] Such sentiments result in a sense of superiority which easily translates into paternalism *vis-à-vis* the underdeveloped world. Modernization theory – as highlighted in the *Zhongguo xiandaihua baogao* – is used to evaluate not only China's progress but that of other states as well. Modernization theory has frequently been subjected to criticism for its Eurocentrism. As Dean C. Tipps notes:

> Though the terminology of contemporary modernization theory has been cleaned up some to give a more neutral impression – it speaks of 'modernity' rather than 'civilization', 'tradition' rather than 'barbarism' – it continues to evaluate the progress of nations, like its nineteenth-century forebears, by their proximity to the institutions and values of Western, particularly Anglo-American societies.[49]

In the case of the *Zhongguo xiandaihua baogao*, the world is represented in hierarchical terms based on the degree of development, and almost reproduces the ethnocentrism displayed by the Western powers during the late nineteenth century, which regarded scientific progress and industrialization along European lines as 'objective' criteria for classifying polities as 'civilized' and 'uncivilized'.[50] The PRC is represented as 'superior' to many African states (and, interestingly, India),[51] being classified as a 'primary developing state' (*chudeng fada guojia*, 初等发达国家), while the latter are classified as 'lacking in development' (*qian fada guojia*, 欠发达国家). Here, one observes a degree of nationalistic celebration of Chinese achievements since the 'reforming and opening up' policies inaugurated by Deng Xiaoping. China is, in a sense, 'on the right track', while others continue to languish in underdevelopment.

Given that China is in the lead in this linear and universal pathway towards modernization, it can present itself as an ideal that those behind should emulate. It is in these statements that we can see elements of paternalistic thinking that reflect 'the sentiment that the Chinese people must tomorrow take over the mission that has been carried by Americans since World War II ... the mission of modernizing and civilizing the world'.[52] Such thinking is characteristic of modernization theories. Tipps points to a substantial element of ethnocentric pride among many US scholars on modernization. These theorists share a widespread attitude of complacency toward American society, and the expansion of American political, military, and economic interests throughout ... Such an atmosphere of complacency and self-satisfaction could only encourage the assumption among social scientists that 'modernity' was indeed an unmixed blessing and that the institutions and values of American society ... represented an appropriate model to be emulated by other, less fortunate societies.[53]

Of course, it is worth noting that there is as yet no concrete evidence that China is engaged in this 'mission of modernizing and civilizing the world', and not all Chinese scholars advocate the propagation of China's experiences of development. Nevertheless, the notion that other underdeveloped states can 'learn' from the PRC's example implies that the Chinese may be prepared to assume the role of the 'teacher' or the 'parent' with superior knowledge, at least *vis-à-vis* the global South.

This impression is only strengthened when one examines a passage in the *Zhongguo xiandaihua baogao*, which states, 'China hopes to reach the level of a developed country by the twenty-first century ... the possibility of catching up with the developed countries is larger if [we] establish partnerships with developing states'.[54] In the table that follows, the Report lists 'candidate partner states' (*zhanlüe huoban de houxuan guojia*, 战略伙伴的候选国家) from which China could learn. In the category of 'level of modernization' and 'innovation in intelligence' (the latter being a hallmark of 'Second Modernization') no developing countries can be found (their worth as 'partners' is in supplying China with natural minerals or labour), implying that, while the Chinese can teach the developing world about development, they have nothing to learn from these states. This hardly seems to match China's supposed desire of '[l]earning from each other and seeking common development' or seeking to 'learn from and draw upon experiences of each other in governance and development'.[55]

One must, however, acknowledge that such views of Chinese superiority are often tempered by the fact that the Western states still occupy the highest position of development (being classified as 'developed states', or *fada guojia*, 发达国家) in the eyes of many Chinese analysts. This is perhaps less the case for those who actively propagate the 'Chinese model' of development as something the rest of the world can follow. Yet, in the case of the *Zhongguo xiandaihua baogao* a tension exists between Chinese ethnocentric pride about their own economic success and a decidedly Western-centric viewpoint of 'progress', as the juxtaposition of China against the more 'advanced' West possibly diminishes the PRC's achievements in development. This is not necessarily a new phenomenon in China: as Xiaomei Chen has noted, there has long been an 'anti-official Occidentalism' discourse that constructs a highly idealized (but no less essentialized) image of the 'West' to critique China's system of governance. It has been circulated among Chinese intellectuals often labelled 'Western' by sheer dint of holding critical views of the Chinese government's policies. In the face of such accusations, Chen argues, 'they had little choice but to assert that the Western Other' – typically decried in more official circles as responsible for the domination and exploitation of China and the rest of the world – 'was in fact superior to the Chinese Self . . . By suggesting that the West is politically and culturally superior to China, they defended their opposition to established "truths" and institutions'.[56] Whether or not the *Zhongguo xiandaihua baogao* and its editors are involved in such implicit resistance to prescribed governmental policy is difficult to ascertain. Nevertheless, it is worth remembering that there remains an influential strand of thought within China which continues to uphold the Western states and their societies as a 'model' of emulation, and in this sense the West remains a highly dualistic entity simultaneously representing 'progress' and 'domination' for the Chinese.

The emergence of paternalistic attitudes towards the developing world can also be attributed to Chinese attitudes towards the 'black race' (*heizhongren*, 黑种人), whose racial features are seen as the very cause of 'underdevelopment'. The adoption of an intellectual framework that draws on modernization theory in China contributes significantly to the notion of racial hierarchies. Pal Nyíri has noted that,

> while the degrees of economic modernity in Hungary or Argentina may be disappointing, their peoples, being white and having low reproduction rates, at least share the 'Western' attributes of high quality. But that view does not hold for others, such as Gypsies in Eastern Europe and, especially, Africans. The public perception of blacks in China is still strongly tinged with a Spencerian idea of racial inferiority; African countries are often described as *both* backward and uncivilized.[57]

Naturally, the quasi-official nature of publications like the *Zhongguo xiandaihua baogao* means they do not contain any blatantly prejudiced views of African peoples. Nevertheless, some surveys have shown that Africans are widely perceived by the Chinese to be lacking in industriousness, to be 'undisciplined, wild, ignorant . . . primitive, uncivilized . . . and [to] lack a capacity for progress'.[58] Given this context, it is unsurprising that many African states are labelled in an arguably derogatory fashion such as 'lacking development'. Again, these sentiments are intensely hierarchical, and reflect paternalistic thinking that China and the 'international community' can teach the underdeveloped world with by means of 'selfless' actions towards 'childlike' polities that are defined along crude racial lines. Such thinking also dovetails with Chinese debates on what a 'responsible great power' is. One Chinese analyst noted that a great power can be considered as 'a powerful country which helps its poorer brothers', leaving little doubt as to the identity of the 'older brother'.[59]

Conclusion

The above discussion has advanced the claim that the PRC's own latent paternalism deriving from ethnocentrism and racism may mean that it is far more willing to tolerate – and even participate in – PKOs with strong social engineering mandates. However, it is worth noting that notions of a universal trajectory of 'democratic' and 'capitalist' development, so often associated with post-Cold-War 'liberal triumphalism', have taken a battering in recent years. US-led military operations in Iraq and Afghanistan have seemingly failed to construct a stable and peaceful domestic order, leading to significant disenchantment among the Western public with the enterprise of transplanting liberal democratic governance overseas. In scholarly circles, apart from obvious criticisms of Eurocentrism in the aforementioned model of 'modernization', the actual efficacy of these policies in both development and PKOs has also been contested by both Chinese and Western commentators.[60] This article thus concludes by considering whether this perceived loss of credibility in universalistic modes of development will lead the PRC to reconsider its paternalistic attitudes *vis-à-vis* the developing world and states that often host PKOs.

The preliminary evidence suggests otherwise. The case of the so-called 'Beijing Consensus' model of development – which is said to pose an alternative to the liberal democratic, capitalist development model propagated by the West – is a case in point. Despite the fact that a significant number of Chinese analysts question whether this concept (which was actually coined by Joshua Cooper Ramo, an analyst based in the West) actually exists,[61] many commentators have enthusiastically taken up the 'Beijing Consensus' as an integral part of Chinese 'soft power' and a potential model for the developing world to follow. Curiously, this is in contradiction to Ramo's argument that one of the key characteristics of the so-called 'Beijing Consensus' is 'self-determination' and a lack of a belief 'in uniform solutions for every situation',[62] which in turn means that the Chinese 'model' of development 'is one that by definition is not ... capable of being transplanted wholesale from the Chinese context to that of other developing states'.[63] The Chinese have hosted meetings such as the 2004 Shanghai 'Conference for Scaling up Poverty Reduction and Global Learning Process', and the assumption that China can offer a 'model' of development for the developing world is never far below the surface in the writings of many Chinese commentators. Liu Jianbo, for instance, states that 'China's rapid economic growth and continuous political stability has no doubt presented itself as a successful model for the developing states, and stimulated enthusiastic attempts by a wide range of African states to learn from and emulate it'.[64]

Even if explicit 'teaching' is not undertaken by the PRC, paternalism remains visible in the literature concerning the 'Chinese model' of economic growth. Chinese scholars make much of the fact that developing states are coming to see the 'Chinese model' of economic growth as an attractive alternative to the so-called 'Washington Consensus'.[65] This can be interpreted as an attempt to demonstrate that,

> [u]nlike Western colon(ial)ists, [the Chinese] do not go about educating or 'reforming' natives, but show them an example of success. This difference underlies the claims of altruism that Chinese officials use to indicate subtly the *moral* superiority of China's economic 'contributions' ... over the more socially interventionist aid schemes of the West.[66]

Such views are reinforced by the publication of laudatory articles by scholars from both China and the developing world praising the 'Chinese model' of development and the PRC's altruism towards the global South.[67] Drawing on the case of Latin America, Sheng Ding states,

> more than any region in the world, Latin America had been a loyal pupil of the Western neoliberal economic development strategy ... [t]he more rigorously the Western economic principles were applied the more disastrous the economic performances ... *Beijing's success in developing its economy on its own path* has made China's developmental model an alternative for many Latin American governments.[68]

The Western powers' waning enthusiasm for transplanting Eurocentric notions of 'legitimate governance' has not yet directly translated into doctrinal changes in PKO mandates. However, the discussion above suggests that even if the Eurocentric models of development currently underpinning PKO mandates are discredited, the PRC could promote its own development experiences through its participation in such operations. Of course, it is important to acknowledge that there is to date very little evidence of this, despite the highly alarmist (and empirically dubious) fears emanating from Western policy circles.[69] Yet, the existence of Chinese paternalist discourses certainly provides some intellectual justification for doing so, and these sentiments stand alongside China's oft-cited adherence to the norm of 'non-interference'. It remains to be seen how China can balance its deep-rooted paternalistic attitude as a 'great power' with its desire to use its growing political power to construct a more 'democratic' international order marked by equality among all states, regardless of levels of development or race. The PRC's PKO policies are set to evolve alongside these internal debates, and will remain an issue emblematic of China's often torturous attempts to adapt to the still Western-dominated international order.

NOTES

1. Department of Peacekeeping Operations (DPKO), 'Ranking of Military and Police Contributions to UN Operations', 30 June 2010 (at: www.un.org/en/peacekeeping/contributors/2010/june10_2.pdf).
2. A useful discussion of China's early views on PKOs can be found in Yongjin Zhang, 'China and UN Peacekeeping: From Condemnation to Participation', *International Peacekeeping*, Vol.3, No.3, pp.3–5; Shogo Suzuki, 'Seeking "Legitimate" Great Power Status in Post-Cold-War International Society: China's and Japan's Participation in PKOs', *International Relations*, Vol.22, No.1, 2008, p.55
3. Pang Zhongying, 'China's Changing Attitude to UN Peacekeeping', *International Peacekeeping*, Vol.12, No.1, 2005, p.87.
4. International Crisis Group (ICG), 'China's Growing Role in UN Peacekeeping', Asia Report 166, 17 Apr. 2009, p.14.
5. Ibid., pp.15–17.
6. Interview with analyst at Chinese Institute of International Studies, Beijing, 23 Apr. 2007; Zhang Huiyu [张慧玉], 'Zhongguo dui lianheguo weihe xingdong de gongxian' [中国对联合国维和行动的贡献] (China's contributions to UN peacekeeping activities), *Wujing xueyuan xuebao* [武警学院学报] (Journal of the Academy of the Armed Police), Vol.20, No.5, 2004, p.32; ICG (see n.4 above), pp.12–14.
7. Suzuki (see n.2 above), pp.55–56
8. See Eva Bertran, 'Reinventing Governments: The Promise and Perils of United Nations Peace Building', *Journal of Conflict Resolution*, Vol.39, No.3, 1995, pp.387–418; Roland Paris, *At War's End: Building Peace after Civil Conflict*, Cambridge: Cambridge University Press, 2004.

9. For an extensive examination of international paternalism, see William Bain, *Between Anarchy and Society: Trusteeship and the Obligations of Power*, Oxford: Oxford University Press, 2003.
10. See Alastair Iain Johnston, 'International Structures and Chinese Foreign Policy', in Samuel S. Kim (ed.), *China and the World: Chinese Foreign Policy Faces the New Millennium*, Boulder, CO: Westview, 1998, pp.73–74; Sophie Richardson, *China, Cambodia, and the Five Principles of Peaceful Coexistence*, New York: Columbia University Press, 2010.
11. For a general critique of this kind, see Phillip Darby, 'Rolling Back the Frontiers of Empire: Practising the Postcolonial', *International Peacekeeping*, Vol.16, No.5, 2009, pp.699–716.
12. See William Pfaff, 'A New Colonialism? Europe Must Go Back into Africa', *Foreign Affairs*, Vol.74, No.1, 1995, pp.2–6; Neta C. Crawford, 'Imag(in)ing Africa', *Harvard International Journal of Press/Politics*, Vol.1, No.2, 1996, pp.30–44.
13. Bonnie S. Glaser and Philip C. Saunders, 'Chinese Civilian Foreign Policy Research Institutes: Evolving Roles and Increasing Influence', *China Quarterly*, No.171, 2002, p.614.
14. See, for instance, Joshua Kurlantzick, *Charm Offensive: How China's Soft Power Is Transforming the World*, New Haven, CT: Yale University Press, 2007; Stefan Halper, *The Beijing Consensus: How China's Authoritarian Model Will Dominate the Twenty-First Century*, New York: Basic Books, 2010.
15. Sheng Hongsheng [盛红生], *Lianheguo weichi heping xingdong falü wenti yanjiu* [联合国维持和平行动法律问题研究] (A Study of Legal Issues in PKOs), Beijing: Shishi chubanshe, 2006, p.22.
16. Interview with analyst at China Foundation for International Strategic Studies, Beijing, 23 Apr. 2007.
17. Ian Taylor, *China's New Role in Africa*, Boulder, CO: Lynne Rienner, 2009, p.23.
18. Bertran (see n.8 above), p.389.
19. DPKO, *United Nations Peacekeeping Operations: Principles and Guidelines*, New York, 2008, p.28.
20. See UN Security Council resolutions: 1925, UN doc., S/RES/1925 (2010), p.6; 1509, UN doc., S/RES/1509(2003); 1919, UN doc., S/RES/1919(2010); 1933, UN doc., S/RES/1933 (2010); and 1912, UN doc., S/RES/1919 (2010), respectively.
21. DPKO (see n.19 above), p.31.
22. Ruth E. Gordon, 'Some Legal Problems with Trusteeship', *Cornell International Law Journal*, Vol.28, No.2, 1995, pp.324–5. Also see Bertran (n.8 above), pp.391–3.
23. Bertran (see n.8 above), p.393.
24. Darby (see n.11 above), p.708.
25. DPKO (see n.19 above), p.28.
26. It is beyond the scope of this article to discuss the debates surrounding the definition of 'failed states'. But see Robert I. Rotberg, 'The New Nature of Nation-State Failure', *Washington Quarterly*, Vol.25, No.3, 2002, pp.85–96. Also see Jean-Germain Gros, 'Towards a Taxonomy of Failed States in the New World Order: Decaying Somalia, Liberia, Rwanda and Haiti', *Third World Quarterly*, Vol.17, No.3, 1996, pp.455–71.
27. Men Honghua [门洪华] and Huang Haili [黄海莉], 'Yingdui guojia shibai de bujiu cuoshi: jian lun Zhongmei anquan hezuo de zhanlüexing' [应对国家失败的补救措施:兼论中美安全合作的战略性] (Responses to save failed states: coupled with a discussion of the strategic dimension of Sino-US security cooperation), *Meiguo yanjiu* [美国研究] (American Studies), No.1, 2004, pp.7–32; Song Dexing [宋德星] and Liu Jinqi [刘金奇], 'Guoji tixi zhong de "shibai guojia" xilun' [国际体系中的"失败国家"析论] (An analysis of 'failed states' in the international system), *Xiandai guoji guanxi* [现代国际关系] (Contemporary International Relations), No.2, 2007, p.35.
28. Song and Liu (see n.27 above), p.35.
29. This point was made in an interview when I posed the question of how China would square practical needs of regional stability with Western neo-imperialism. Interview with analyst at Chinese Institute of International Studies, Beijing, 23 Apr. 2007.
30. For a detailed treatment on this, see Shogo Suzuki, *Civilization and Empire: China and Japan's Encounter with European International Society*, London: Routledge, 2009.
31. See Michael Adas, *Machines as the Measure of Men: Science, Technology, and the Ideologies of Western Dominance*, Ithaca, NY: Cornell University Press, 1989.
32. Miwa Hirono, *Civilizing Missions: International Religious Agencies in China*, London: Palgrave Macmillan, 2008, p.27. Note that traditional Chinese conceptualizations of civilization were also unitary and progressive.
33. See Adrian Leftwich, 'Governance, Democracy and Development in the Third World', *Third World Quarterly*, Vol.14, No.3, 1993, pp.605–24; Carolyn Baylies, '"Political Conditionality" and Democratization', *Review of African Political Economy*, Vol.22, No.65, 1995, pp.321–37.

34. See table supplied in *Zhongguo xiandaihua zhanlüe yanjiu keti zu* [中国现代化战略研究课题组] (Committee on the Strategy of China's Modernization), *Zhongguo kexueyuan zhongguo xiandaihua yanjiu zhongxin* [中国科学院中国现代化研究中心] (Centre for China's Modernization, Chinese Academy of Sciences), *Zhongguo xiandaihua baogao 2008: guoji xiandaihua yanjiu* [中国现代化报告 2008：国际现代化研究] (China Modernization Report 2008: A Study of International Modernization), Beijing: Beijing daxue chubanshe, 2008.

35. Elena Barabantseva, *Overseas Chinese, Ethnic Minorities and Nationalism: Decentering China*, London: Routledge, 2011, p.71.

36. See Zhongguo xiandaihua zhanlüe yanjiu keti zu, Zhongguo kexueyuan zhongguo xiandaihua yanjiu zhongxin (n.36 above), pp.320–409.

37. Dean C. Tipps, 'Modernization Theory and the Comparative Study of Societies: A Critical Perspective', *Comparative Studies in Society and History*, Vol.15, No.2, 1973, p.204.

38. Pál Nyíri, 'The Yellow Man's Burden: Chinese Migrants on a Civilizing Mission', *China Journal*, No.56, Jul. 2006, p.84 (emphasis added).

39. Hirono (see n.32 above), p.21.

40. This point is also supported by Barabantseva (see n.35 above), p.6.

41. Richardson (see n.10 above), p.162.

42. Interview with analyst at Chinese Institute of International Studies, Beijing, 23 Apr. 2007.

43. On this point, see Wu Xinbo, 'Four Contradictions Constraining China's Foreign Policy Behavior', *Journal of Contemporary China*, Vol.10, No.27, 2001, pp.293–4.

44. See for instance Kurlantzick (n.14 above).

45. For a detailed exploration of this point, see Gerry Simpson, *Great Powers and Outlaw States: Unequal Sovereigns in the International Legal Order*, Cambridge: Cambridge University Press, 2004.

46. See Suzuki (n.2 above).

47. Peter Van Ness, 'China as a Third World State: Foreign Policy and Official National Identity', in Lowell Dittmer and Samuel S. Kim (eds), *China's Quest for National Identity*, Ithaca, NY: Cornell University Press, 1993, p.213.

48. Ibid. The contradictions between China's self-image as both 'great power' and 'poor country' are also analysed by Wu Xinbo (see n.43 above), pp.293–4.

49. Tipps (see n.37 above), p.206.

50. Adas (see n.32 above).

51. See Figure 5–3, *Zhongguo xiandaihua zhanlüe yanjiu keti zu, Zhongguo kexueyuan zhongguo xiandaihua yanjiu zhongxin* (n.34 above), p.274.

52. Nyíri (see n.38 above), p.106

53. Tipps (see n.37 above), pp.208–9.

54. Zhongguo xiandaihua zhanlüe yanjiu keti zu, Zhongguo kexueyuan zhongguo xiandaihua yanjiu zhongxin (see n.34 above), p.223.

55. Speech by Du Xiaocong of the Chinese Permanent Mission to the UN, 'China's Role in Africa' (at: www.focac.org/eng/zfgx/dfzc/t689653.htm).

56. Xiaomei Chen, 'Occidentalism as Counterdiscourse: "He Shang" in Post-Mao China', *Critical Inquiry*, Vol.18, No.4, 1992, p.691.

57. Nyíri (see n.38 above), p.103.

58. Barry Sautman, 'Anti-Black Racism in Post-Mao China', *China Quarterly*, No.138, 1994, p.434. Interestingly, the comments cited above came from university students, who might be expected to demonstrate a greater appreciation of non-Chinese culture and peoples, as well as sensitivity to racism. A comprehensive study of race in China is provided by Frank Dikötter, *The Discourse of Race in Modern China*, Stanford, CA: Stanford University Press, 1992.

59. Interview with analyst at China Institute of Contemporary International Relations, Beijing, 19 Apr. 2007.

60. See Sigrun I. Skolgy, 'Structural Adjustment and Development: Human Rights – an Agenda for Change', *Human Rights Quarterly*, Vol.15, No.4, 1993, pp.763–70; Roland Paris, *At War's End*, pp.151–78; Ngaire Woods, 'Whose Aid? Whose Influence? China, Emerging Donors and the Silent Revolution in Development Assistance', *International Affairs*, Vol.84, No.6, 2008, pp.12–14.

61. See for instance Zhan Yijia [詹奕嘉], 'Zhongguo shi ruan shili daguo ma?' [中国是软实力大国吗] (Is China a soft great power), *Shijie zhishi* [世界知识] (World Knowledge), No.20, 2006, p.5; Zhang Jianjing [张剑荆], '"Beijing gongshi" yu zhongguo ruan shili de tisheng' ["北京共识"与中国软实力的提升] (The 'Beijing Consensus' and the rise of China's soft power), *Dangdai shijie yu shehui zhuyi* [当代世界与社会主义] (Contemporary World and Socialism),

No.5, 2004, p.10. I have explored this issue further in Shogo Suzuki, 'Chinese Soft Power, Insecurity Studies, Myopia and Fantasy', *Third World Quarterly*, Vol.30, No.4, 2009, pp.779–93.
62. Johua Cooper Ramo, *The Beijing Consensus*, London: Foreign Policy Centre, 2004, pp.4,12.
63. Shaun Breslin, 'Understanding China's Regional Rise: Interpretations, Identities and Implications', *International Affairs*, Vol.85, No.4, 2009, p.827.
64. Liu Jianbo [罗建波], 'Ruhe youhua zhongguo heping jueqi de guojia xingxiang' [如何优化中国和平崛起的国家形象] (How should China's image of peaceful rise be optimized?), in Men Honghua [门洪华] (ed.), *Zhongguo: ruanshili fanglüe* [中国：软实力方略] (China: Soft Power Strategy), Hangzhou: Zhejiang renmin chubanshe, 2007, p.251.
65. See, for instance, Sheng Ding, 'To Build a "Harmonious World": China's Soft Power Wielding in the Global South', *Journal of Chinese Political Science*, Vol.13, No.2, 2008, p.207.
66. Nyíri (see n.38 above), p.104 (original emphasis).
67. See, for instance, Li Anshan [李安山], 'Wei zhongguo zhengming: zhongguo de feizhou zhanlüe yu guojia xingxiang' [为中国正名：中国的非洲战略与国家形象] (Establishing a name for China: China's Africa strategy and national image), *Shijie zhengzhi* [世界政治] (World Politics), No.4, 2008, pp.6–15; Luo Jianbo [罗建波], 'Ruhe lijie zhongfei xinxing zhanlüe huoban guanxi' [如何理解中非新型战略伙伴关系] (How should China and Africa's new strategic partnership be understood), *Guoji luntan* [国际论坛] (International Forum), Vol.9, No.5, 2007, pp.31–6.
68. Ding (see n.65 above), p.207 (emphasis added).
69. Ramo (see n.62 above); Halper (see n.14 above). For a counter-point, see Suzuki (n.61 above).

A Responsible Power? China and the UN Peacekeeping Regime

COURTNEY J. RICHARDSON

The People's Republic of China asserts that it is a responsible power in international affairs, emphasizing its participation in UN peacekeeping as evidence of its exemplary behaviour. In order to uncover what 'responsible power' means in the context of Chinese participation in peacekeeping, this article analyses the motivations and barriers that shape China's peacekeeping deployments. The term 'responsible power' has value not only because it is flexible, capturing China's ambivalence regarding peacekeeping, but also because 'responsible power' enables China to frame the discourse regarding its foreign and security policy. It appears that for the near future, China remains committed to modest engagement in peacekeeping. The article concludes that China has the potential to foster an ever more constructive role in the UN peacekeeping regime. However, in order to effectively engage China, a deeper understanding of the policy priorities of Chinese foreign policy actors is needed.

China is involved in peacekeeping at the UN on multiple levels: as a delegate in discussions on peacekeeping affairs of the day; as a permanent member of the Security Council, shaping resolutions and mandating peacekeeping missions; as a financial contributor to the peacekeeping budget; and as a troop and police contributor, deploying an array of personnel to peacekeeping missions. By going beyond its initially minimalist involvement to more active engagement in the UN peacekeeping regime, China has demonstrated a more holistic commitment to peacekeeping.

Yet, peacekeeping presents particular pressures for China. Peacekeeping is a high-profile, cross-cutting matter, weaving together several issues, from China's push for resources abroad, to its relationships with other states, to its projection of military power. Moreover, with China's growing peacekeeping presence, greater attention is called to other issues in the purview of its foreign and security policy. Furthermore, as China becomes more visible in peacekeeping, expectations grow for China to show dexterity in policy areas on which it was formerly mute or inflexible. Also, unlike states that have alternative security platforms to deploy peacekeepers, through NATO or the EU for instance, China remains committed to engaging in the UN peacekeeping regime as its sole mechanism to bolster international peace and security.[1] UN peacekeeping has entered a 'consolidation phase',[2] with the downsizing of missions in the Democratic Republic of Congo, Chad and the Central African Republic. However, it is clear that the demand for peacekeeping will not subside, and the UN continues to welcome and encourage China to increase its troop contributions.[3] With these pressures and hopes for China's role in peacekeeping, it is unsurprising that China is responding carefully.

Over the last thirty years, China has become more confident of its position in international society and more willing to engage abroad.[4] And since the 1980s Chinese foreign policy has generally reflected Deng Xiaoping's verdict that the international environment is relatively stable, enabling China to focus on domestic development. The careful gauging and amendment of authoritative statements (*tifa*, 提法), such as 'harmonious world', 'peaceful rise' and 'responsible power', for example, are used to capture China's strategic outlook and emphasize the country's commitment to a peaceful international environment.[5]

In trying to ascertain Chinese motivations for participation in the UN peacekeeping regime, it is useful to pay attention to the language China uses to describe its role in peacekeeping, as language is a two-way mirror – indicating Chinese preferences for how China should be perceived, while revealing concerns over misperceptions of China.[6] The focus of this article is on one *tifa* in particular: 'responsible power' (*fuzeren de guojia*, 负责任的国家). As this article highlights, the term serves China well – simultaneously countering critics, while providing a cohesive explanation for Chinese activities. Responsible power also reflects ambivalence about the greater peacekeeping debate concerning the nexus of intervention, state sovereignty and the use of force.

For various reasons, the article focuses only on *deployments* to UN peacekeeping, as opposed to other means that China has to engage in the peacekeeping regime, such as inter-state diplomacy. First, it is in troop deployment that states are confronted with questions about discriminating between low-level spoilers and significant threats to local peace; how to recognize and prevent threats to the protection of civilians; and how to operate with foreign militaries. Second, troop deployments are seen as one of the most legitimate means to support peacekeeping, as peacekeepers have to interpret mandates in terms of an implementable plan for fostering peace. Peacekeeping experience signals that states have participated in the collective burden of fostering international security. Third, through troop deployments states gain a practical understanding that can inform their experience in mandate discussions, finance debates and other policy fora. For all these reasons, deployment is of particular interest and, as this article explains, deployment can present one of the most problematic means for China to engage in peacekeeping.

Responsible Power

'Responsibility' is a term much in vogue in international relations, with 'responsible sovereignty',[7] 'responsibility to protect'[8] and 'sovereignty as responsibility'[9] part of the current international relations lexicon. However, the Chinese understanding of 'responsible power' is cast in a different light. China repeatedly invokes the term in framing its involvement in UN peacekeeping.[10] For example, in a September 2006 interview, the Deputy Chief of General Staff of the People's Liberation Army (PLA) described China's involvement in the UN peacekeeping regime as follows:

> China is a peace-loving country. In addressing grave issues involving peace and security, we are a responsible country ... Chinese peacekeeping activities demonstrate our country's image as a responsible superpower. The quality of our troops is highly praised by international organizations and other countries [and] in the course of our peacekeeping activities under the UN Charter, China sets a glorious example.[11]

A popular misconception is that the Chinese use of the term 'responsible power' was sparked by US Secretary of State Robert Zoellick in 2005, when he exhorted China to become a 'responsible stakeholder' in international affairs. Earlier usage of the term can be found, though. For example, Premier Zhu Rongji noted in 1999 that 'China was not only a responsible economic player but also a political one in upholding justice and peace'.[12] Scholars note that the term 'responsible power' is malleable and that the standards for defining a responsible power are context specific and in the eye of the beholder.[13] Moreover, it is unclear whether 'responsible power' is a statement of intent to achieve that status or a statement that China has already attained such a position.[14] However, perhaps the term 'responsible power' has value precisely because it is a rhetorical device that is evocative without being restrictive.

There are four benefits of using the term in China's discussion of its peacekeeping effort. First, China is able to proactively frame the discourse regarding its role in peacekeeping, instead of having conceptions of peacekeeping and China's role dictated to it. China is thereby shaping perceptions and expectations of its position in the UN peacekeeping regime and the international system. 'Responsible power' also facilitates China's transition to great-power status with as little disruption as possible.[15] To this end, 'responsible' power serves as a one-size-fits-all message for various audiences: redefining China's role in relation to the other major states on the Security Council; assuring host governments and local populations that a Chinese presence should be seen as positive; and shaping Chinese domestic opinion on the duties that China has abroad.

Second, in using that term China is able to be part of the international system, while remaining somewhat aloof from Western notions of the so-called 'international community'. China presents itself as a non-Western, non-imperialist developing state that is a permanent member of the Security Council, able to fund missions and deploy high-value 'enabler units' (engineering, logistics and medical teams). Thus 'responsible power' is part of China's rhetorical effort to gain recognition as a 'legitimate great power', though on its own terms.[16]

The English School of international relations asserts that great powers bear more responsibility than other states for the upkeep of international society and that these

> Powers [are] recognized by others to have, and conceived by their own leaders and peoples to have, certain special rights and duties. Great powers, for example, assert the right, and are accorded the right, to play a part in determining issues that affect the peace and security of the international system as a whole. They accept the duty, and are thought by

others to have the duty, of modifying their policies in the light of the managerial responsibilities they bear.[17]

Thus, in return for the acceptance by smaller states that great powers will actively protect the core norms of international society, great powers are expected to take on a more active role in the maintenance of international affairs. There is a degree of acceptance by smaller states of the status of these larger states, and therefore the actions of the latter are in theory empowered with legitimacy.[18]

However, smaller states have not always conferred legitimacy willingly, and neither is there total satisfaction with the power structure among states in the international system. To this extent, 'responsible power' is a useful artifice: it enables China to be part of the world order, while still keeping it safely apart from 'irresponsible activities' deemed to be too interventionist or spearheaded by liberal Western states in the name of the 'international community', enabling China to appeal to these smaller states that supposedly confer legitimacy upon the great powers.

Third, the term 'responsible power' enables China to semantically update its critique of the existing international order to resonate with evolving conceptions of the system. 'Responsible power' is part of an effort to make sense of China's place in the post-1945 international system, of which China was not a founding architect. China's perceptions regarding international politics have changed significantly since the founding of the People's Republic of China in 1949: when China was a socialist state allied to the Soviet Union; then as a revolutionary state challenging both the United States and the Soviet Union as imperialist superpowers; then working towards normalizing relations with both those powers as part of a (sometimes tentative) integration into the international system. With these changes in perceptions of the world, China has updated its explanations of world politics: from how Western imperialism victimized the Chinese people; to how capitalism divided the world unjustly; to how China should keep its head down but address the need to modernize energetically. To this end, terms like 'responsible power' are not only artefacts of the image that China wants to project of itself, but part of its means of doing so.

Fourth, 'responsible power' allows China to note that it is an atypical great power, emphasizing its 'peaceful development' and intention not to destabilize international politics for the sake of its own narrow national interests. A statement by a well-regarded PLA strategic thinker, Maj. Gen. Peng Guangqian, highlights this point implicitly: '[u]nlike some Western countries, China does not take advantage of peacekeeping to push national interests in other countries'.[19] In other words, responsible power is an implicit critique of the sole global superpower, the United States.

'Responsible *great* power' (*fuzeren de daguo*, 负责任的大国) is a less frequently used term, referring to China as one of the great powers. Separating the two terms of 'responsible power' and 'responsible great power' reflects *where* China positions itself – either as a state that is acting responsibly in its relations with all states in the international system, or as a state acting responsibly from the privileged vantage point of being a great power. 'Responsible great power' also hints at conversations regarding 'comprehensive national power' (*zonghe guoli*, 综合国力), China's approach in quantifying state power and comparing its standing with other states. Use of the term 'responsible great power' specifies China's positioning and the self-designation precludes discussion about the nature of China's rise.

Chinese Peacekeeping Deployments

China is very specific in its peacekeeping deployments: dispatching 'enabler units'; individual police and individual liaison officers; and formed police units (forces of greater utility because they train, deploy and operate in the field as a team). These troops are typically more challenging for the UN Secretariat to source, since most militaries from developing states do not have these high-value capabilities. Moreover, China started increasing its troop contributions and began concerted engagement in the UN peacekeeping regime at a time of severe overstretch in UN operational capacity. Chinese participation in the UN–AU (African Union) Hybrid Mission in Darfur (UNAMID), the UN Interim Force in Lebanon (UNIFIL) and the UN Organization Mission in the Democratic Republic of Congo (MONUC), for example, supported high-profile, large-scale missions short of desperately needed enabler units, giving enhanced support to Chinese statements about 'responsible power'.[20]

Chinese peacekeepers are regarded as showing more acceptance of the fluid nature of their deployment and a willingness to use their capabilities to execute tasks beyond those initially requested.[21] There is now a dedicated Office for Peacekeeping Affairs within the PLA and a Peacekeeping Division within the Ministry of Public Security, staffed increasingly with officers with experience in both the UN Secretariat and peacekeeping missions.[22] Between the Ministry of Public Security and the PLA, China now maintains three peacekeeping training centres. China continues to lobby for more officers at the UN Secretariat and in senior positions in the field: in September 2007, PLA Maj. Gen. Zhao Jingmin was the first Chinese officer to be appointed as force commander of a UN peacekeeping mission, when he assumed responsibilities for the military-related tasks of the UN Mission for the Referendum in Western Sahara (MINURSO).[23] In January 2011, PLA Major General Chao Liu was appointed force commander of the UN Peacekeeping Force in Cyprus (UNFICYP).[24]

Given China's focus on more development-oriented activities such as drilling waterholes and delivering healthcare, China is yet to deploy blue-helmeted peacekeepers. However, statements indicate that this may change. The Chinese offered 1,000 troops to the UNIFIL mission in September 2006,[25] though the UN encouraged China to continue deploying enabler units. In July 2010, the PLA noted that in order to deploy infantry troops abroad Chinese decision-makers would 'take into account our national defence policy, which is defensive in nature, the international community's response, as well as our troops' capability'.[26] Such conditions reflect two subtle points. First, the PLA is aware of the need not to foster negative perceptions of a resurgent China. Second, the PLA is aware that the potential costs of underperformance in the field fall on their shoulders.

Motivations for Engagement in the UN Peacekeeping Regime

Chinese peacekeeping activities are rooted in a wide variety of motivations, which include gaining operational experience, addressing economic and security concerns, responding to domestic pressures, military diplomacy and a reorienting of China's role in international society.

Peacekeeping provides a means for China to gain operational experience in conflict zones, which is important for a military that has not deployed abroad since the Sino-Vietnamese War in 1979. Chinese peacekeepers work with new technologies, learn new skills and also gain experience of co-deploying with foreign militaries in complex missions in difficult environments.[27] Peacekeeping deployments also present the Chinese with the opportunity to build their links with the defence community of the host state. There is evidence that China is rotating military officers with prior experience as military attaché officers into missions on the same continent, so that these officers can deepen their regional expertise. Other military officers have served on multiple missions in the field, graduating to mid- and high-level positions in mission areas and UN headquarters, where they work on policy and planning issues.[28] Thus, peacekeeping deployment complements training activities and annual peacekeeping exercises.

China participates in peacekeeping training exercises and professional development exchanges with other militaries, and is now progressing to leadership exchanges.[29] For example, China co-hosted the 'Peacekeeping Mission' exercises with Mongolia in July 2009, when officers from both states participated in peacekeeping drills. China's three peacekeeping training centres also host foreign exchanges. The PLA Peacekeeping Centre in China hosted a Senior Commander Training Course for PLA generals in the summer of 2010, where military leaders discussed such issues as humanitarian access, protection of civilians and 'robust peacekeeping'.[30] By advancing discussions, the PLA is promoting further dialogue and sharpening its own understanding of these complex matters.

It is often assumed that there is a direct correlation between economic incentives and peacekeeping deployment. Indeed, the press reports that 'Chinese peacekeeping troops also collaborate with Chinese institutions and organizations in the country of residence to protect the rightful interests of Chinese people and companies'.[31] Coupled with a willingness to work with less democratic regimes, and a conservative, principled stance regarding intervention, there is an assumption that Chinese peacekeeping activities facilitate China's search for foreign resources. However, research indicates that such a relationship between economic activity and peacekeeping participation is more nuanced than might appear.[32] It is unclear whether there is a single Chinese position regarding peacekeeping-related deployments, with reports noting the more forward-leaning posture of the Ministry of Foreign Affairs compared with the more cautious position of the PLA.[33] Indeed, the positions between the two agencies differed to such an extent that bureaucratic wrangling is known to have slowed down China's deployment to the multinational anti-piracy mission off the Gulf of Aden in December 2008.[34] Moreover, the Chinese decision-making structure, with its emphasis on deliberation and consensus-building, makes policy formulation and implementation a laborious and time-consuming process.[35] With government agencies, ministries and business entities operating abroad in conflict zones and developing states, it is likely that the decision-making space will become even more cluttered.[36] Admittedly, peacekeepers are wary of misconduct that could negatively affect China's bilateral relationship with the host government. However, such concerns are not peculiar to Chinese peacekeepers; other countries, too, caution troops to be cognizant of the political effects of their actions.

Perhaps a more fruitful way to approach the matter of economic incentives and peacekeeping is to recognize that as more Chinese nationals live overseas and as economic activities develop abroad, China may find it useful to expand foreign engagement beyond economic and political means to encompass a security element.[37] The Ministry of Commerce estimates that at the close of 2009 there were over five million Chinese citizens working abroad.[38] Reported incidents of Chinese workers under threat in Ethiopia, Sudan, Somalia and elsewhere pushed China to develop initiatives to deal with the safety and security of its nationals abroad. Given the overlap between these insecure areas and peacekeeping locales, it is reasonable to assume that deploying peacekeeping personnel would underpin Chinese commitments to local peace activities. However, it remains to be seen whether China will serve as a broader stabilizing presence in insecure places, or whether China's priority will be to send a security presence only to protect its own nationals and narrower national interests.

Peacekeeping is also an instrument for responding to domestic pressures for action when Chinese nationals are attacked abroad. Outcry in the 'blogosphere' following the 4 June 2007 attacks on Chinese seamen by Somali pirates was a driver for deploying the PLA Navy to anti-piracy missions off the Gulf of Aden as authorized by the UN Security Council.[39] There were expectations not only that China could do something to protect its people, but that China *should* take action.[40] Thus, peacekeeping is another means for China to be proactive and to address domestic opinion, while further strengthening the state's relationship with the Chinese public.

Peacekeeping is part of China's military diplomacy, used to counter-balance Western power and to counter negative perceptions of Chinese military spending, modernization and force projection.[41] Chinese foreign policy actors therefore seek to ensure acceptance of China as a benign military power, countering perceptions of 'the China threat' or 'Chinese imperialism'. To this end, peacekeeping is a low-cost, high-return activity: instead of repeating desires for mutual peace, harmony and coexistence, peacekeepers demonstrate a commitment to world peace and development through their activities in peacekeeping missions.[42] In emphasizing the numerous service recognition medals from host states and UN officials, foreign policy actors implicitly highlight China's commitment to mutual benefit in working with host states. Moreover, Chinese troop contributions are not 'blue helmets' *per se* but 'blue berets', peacekeepers who provide more human-security-oriented functions – training local police, providing public security, reforming security and legal processes, paving roads, treating patients in field hospitals – in that sense, Chinese peacekeepers are citizen diplomats projecting a softer image of Chinese power, countering negative perceptions of Chinese military strength.[43]

Chinese deployments to UN peacekeeping also enable China to reorient its position internationally by staking out a position for China as a potential alternative to the United States as 'global policeman'.[44] As China is not occupied with fighting two major wars or hampered by restrictive command and control requirements, it has more flexibility to deploy personnel in peacekeeping. With more room to manoeuvre, China has the potential to carve a new role for itself internationally.

Obstacles to Engagement in the UN Peacekeeping Regime

Involvement in peacekeeping is not a cost-free venture for China. Indeed, Chinese forces inter-operate with multinational forces, addressing complex mandates in often physically unsafe environments. Concerns arise not just about the safety of the peacekeepers, in that they could be fired upon by spoilers, but also that Chinese personnel could have to return fire. Fears about shooting nationals of the host state while in the field, and the potential negative repercussions on other local Chinese initiatives, have led observers to note the typically restrictive Chinese interpretation of their rules of engagement and tactics.[45] These concerns are understandable and evidently significant for China. Since peacekeeping means committing troops abroad, China is reluctant to take up any activity that may promote perceptions of a Chinese 'fire-breathing dragon', encroaching on spheres of interest and projecting its force abroad too freely. When the Chinese deployed to the UN Stabilization Mission in Haiti (MINUSTAH), commentary focused on three issues: the deployment of Chinese formed police units abroad; the deployment to a host state that has official relations with Taipei; and the fact that China was entering the sphere of influence traditionally monitored by the United States.[46] Thus, deployments have to portray China as a 'helpful fixer' without fuelling concerns about a rising, expansionist China.

Another group of concerns relates to the potential repercussions that China could face if its peacekeepers are seen as less than ably executing their tasks on mission. These worries are driven in part by concerns to protect China's reputation abroad and in part by the need for the PLA and the state to be seen as contributing to Chinese prosperity and security in a period of relative calm in Chinese foreign policy. Perceptions of Chinese peacekeepers as less than competent could erode the PLA's justification of budgetary growth to fund military transformation, especially at a time when there are few traditional security threats to the Chinese state.

It is unclear also what position peacekeeping holds in Chinese priorities. As an extension of President Hu's call for the PLA to execute 'new historic missions' (*xin de lishi shiming*, 新的历史使命),[47] the PLA is to execute 'diversified military tasks' (*duo yanghua junshi renwu*, 多样化军事任务) on behalf of the Chinese people and the state. The white paper *China's National Defense in 2008* notes that the PLA conducts military operations other than war and lists Chinese troop and police contributions to UN peacekeeping operations.[48] Analysts note that there is no formal definition of non-traditional security in Chinese government security literature, though there is an expansive list of transnational threats and transnational issues.[49]

Lastly, in discussing and debating peacekeeping in the UN Security Council, the Special Committee on UN Peacekeeping Operations, the UN Working Group for Peacekeeping Operations and other international fora, China is increasingly confronting some of the most troublesome and contentious issues such as the peacekeeping–peacebuilding nexus and the nature of genocide and human rights promotion. Over time, engaging in the peacekeeping discourse and deploying troops abroad may constrain China's room to manoeuvre with regard to other foreign policy activities. Indeed, news reports note the potential pressures on China's ability to enhance relationships with sub-state parties in the run-up to the 2011 North–South Sudan referendum, given China's explicit support of the government in Khartoum in consultations over peacekeeping affairs in that country.[50]

Conclusion: 'Responsible Power' in the Context of UN Peacekeeping

At this juncture, there are three strategic-level questions regarding China's trajectory in the UN peacekeeping regime. First, it remains to be seen whether China will modify its interpretation of 'responsible power' based upon its growing assertiveness in foreign affairs. It is uncertain whether China will grow into a 'helpful fixer' role, with modest increases in its enabler unit contributions, defining 'responsible power' by the Chinese hallmark of kilometres of paved roads and number of patients treated in field hospitals, or whether China will shed its troop commitments in favour of mandate design, financial contributions and behind-the-scenes dealings – tasks typical of the other permanent members of the UN Security Council.

Second, as China addresses different audiences with its responsible power message, it faces tensions in addressing domestic priorities against requests for participation in peacekeeping. Natural disasters and the ensuing humanitarian relief and recovery operations, such as those following the 2008 Wenchuan earthquake and the 2008 blizzards, and international events like the 2010 Shanghai World Expo and the 2008 Olympic Games, highlight the role of the PLA and Ministry of Public Security in addressing both the needs of the people and securing the state. With some of China's most experienced and well-trained soldiers and some of their most expensive assets (such as advanced field hospitals) in use abroad, peacekeeping contributions could be perceived as competition and not a complementary activity for scarce government resources. Even if increased engagement abroad is perceived as a means to support domestic development, for the foreseeable future it is arguable that domestic priorities will trump foreign policy efforts, and thus the readiness of China to proactively participate in international affairs will be moulded by domestic priorities.[51]

Third, though peacekeeping may be an important, if unessential, task for China, the limits of China's responsible-power approach remain to be seen. Though China has a well-known, longstanding opposition to intervention, it is unclear what this implies for its role in peacekeeping. In other words, will such a stance of non-intervention change after repeated Chinese participation in peacekeeping missions that attempt to promote better governance, rule of law, judicial reform and other statebuilding activities in the host state? Indeed, it is unclear whether China will ultimately attempt to reconcile its rhetoric and practice.

In conclusion, the term 'responsible power' sheds light on the concerns that China has regarding UN peacekeeping commitments. It appears that China remains committed to engaging in the UN peacekeeping regime, but it is reasonable to expect China to reduce contributions if its peacekeepers are perceived as detrimental to China's reputation as a peaceful state or if China faces pressing domestic needs. Although China has the potential to foster an ever more constructive role in the UN peacekeeping regime, in order to effectively engage China, a deeper understanding of the policy priorities of Chinese foreign policy actors is needed.

ACKNOWLEDGEMENTS

My thanks to Miwa Hirono, Ian Johnstone, Marc Lanteigne and Alan M. Wachman for their comments on earlier drafts of the article.

NOTES

1. For example, in response to statements welcoming Chinese participation in NATO missions in Afghanistan, Foreign Ministry spokesman Qin Gang stated, 'Except for the UN peace-keeping missions approved by the UN Security Council, China never sends a single troop abroad. It's out of the question to send Chinese troops to International Security Assistance Force (ISAF) in Afghanistan'. See 'Foreign Ministry Spokesperson Qin Gang's Remarks on the So-Called Issue of China Contributing Troops to ISAF in Afghanistan', 18 Nov. 2008 (at: www.fmprc.gov.cn/eng/xwfw/s2510/t522607.htm).
2. 'UN Peacekeeping in Consolidation Phase, Says Top Official', *UN News Centre*, 6 Aug. 2010 (at: http://unclef.com/apps/news/story.asp?NewsID=35558&Cr=le+roy&Cr1=).
3. For example, 'Annan Urges Greater Peacekeeping Role for China', *United Nations Radio*, 12 Oct. 2004 (at: www.unmultimedia.org/radio/english/detail/45480.html); 'UN Official Lauds China's Contribution to Peacekeeping Efforts', *People's Daily Online*, 30 July 2010 (at: http://english.peopledaily.com.cn/90001/90776/90883/7087261.html).
4. Analyses of the changes of Chinese foreign and security policy include Evan S. Medeiros and Taylor M. Fravel, 'China's New Diplomacy', *Foreign Affairs*, Vol.82, No.6, 2003, pp.23–35; Avery Goldstein, *Rising to the Challenge: China's Grand Strategy and International Security*, Stanford, CA: Stanford University Press, 2005; Bates Gill, *Rising Star: China's New Security Diplomacy*, Washington, DC: Brookings Press, 2007; Evan S. Medeiros, *China's International Behavior: Activism, Opportunism and Diversification*, Washington, DC: RAND, 2009.
5. See Bonnie S. Glaser and Evan S. Medeiros, 'The Changing Ecology of Foreign Policy-Making in China: The Ascension and Demise of the Theory of "Peaceful Rise"', *China Quarterly*, Vol.190, 2007, pp.291–310.
6. For a discussion of language as an indicator of government concerns, see ibid.
7. Bruce Jones, Carlos Pascual and Stephen John Stedman, *Power & Responsibility: Building International Order in an Era of Transnational Threats*, Washington, DC: Brookings Press, 2009.
8. International Commission on Intervention and State Sovereignty, *The Responsibility to Protect: Report of the International Commission on Intervention and State Sovereignty*, Ottawa: International Development Research Centre, 2001.
9. Donald Rothchild, Francis M. Deng, I. William Zartman, Sadikiel Kimaro and Terrence Lyons, *Sovereignty as Responsibility: Conflict Management in Africa*, Washington, DC: Brookings Press, 1996; Francis M. Deng, 'Reconciling Sovereignty with Responsibility: A Basis for International

Humanitarian Action', in John Harbeson and Donald Rothchild (eds), *Africa in World Politics: Post-Cold War Challenges*, Boulder, CO: Westview Press, 1995, pp.295–310.

10. For example, in *China's Foreign Affairs*, an annual compendium of the Policy Planning section of the Foreign Ministry, it is noted that, 'always valuing and supporting PKO consistent with the UN Charter, China has gradually expanded its involvement in these endeavors and thus projected an image of a peace-loving and responsible major country'. *China's Foreign Affairs 2005*, China: World Affairs, 2005, p.422.

11. 'Zhongguo yuanxiang pai yizhi zhuangjiabing canjia lianheguo zhuli weihe budui' [中国原想派一支装甲兵参加联合国驻梨维和部队] (China had first planned to send military troops to participate in United Nations peacekeeping mission In Lebanon), *Xinhua News*, 28 Sept. 2006 (at: http://news.xinhuanet.com/world/2006-09/28/content_5148415.htm), cited in Bonny Ling, 'China's Peacekeeping Diplomacy', *China Rights Forum*, Vol.47, No.1, 2007, p.48.

12. Pang Zhongying, 'China's Changing Attitude to UN Peacekeeping', *International Peacekeeping*, Vol.12, No.1, 2005, p.97.

13. Rosemary Foot, 'Chinese Power and the Idea of a Responsible State', *China Journal*, No. 45, 2001, pp.1–19.

14. Shih Chih-Yu, 'Breeding a Reluctant Dragon: Can China Rise into Partnership and Away from Antagonism?', *Review of International Studies*, Vol.31, No.4, 2005, pp.755–74.

15. I thank Marc Lanteigne for this point.

16. Shogo Suzuki, 'Seeking "Legitimate" Great Power Status in the Post-Cold War International Society: China's and Japan's Participation in UNPKO', *International Relations*, Vol.22, No.1, 2008, pp.45–63.

17. Hedley Bull, *The Anarchical Society: A Study of Order in World Politics*, 3rd edn, New York: Columbia University Press, 2002, p.196.

18. Ibid.

19. Cheng Guangjin, 'Chinese Combat Troops "Can Join UN Peacekeeping" ', *China Daily*, 7 July 2010 (at: www.chinadaily.com.cn/china/2010-07/07/content_10073171.htm).

20. I thank Richard Gowan for this point.

21. Interview with UN official, New York, Aug. 2010.

22. This paragraph draws in part from Courtney J. Richardson, 'China's Growing Involvement in Global Peacekeeping', in Center on International Cooperation, *Annual Review of Global Peace Operations 2010*, Boulder, CO: Lynne Rienner, p.105.

23. 'Secretary-General Appoints Major General Zhao Jingmin of China as Force Commander for Western Sahara Mission', UN press release, UN doc., SG/A1089 BIO/3918, 28 Aug. 2007 (at: www.un.org/News/Press/docs//2007/sga1089.doc.htm).

24. 'Chinese General to Lead UN Peacekeeping Force', *The Straits Times*, 14 Jan. 2011.

25. 'China Ups Lebanon Force to 1,000', *BBC News*, 18 Sept. 2006 (at: http://news.bbc.co.uk/2/hi/asia-pacific/5355128.stm).

26. Cheng (see n.19 above).

27. Philippe D. Rogers, 'China and United Nations Peacekeeping Operations in Africa', *Naval War College Review*, Vol.60, No.2, 2007, pp.73–92.

28. Huang Shan, 'A Decade of China's Peacekeeping Missions', 18 Jan. 2010 (at: www.china.org.cn/world/haitiquake/2010-01/18/content_19262239.htm).

29. Zhang Ping, 'Remarks on the Chinese People's Liberation Army's Participation in UN Peacekeeping Operations', at conference on 'Multidimensional and Integrated Peace Operations: Trends and Challenges', Beijing, Mar. 2007 (at: www.regjeringen.no/upload/UD/Vedlegg/FN/Multidimensional%20and%20Integrated/Chinese%20Ministry%20of%20Defence%20%20PLA%20Participation%20in%20UNPO.doc).

30. Li Mu, 'China Holds High-Level UN Peacekeeping Training Class', *People's Daily Online*, 21 Sept. 2010 (at: http://english.peopledaily.com.cn/90001/90776/90786/7147474.html).

31. Huang Shan (see n.28 above).

32. Erik Lin-Greenberg, 'Blue-Helmeted Dragons: Explaining China's Participation in United Nations Peace Operations', MA thesis, Massachusetts Institute of Technology, 2009; email correspondence with author.

33. International Crisis Group, 'China's Growing Role in UN Peacekeeping', *Asia Report*, No.166, 2009. p.26.

34. Ibid.

35. Bates Gill, 'New Directions in Chinese Security Policy', paper at conference on 'Chinese and American Approaches to Non-traditional Security Challenges: Implications for the Maritime Domain', Newport, RI, 4 May 2010, p.9. One possible outline of the Chinese decision-making process regarding peacekeeping is offered in International Crisis Group (see n.33 above), p.26.

36. Linda Jakobson and Dean Knox, 'New Foreign Policy Actors in China', Stockholm International Peace Research Institute Policy Paper No.26, Sept. 2010.
37. Andrew Ericksson and Gabe Collins, 'Looking after China's Own: Pressure to Protect PRC Citizens Working Overseas Likely to Rise', *China Signpost*, No. 2, 2010 (at: www.andrewerickson.com/2010/08/china-signpost%C2%A9-%E6%B4%9E%E5%AF%9F%E4%B8%AD%E5%9B%BD-looking-after-china%E2%80%99s-own-pressure-to-protect-prc-citizens-working-overseas-likely-to-rise/).
38. Ibid.
39. Interview with international policy analyst, Sydney, July 2009. Also see Wang Cong, 'China to Send Navy to Fight Somali Pirates', *Xinhua News*, 18 Dec. 2008 (at: http://news.xinhuanet.com/english/2008-12/18/content_10525310.htm).
40. Interview with international policy analyst, Beijing, Dec. 2008.
41. Bates Gill and Chin-Hao Huang, 'China's Expanding Role in Peacekeeping: Prospects and Policy Implications', Stockholm International Peace Research Institute Policy Paper No.25, Nov. 2009; Cynthia Watson, 'The Chinese Armed Forces and Non-traditional Missions: A Growing Tool of Statecraft', *China Brief*, Vol.9, No.4, 2009, pp.9–12.
42. Bates Gill and Chin-Hao Huang, 'China's Expanding Presence in UN Peacekeeping Operations and Implications for the United States', in Roy Kamphausen, David Lai, and Andrew Scobell (eds), *Beyond the Strait: PLA Missions Other than Taiwan*, Philadelphia, PA: Strategic Studies Institute, 2009, p.106.
43. Ling (see n.11 above).
44. 'China: Peacekeeping and the Responsible Stakeholder', 28 Aug. 2007 (at: http://www.stratfor.com).
45. Interview with UN official, New York, July 2010.
46. For example, see Chietgj Bajpaee, 'Chinese Energy Strategy in Latin America', *China Brief*, Vol.5, No.14, 2005, pp.1–2.
47. For more detail, see James Mulvenon, 'Chairman Hu and the PLA's New Historic Missions', *China Leadership Monitor*, No.27, 2008, pp.1–11.
48. Information Office of the State Council of the People's Republic of China, *China's National Defense in 2008*, 2009.
49. Susan L. Craig, *Chinese Perceptions of Traditional and Nontraditional Security Threats*, Philadelphia, PA: Strategic Studies Institute, 2007.
50. Jonathan Manthorpe, 'China Works a Chinese Puzzle as Sudan Prepares to Split', *Vancouver Sun*, 29 July 2010 (at: www.vancouversun.com/news/Beijing+works+Chinese+puzzle+Sudan+prepares+split/3295101/story.html).
51. Gill (see n.35 above), p.9.

The Responsibility to Protect and China's Peacekeeping Policy

SARAH TEITT

When the term 'responsibility to protect' (R2P) was introduced in 2001, it was conceived as signifying a framework primarily aimed at legitimizing the use of force against states to protect populations from egregious abuse. China initially condemned the principle, then later endorsed R2P at the 2005 World Summit and reaffirmed its endorsement in the UN Security Council. This article examines the shift in China's position, which seems to run counter to China's stance on sovereignty, non-interference and the use of force. It asserts that China has gradually sought to distance the R2P principle from military action taken without the consent of the host state, and to limit the impact of R2P on robust civilian protection in consent-based UN peacekeeping. In doing so, China has adeptly managed to avoid some of the image costs of obstructing the UN effort to prevent and respond to atrocities, without ceding ground on its core peacekeeping policies and priorities.

When Chinese President Hu Jintao joined other heads of state and government in the unanimous endorsement of the responsibility to protect (R2P) at the 2005 World Summit, he indicated China's support for international efforts to take better and more reliable action to protect populations from mass atrocity crimes. Advocates of R2P attest that, by endorsing the principle, China pledged to protect populations from genocide, war crimes, ethnic cleansing and crimes against humanity within its own borders, and to assist other states in upholding their own prevention and protection obligations.[1] China further indicated that it is prepared to respond collectively through the UN Security Council to take 'timely and decisive action', including Chapter VII enforcement measures as a last resort, when a state is manifestly failing to protect its population from grave abuse. In addition to supporting prevention efforts, this R2P commitment raises expectations that China and other members of the Security Council will agree to authorize military missions to provide protection to beleaguered populations when peaceful, diplomatic or humanitarian measures are unable to thwart the most odious of mass human rights violations. The World Summit R2P endorsement was reaffirmed in UN Security Council Resolution 1674 (2006), a consensus resolution on the protection of civilians (POC) in armed conflict, which passed with China's support.

Although China's constructive and cooperative engagement in UN peacekeeping over the last decade is now widely recognized, China's support for, or in the very least acquiescence in, the UN endorsement of R2P seems to test the limits of its flexibility on sovereignty and non-interference. Pang Zhongying argues, for example, that China is moving towards a 'new paradigm' that sometimes accepts international intervention in the domestic affairs of states to respond to humanitarian crises, yet he asserts that China does 'not endorse the new Western-initiated and promoted idea of the "Responsibility to Protect"'.[2] This is a curious assessment, as R2P advocates hail from Western and non-Western states alike, and Pang draws direct attention to the multiple occasions on which China has unmistakably agreed to the inclusion of R2P in UN documents (as noted, in the World Summit Outcome Document and resolution 1674, but also, *inter alia*, in Security Council Resolution 1894 [2009] and the 2004 Report of the UN Secretary-General's High Level Panel, which included a senior Chinese official).[3] Moreover, despite his assertion that China does not endorse R2P, Pang suggests that Chinese analysts have gradually recognized R2P as a bridge between those who claim a right to intervene coercively to protect populations and others who continue to place great normative and political purchase in sovereignty and non-intervention.[4]

This article sheds light on the apparent contradiction in China's simultaneous acceptance of and resistance to the R2P principle. It first examines how China's position on R2P changed from outright condemnation and strong criticism when the International Commission on Intervention and State Sovereignty introduced the concept in 2001, to a more tempered position at the 2005 World Summit. Although China was wary of the potential for R2P to strengthen justifications for coercive intervention, it opted to divorce R2P from non-consensual force rather than obstruct the UN endorsement of the principle. China thereby avoided the risk of being accused of condoning genocidal violence and demonstrating a callous disregard for human misery without abdicating ground on its core peacekeeping policies and priorities. The article then analyses some of the ways in which China continues to limit the ability to follow through on the Summit R2P commitment, by restricting the development of UN doctrine to guide the protection of civilians in consent-based UN peacekeeping operations. In the final section, the article reflects on what China's stance on R2P reveals about its international standing in contemporary international relations. In many respects, China has approached R2P as the consummate middle power: China has adeptly avoided directly challenging what it perceives to be the Western normative order underpinning R2P in a manner that might repudiate China's self-professed responsible engagement in UN peacekeeping arrangements. At the same time, China has leveraged its relationship with like-minded states to limit the prospect of R2P directly undermining its resistance to non-consensual intervention, or to utterly discredit its commitment to enhancing civilian protection through political negotiations rather than enforcement measures.

China and the Evolution of R2P: From Condemnation to Reluctant Engagement

China was initially highly critical of R2P when the principle was first introduced in the 2001 *Report of the International Commission on Intervention and State Sovereignty* (ICISS). The Commission was established in response to UN Secretary-General Kofi Annan's challenge to produce options for averting a situation similar to Rwanda in 1994, when states failed to intervene to prevent 800,000 deaths during a 100-day genocide, and Kosovo in 1999, when the Security Council was unable to fulfil its role as the final arbiter on the use of force due to NATO's determination to deploy regardless of UN approval. Annan characterized the issue as a problem of reconciling what had come to be perceived as competing demands on the UN system: upholding Charter obligations to respect state sovereignty and taking action to protect populations from grave human rights abuses. Rather than simply lobbying support for non-consensual intervention, commissioners sought to consult with a wide and diverse set of opinions to seek common ground, as they saw it, to overcome the policy impasse on the use of protective force. They averred that '[t]he kind of intervention with which we are concerned ... is action taken *against* a state or its leaders, *without its or their consent*, for purposes which are claimed to be humanitarian or protective'.[5] Although China had demonstrated flexibility in its stance on non-intervention and constructively engaged in consent-based peacekeeping in internal conflicts throughout the 1990s, it retained its staunch opposition to non-consensual force and had denounced the purported humanitarian grounds for NATO's intervention in Kosovo. Ambitiously, the commission was seen to be directly confronting the core of China's allegiance to state sovereignty and conservative reading of the UN Charter's non-interference principle.

The Commission held a series of regional and national roundtable consultations, the penultimate of which took place in Beijing in mid-June 2001 (followed by a roundtable in St Petersburg two days later). During the Beijing consultation, representatives of China's foreign policy community launched a damning critique of humanitarian intervention. Chinese analysts and policymakers argued that the Western assumptions underlying the use of force for 'moral or conceptual reasons' are 'questionable and dangerous', and maintained that so-called humanitarian justifications are applied inconsistently and used as window dressing to justify illegitimate interference. They rejected outright the term 'intervention', and instead suggested that military force with humanitarian objectives should be labelled 'assistance'.[6] The preference for the term 'assistance' reflected China's opposition to coercive intervention. The Chinese delegates present at the consultations stated in no uncertain terms that the '[c]onsent of conflicting parties concerned to a third party's involvement is a precondition for taking humanitarian actions'.[7] On this basis, the Chinese ICISS roundtable participants maintained that military assistance should be authorized in accordance with the UN Charter through the Security Council, be conducted in a neutral, impartial manner and abide by the principle of the non-use of force except in self-defence. The opinions voiced in this consultation were not an anomaly, but were consistent with several of China's policy statements that conveyed its great aversion to resorting to force even when a government is implicated in the widespread abuse of its citizens.

The Commission's final report at the end of 2001 glossed over some of the reservations emanating from the consultation in Beijing. While the report acknowledged Chinese participants' insistence that peace enforcement measures should have explicit UN Security Council authorization, it did not adequately reflect the adamant opposition to the use of force for humanitarian protection against the will of the host state. The basic premise of the report maintained that (a) state sovereignty implies a responsibility for state authorities to protect their people, and (b) when a state is unwilling or unable to halt or avert serious harm on the scale of mass killings or ethnic cleansing, 'the principle of non-intervention yields to the international responsibility to protect'.[8] The report proposed a continuum of measures for the international community to address grave human rights abuses, which included the responsibility to prevent, react and rebuild. UN member states were charged with the responsibility to address the causes of conflict; to react to a state's inability or unwillingness to curb wide-spread abuse, by imposing sanctions, initiating international prosecutions and, in extreme cases, intervening with military force; and to rebuild societies after mili-tary intervention.[9] The majority of the report was dedicated to proposing clear rules, procedures and criteria for determining whether and how UN member states should coercively intervene to protect populations. In forwarding these rec-ommendations, the report implied that by virtue of holding consultations in every region and enjoying the unanimous endorsement of esteemed commissioners from diverse backgrounds, consensus had been forged on the use of force *against* state authorities in extreme cases. The objections raised in Beijing, at least, did not bear out this conclusion. Thus, when the Commissioners put forward claims that their 'path-breaking report' had made headway on establish-ing the legitimacy of military intervention when necessary, it did so without China's clear support for these principles.[10]

While it is important to point out Chinese resistance to some of the rec-ommendations contained in the ICISS Report, China's stance on non-consensual force should not to be mistaken for its wholesale rejection of R2P, particularly given that the commissioners avowed that prevention is the most important aspect of the principle. Of course, the notion that prevention was at the heart of R2P may have appeared credible to Chinese analysts had the lion's share of the report been dedicated to sophisticated policy recommendations for prevention measures rather than guidelines for coercive intervention. Nevertheless, the Com-mission gained vital ground in moving from the semantics of 'humanitarian inter-vention' to 'the responsibility to protect'. The shift was meant to recalibrate the policy dilemma from being an issue of the rights of outsiders to intervene to one of the responsibility of governments to protect vulnerable populations. As Pang notes, this shift was gradually welcomed by Chinese analysts, who responded favourably to the attempt to carve out a middle ground between states that emphasize the value of sovereignty and the hazards of military inter-vention versus others that focus on the potential pitfalls of a tepid international response in the face of state-sponsored violence.[11] In looking anew at the policy dilemma, ICISS consultations revealed that even states such as China that remain rhetorically committed to non-interference agreed that state sover-eignty entails a responsibility to protect populations from mass atrocities, and that UN member states should be committed to preventing and appropriately responding to gaps in protection. While this may appear to be a modest accom-plishment relative to the Commission's aspiration to reach an agreement on taking military action to halt atrocities, the report moved the debate forward by disassociating sovereignty from non-interference, and instead linking it to a state authority's responsibility to ensure that its populations live free from extreme abuse.

As momentum gathered for official UN endorsement of R2P, China chose to quietly assert its resistance to non-consensual military action rather than obstruct the adoption of the principle. When the ICISS Report was discussed in the Security Council's annual retreat in May 2002, China rejected the prospect for interventions not authorized by the Security Council and insisted that the Council maintain final authority over decisions pertaining to the use of force.[12] China's insistence on this matter ensured that its reservations on coercive intervention would not be easily dismissed. Even with clear affirmation of the Security Council's authority, China remained reluctant to endorse R2P at the UN, particularly after the Secretary-General's 2004 High Level Panel (HLP) characterized R2P as an 'emerging norm' to guide the use of collective force to halt atrocities.[13] Annan, however, recognized that equating R2P to the use of protective force did not bode well for gathering global endorsement of the principle in the light of scepticism after Western interventionism and the US invasion of Iraq. Flagging that he was 'aware of the sensitivities involved in this issue', which presumably included China's resistance to a more permissive framework for military intervention, Annan deviated from the HLP endorsement of R2P as a norm guiding military action. Rather than including R2P in the same section as the use of force, Annan endorsed R2P under the section on the Rule of Law, under the heading 'Freedom to Live in Dignity' in his 2005 report, 'In Larger Freedom'.[14] This separation marked the beginning of a gradual shift from pitching R2P as primarily a matter of taking military action in response to widespread killing or ethnic cleansing to a more nuanced framework to delineate each state's responsibility for preventing and responding to mass atrocities. This move rendered the principle less antagonistic to China's international policy and paved the way for it to consider endorsing R2P at the 2005 World Summit.

Before the Summit, the Chinese government's 'Position Paper on UN Reform' (2005), articulated policy on R2P under the heading 'Rule of Law, Human Rights and Democracy', rather than in the section on 'Security Issues' (which included headings on internal conflict, sanctions, the use of force, and peacekeeping).[15] China acknowledged that, 'When a massive humanitarian crisis occurs, it is the legitimate concern of the international community to ease and defuse the crisis.' However, the Position Paper went on to state that any response to crises should strictly conform to the UN Charter and 'respect the opinions of the country concerned and regional organisations'. Military responses were only implicitly referenced in relation to R2P at the end of the section, where China called for 'more prudence in considering enforcement action'.[16] As the Position Paper was released with the intention of clarifying China's position on topics under discussion at the Summit, it is fair to suggest that China's stance on military intervention to protect populations, particularly action taken *against* the will of the host state, had not significantly changed. China maintained that national authorities should assume primary protection responsibilities, Security Council action should respect the will of the host state and more focus should be on prevention and peaceful conflict resolution.[17]

Contrary to expectations, China did little to obstruct the Summit's endorsement of R2P, under the proviso that it would affirm the authority of the UN Security Council and refrain from including criteria or guidelines for military action. After careful review of the wording of the three paragraphs related to R2P, China joined in endorsing them and vowing to act in accordance with the principles.[18] According to the World Summit Outcome Document (WSOD), each state bears the responsibility to protect its population from genocide, war crimes, ethnic cleansing and crimes against humanity, including the prevention of such crimes and their incitement. World leaders further agreed that each state bears the responsibility to generate and deploy appropriate diplomatic, humanitarian and other peaceful measures to assist states in protecting imperilled populations. As a last resort, member states determined that the UN stands prepared to take collective action on a case-by-case basis under Chapter VII of the Charter, with regional organizations if appropriate, when state authorities are manifestly failing to protect their population from genocide, war crimes, ethnic cleansing and crimes against humanity. In January 2009 Secretary-General Ban Ki-Moon issued a report on implementing R2P which carefully unpacked the World Summit agreement into three pillars:

1. The primary responsibility of each state to protect its population from genocide, war crimes, ethnic cleansing and crimes against humanity, and from the incitement of such things.
2. The responsibility of the international community to assist states to uphold their associated prevention and protection obligations.
3. The responsibility of the international community to respond in a 'timely and decisive manner' when a state is 'manifestly failing' to protect its populations from the four mass atrocity crimes.[19]

As Alex Bellamy notes, much of the commentary on R2P following the UN General Assembly endorsement misunderstood the way the concept had evolved and changed from the ICISS Report to the 2005 Summit, some pundits citing the WSOD as evidence of an emerging norm providing legal justification for humanitarian intervention.[20] Yet, in part due to China's resistance, nowhere in the WSOD is there a provision that justifies the use of force beyond the conditions of the UN Charter, a procedure that would allow for unilateral or coalition action without the authorization of the UN Security Council, or a presupposition that force is the appropriate or necessary response in every case of atrocity.[21] Assumptions that there was ever a global consensus on R2P beyond this agreement led David Vesel to assert that the early architects of R2P had fallen into the solidarist tendency to 'overestimate the extent to which the protection of human rights has become internationally accepted over other order-enhancing measures', and to make 'modest claims' the basis of 'extreme conclusions'.[22] With persistent (mis)representations of R2P as a norm legitimizing coercive intervention, it is understandable that China is cautious about the principle. Although it had endorsed R2P, China initially resisted efforts to affirm R2P in the Security Council. Only after months of negotiation did China relent to R2P being included in Resolution 1674 (2006) on the condition that the resolution did not explicitly link R2P with military action, and was limited to a reaffirmation of paragraphs 138–40 of the WSOD. Later, China abstained on Resolution 1706 (2006) on Darfur, which was the first country-specific resolution to reference R2P.[23]

From the introduction of the term in 2001 to its 2005 endorsement, to subsequent debates in the General Assembly, China has resisted the association between R2P and coercive intervention. China's unwillingness to accept anything but a vague link between R2P and the use of force for human protection made it possible for China to endorse R2P without fundamentally altering its position on non-consensual intervention. Yet it is important to note that China has consistently refrained from openly and emphatically denouncing the R2P principle. Chinese statements on R2P in UN settings do not reject the notion that state sovereignty entails not only external rights but also internal obligations. Chinese representatives to the UN affirm that the Security Council bears a responsibility to take action to address humanitarian crises, even on the domestic terrain of sovereign states.[24] Instead of simply defending a static concept of sovereign inviolability which would preclude international interference in intrastate humanitarian crises, China has sought to limit the definition of and expectations set by R2P. In its limited contestation, China preserved the vestiges of its once firm stance on non-interference – the requirement of host state consent for collective international military deployment – without appearing to completely turn a blind eye to mass atrocities.

China continues to adopt this cost-avoiding position in relation to implementing R2P, particularly in relation to developing guidelines for UN peacekeepers to protect populations under threat. As Susan C. Breau notes, the impact of R2P on consent-based UN peacekeeping operations centres on the willingness of UN missions to carry out 'robust' protection mandates to use force at a tactical level to protect civilians.[25] As including POC in consent-based peacekeeping does not directly confront the sensitivities China associates with non-consensual intervention, and as China has supported Chapter VII mandates with POC tasks on multiple occasions, one could assume that enhancing robust protection capabilities under the auspices of UN peacekeeping would be a less contentious starting point for China to support efforts to offer physical protection to populations under the threat of atrocities. The following section exposes some of the challenges to this assumption by analysing China's position on the extent to which UN peace operations should be authorized to use force to protect civilians.

R2P, POC and China's UN Peacekeeping Policy

China has adopted a cautious approach to enhancing POC in UN peacekeeping, emphasizing that national authorities should assume primary protection responsibilities; that Security Council action should respect the territorial integrity and will of the host state; and that more focus should be on prevention and peaceful conflict resolution.[26] In line with this policy, in the July 2010 Security Council debate on the POC, China's delegate noted,

> Adhering to the three principles of the consent of the country concerned, impartiality and the non-use of force except in self-defence is the key to the success of peacekeeping operations. Any deviation from those basic principles will cause more conflicts and problems, even to the point of jeopardizing the success of the peacekeeping operation concerned, rather than help to protect civilians.[27]

While this statement for the most part mirrors the UN 'Principles and Guidelines' of January 2008, which assert that consent, impartiality and the non-use of force remain the cornerstone of UN peacekeeping, the 'Principles and Guidelines' state that force may be used in self-defence as well as the defence of the mandate.[28] As the above quote illustrates, Chinese representatives at the UN and in other international settings notably refrain from expressly including the latter qualifier.[29]

Notwithstanding its reservation on the use of force, China has been actively engaged in deliberations on the role of UN peacekeeping missions to deter and defend attacks against civilian populations since the Council first took up POC as a thematic issue in February 1999. China endorsed Resolution 1265, which expressed the Council's willingness to examine how peacekeeping operations could assist in civilian protection.[30] The following year, in April 2000, China joined the unanimous Council endorsement of Resolution 1296, which noted that 'the deliberate targeting of civilian populations or other protected persons and the committing of systematic, flagrant and widespread violations of international humanitarian and human rights law in situations of armed conflict may constitute a threat to international peace and security'.[31] Over the last decade the Council has explicitly mandated ten UN peacekeeping missions to take necessary measures, including force, to 'protect civilians under imminent threat of physical violence'.[32] In each case, China has voted in favour, namely: UN Mission in Sierra Leone, UN Organization Stabilization Mission in the Democratic Republic of Congo (MONUC), UN Mission in Liberia, UN Operation in Burundi, UN Stabilization Mission in Haiti, UN Operation in Côte d'Ivoire, UN Mission in Sudan, UN Interim Force in Lebanon, African Union (AU)/UN Hybrid Operation in Darfur and UN Mission in the Central African Republic and Chad. China likewise endorsed POC Resolutions 1674 (2006) and 1894 (2009), both of which reaffirmed R2P. Resolution 1674 reaffirmed the practice of ensuring that UN peacekeeping missions included POC provisions and prioritized protection when making decisions on the use of available capacity and resources, while Resolution 1894 requested the Secretary-General to develop an operational concept for POC in peacekeeping operations. It is worth noting as well that China endorsed Resolution 1820 (2008), which recognized that rape and other forms of sexual violence can constitute atrocity crimes, and requested the Secretary-General to develop guidelines for UN peacekeeping operations to better protect women and girls from sexual violence. Later that year, in response to deteriorating security and increased attacks on civilians in the Kivus (Democratic Republic of Congo), China joined the Council's unanimous endorsement of Resolution1856 to revise MONUC's robust mandate to place the highest priority on protecting civilians. It is fair to say, then, that China and others Security Council members have repeatedly, if not consistently, determined a role for peacekeeping missions to bolster civilian protection both at the thematic level and in establishing and renewing country-specific operations.

Despite a series of mandates that authorize peacekeepers to use force to protect civilians, peacekeeping missions have not managed to consistently protect populations under attack. UN peacekeepers remain ill-prepared to deter violence against civilians, contrary to international and local expectations raised by R2P. The Department of Peacekeeping Operations (DPKO) and Department of Field Support (DFS) released a 'non-paper' entitled 'A New Partnership Agenda: Charting a New Horizon for UN Peacekeeping' in July 2009 which brought to light the protection challenges that UN peacekeeping operations confront. While much can be said about the gap between expectations and resource allocation, the non-paper arguably highlighted more fundamental shortcomings. There is presently no shared understanding of the scope and function of robust peacekeeping, nor is there a consensus on what can and should be done to protect civilians.[33] Subsequent efforts have been made to establish the necessary doctrine, training and resources needed to fulfil protection mandates to address these obstacles. Such efforts include an independent study for the DPKO and Office for the Coordination of Humanitarian Affairs (OCHA) (*Protecting Civilians in the Context of UN Peacekeeping Operations: Successes, Setback and Remaining Challenges* [November 2009]), UNSC Resolution 1894 (November 2009) and the report of the General Assembly's Special Committee on Peacekeeping Operations (March 2010).[34] The Secretariat has adopted many of the recommendations to develop: the DPKO/DFS 'Lessons Learned Note on the Protection of Civilians in UN Peacekeeping Operations: Dilemmas, Emerging Practices and Lessons Learned'; 'Draft DPKO/DFS Concept Note on Robust Peacekeeping'; and 'Draft DPKO/DFS Operations Concept on POC in UN Peacekeeping Operations'.[35] While these developments are significant, they fall short of addressing the core dilemma that 'New Horizon' highlighted – the absence of a shared understanding or clear consensus on what UN peacekeeping missions ought to be doing to protect civilians.

China's tepid response to the attempts to develop POC doctrine is indicative of this underlying challenge. In the August 2009 Security Council peacekeeping debate following the release of 'New Horizon', the Chinese delegate emphasized that '[p]eacekeeping operations must exercise caution in the use of force and avoid excessive emphasis on military options. Given the ongoing divergence of views on mandating peacekeeping operations to protect civilians, further in-depth discussions on that issue will be necessary'.[36] Later, in October 2009, Chinese representative Liu Zhenmin stressed that robust peacekeeping and POC remain 'sensitive' and asserted that 'full consultations among Member States with a view to reaching consensus' were needed in order to implement the Secretariat's recommendations for developing concept notes and operational guidance on these issues.[37] Then, in November 2009, China's Ministry of National Defence invited Under Secretary-General for Peacekeeping Operations

Alain Le Roy to meet military officials and Red Cross representatives for a four-day discussion in Beijing on the direction of UN peacekeeping. In addressing the symposium, Vice Foreign Minister He Yafei characterized the 'mandate to protect civilians and robust peacekeeping' as 'emerging theories' (despite a decade of Security Council engagement on POC), and claimed that equal importance should be attached to 'the development and innovation of traditional theories such as conflict prevention, dispute mediation, crisis management and post-conflict peacebuilding'.[38] Unlike other delegations that have expressed concern that traditional peacekeeping principles are unable to meet the challenges of peacekeeping environments and offer support for recommendations to clearly define and further develop the role of UN peacekeepers in civilian protection, China has been hesitant to endorse such proposals and maintains that the new peacekeeping doctrine should be based on traditional peacekeeping principles.[39]

China's resistance to deepening the Council's engagement on POC is further noted in its unwillingness to support the informal Security Council Expert Group on the POC.[40] The Secretary-General recommended that the group be established in his October 2007 POC report. In elaborating on the proposed scope and mandate of the expert group in his May 2008 address to the UN Security Council, John Holmes, Under Secretary-General for Humanitarian Affairs and Emergency Relief Coordination, noted that the group is essential to the Security Council's ability to adopt a consistent approach to taking action against 'horrific crimes'.[41] The proposal envisaged an 'informal forum' of experts from each Council member state to hold 'transparent, systematic and timely consultations on POC concerns, particularly, but not only, in the context of the establishment or renewal of peacekeeping mandates'.[42] China opposed the establishment of the group on the basis that POC should not be considered in isolation from the peace process and political situation, and is better addressed on a case-by-case basis as part of country-specific considerations.[43]

There is merit in China's caution that POC action should cater to the specific conflict environment and support political solutions rather than be viewed as a solution in its own right. However, China's position does not adequately account for the Security Council's struggles to consistently address gaps in protection across different peacekeeping missions and crisis situations, which in the past China has argued reflects double standards.[44] Moreover, China did not choose to view the expert group as a potential redress for its critique, nor did China couple its resistance to establishing the group with constructive proposals for ensuring that POC is complementary to, not a replacement for, political negotiations. Instead, China initially resisted efforts to even discuss the Secretary-General's recommendations on POC, making it difficult for members to agree on even an informal working group.[45] The Council deferred the recommendation to establish an expert group on civilian protection until early 2009, when some of the tension was resolved by determining that the group would have only an informal mandate to consider protection issues in relation to existing peacekeeping operations. Accordingly, the group convenes when a peacekeeping mandate with a POC dimension comes up for renewal, and can invite OCHA to provide recommendations on renewing the mandate with due regard for the updated 'Aide-Memoire on POC in Armed Conflict'.[46]

To some extent, the existence of the Expert Group is an indication that POC is becoming entrenched as a UN peacekeeping priority. It also signals that Council members, China not least among them, have dropped some of their reservations and are prepared to engage more consistently on POC. However, the mandate to only address situations already on the Council's formal agenda precludes the group convening to offer recommendations on emerging protection crises. Even with this modest mandate, China has refrained from ever joining the consultations, which is seen as an attempt to resist formalizing and further developing the group's agenda.[47]

China's lukewarm and sometimes adversarial position on the Council's engagement with civilian protection suggests that, despite its endorsement of missions with POC mandates, China is uncomfortable with the priority placed on authorizing missions to protect local populations. When POC was first being introduced on the Council's agenda, Secretary-General Kofi Annan commended the Council for taking up the issue, noting that it reflected 'a growing recognition that our first duty in any conflict is to protect innocent civilians ... [This] is our most important obligation under the Charter'.[48] Although China has supported POC resolutions, it has not shared Annan's opinion that civilian protection is the Security Council's top priority, even in extreme cases. Chinese delegates consistently emphasize the cessation of violent conflict as the most pressing obligation, so that while force *may* be justifiable to protect civilians, it is not the primary or even the most important response. China has since become more assertive, as evidenced in the August 2010 open debate on peacekeeping operations. There, China's Deputy Permanent Representative to the UN, Ambassador Wang Min, noted that the political process in Darfur continued to falter three years after the authorization of UNAMID's robust protection mandate, which had led the Council to request UNAMID to, among other things, 'prioritize the promotion of the political process in Darfur'.[49] Notably, Wang did not make explicit reference to the other two priorities of the mandate – providing civilian protection and humanitarian access in Darfur. This statement captures China's position: it acknowledges that the Security Council has a responsibility not to shirk from addressing extreme attacks on civilian populations, accepts that POC will be a task for peacekeepers, but emphasizes that the overarching priority is not protecting civilians under imminent physical threat or the delivery of life-saving humanitarian aid, but to end conflict through political negotiations.

As alluded to above, for China, physical protection cannot be viewed in isolation from other factors. Although R2P is concerned with prevention, response and post-conflict peacebuilding, it is most often associated with greater impetus to provide physical protection to populations. China is less than enthusiastic about an 'emerging norm' that supports the prominent place POC and robust peacekeeping have taken in the 'New Horizon' for UN peacekeeping. China voices concern that such focus favours enforcement measures over political engagement and conflict management over prevention, which may result in an increased and unachievable demand for more, and more robust, operations.[50]

Instead, China posits that the bulk of the Security Council's efforts should support the peace initiatives of regional and sub-regional organizations, including the consideration of early interventions. As an indication of its preference for political solutions to conflict, in December 2009 China donated US$700,000 to the UN peacekeeping fund to support mediation efforts. US$500,000 was earmarked for the Trust Fund for the AU–UN Joint Mediation Support Team for Darfur to support the political process (China had already contributed US$500,000 to the fund in March 2008), and US$100,000 was provided to both the Trust Fund for Preventive Action and the trust fund that supports UN preventive diplomacy and political mediation. At that time, China ranked seventh among UN members in financial contributions to peacekeeping.[51] With this in mind, advocates of R2P would do well to recognize China's alternative perspective on and contribution to civilian protection if they hope to constructively engage China in efforts to address gruesome violence against populations in situations already on the Security Council's agenda, or other ones that ought to be.

Conclusion

This analysis does not mean to suggest that China will block future discussion on R2P, or discontinue the trend of agreeing to mandate UN peacekeeping missions to protect civilians when host states consent or even in situations that have deteriorated to the point that there is no recognizable authority whose consent would matter. Nor does it contend that China will significantly obstruct the development of doctrine, training and logistical support for UN peacekeepers to carry out mandated protection tasks. It does, however, offer insights into the manner in which China has contested and shaped rather than obstructed the development of R2P, despite China's initial harsh condemnation of the principle. In seeking to distance R2P from military action taken against states, China limited the potential for R2P advocates to attempt to use the World Summit endorsement as a lever to lobby – or, worse, bypass – a deadlocked Security Council to authorize coercive military action to protect populations from state-sponsored mass killings. Even in consent-based peacekeeping, China has resisted efforts for the DPKO to prioritize civilian protection by consistently constraining, but not altogether rejecting, doctrinal development on the use of force for civilian protection.

China's resistance to, rather than outright condemnation of, R2P suggests that China remains hesitant to assert its position and be seen to be undermining normative and policy developments aimed at protecting populations from egregious harm. Perhaps to deflect criticism that it is reneging on the UN's R2P commitment, China has at times defended its opposition to authorizing coercive measures – to address, for example, grave human rights abuses in Darfur, Myanmar and Zimbabwe – on grounds other than sovereignty-buttressing rhetoric. In these cases, rather than simply contending that humanitarian crises are an internal affair of the sovereign state, China has proposed that protection is best achieved through political settlements rather than coercive protection measures. Interestingly, China has repeatedly drawn attention to the coherence between its position and the stance of regional organizations and other members of the

Global South. In declaring its solidarity with other, like-minded nations, and avoiding direct challenges to what is perceived as a Western normative order, China acts as the consummate middle power seeking to avoid the full brunt of (Western) consternation and to dispel concerns that as China emerges as a global power it will usurp its Council seat to serve as 'tyranny's safeguard' (see the introduction to this issue by Miwa Hirono and Marc Lanteigne). At the same time, China's attempt to align its position with the concerns of the Global South limits the cost of resistance and undercuts the normative and political terrain for R2P to justify military intervention.

On the one hand, China's position on R2P might offer evidence of China's sophisticated and adept diplomacy to appear cooperative and conciliatory without ceding ground on its vital interest to preserve sovereignty and restrict interventionist claims. On the other, it demonstrates China's willingness to engage in new developments in UN peacekeeping despite its reservations, which so often fall on deaf ears or are presumed to be a recalcitrant rather than a divergent position. In many respects, China's resistance rather than obstructionism is a diplomatic gamble, as expectations raised by R2P may pose challenges for China as it seeks to balance a desire to uphold an image of being a responsible power, through involvement in UN peacekeeping, with simultaneously contesting the defining parameters of that responsibility. The fact that China has not patently obstructed or denied R2P means that the principle exists and to some degree flourishes. By its very existence in UN documents and public rhetoric, R2P raises the image costs of China's resistance to measures to prioritize civilian protection in the future development of UN peacekeeping policy, which China is reluctant to endorse. As R2P becomes more entrenched in UN debates and programming, China may be required to do more to ensure that it is less necessary to resort to military action to halt atrocities if it is to make a credible claim to responsible international citizenship through participating in UN peacekeeping arrangements.

ACKNOWLEDGEMENTS

My thanks go to Miwa Hirono, Marc Lanteigne, Michael Pugh and Alex Bellamy for their astute comments, and to the Asia Pacific Centre for the Responsibility to Protect for supporting this research.

NOTES

1. See, e.g., statements by the Asia Pacific Centre for the Responsibility to Protect and the International Coalition for the Responsibility to Protect (at: http://r2pasiapacific.org and www.responsibilitytoprotect.org).
2. Zhongying Pang, 'China's Non-intervention Question', *Global Responsibility to Protect*, Vol.1, No.2, 2009, pp.238–9.
3. The bulk of the literature on R2P traces its intellectual and political origins to the work of Francis Deng (a Sudanese national) in the 1990s on 'sovereignty as responsibility' (the notion that state sovereignty entails both external rights and internal obligations), and Article 4(h) of the Constitutive Act of the AU, which grants the AU the right to intervene in members states in cases of genocide, war crimes and crimes against humanity (at: www.africa-union.org/root/au/Aboutau/Constitutive_Act_en.htm). See Francis Deng, 'Frontiers of Sovereignty', *Leiden Journal of International Law*, Vol.8, No.2, 1995, pp.249–86; Francis Deng, Sadikiel Kimaro, Terrence

Lyons, Donald Rothchild and I. William Zartman, *Sovereignty as Responsibility: Conflict Management in Africa*, Washington, DC: Brookings Institution, 1996.

4. Pang (see n.2 above), p.240.
5. ICISS, *The Responsibility to Protect*, Ottawa: International Development Research Centre, 2001, p.8 (emphasis added).
6. ICISS, *Research and Consultations: Supplementary Volume to The Responsibility to Protect*, Ottawa: International Development Research Centre, 2001, p.392.
7. Ibid., p.393.
8. ICISS, (see n.5 above), synopsis.
9. Ibid., p.xi.
10. Ibid., pp.xi, 11.
11. Pang (see n.2 above), p.240.
12. Alex J. Bellamy, *Responsibility to Protect: The Global Effort to End Mass Atrocities*, Cambridge: Polity, 2009, p.67.
13. 'A More Secure World: Our Shared Responsibility', Report of the Secretary-General's High Level Panel on Threats, Challenges and Change, UN doc., A/59/566, 2 Dec. 2004, para.203, p.66. Curiously, the Chinese representative on the panel did not reject the association between R2P and the use of protective force.
14. 'In Larger Freedom: Towards Development, Security and Human Rights for All', Report of the Secretary-General, UN doc., A/59/2005, 21 Mar. 2005, p.35; Alex J. Bellamy, 'Whither the Responsibility to Protect? Humanitarian Intervention and the 2005 World Summit', *Ethics and International Affairs*, Vol.20, No.2, 2006, p.157.
15. Ministry of Foreign Affairs of the People's Republic of China, 'Position Paper of the People's Republic of China on the United Nations Reforms', 7 June 2005 (at: www.mfa.gov.cn/eng/wjb/zzjg/gjs/gjsxw/t199318.htm).
16. Ibid.
17. 'Cross-Cutting Report: Protection of Civilians No.4', *Security Council Report*, 30 Oct. 2009, p.20 (at: www.securitycouncilreport.org/atf/cf/{65BFCF9B-6D27-4E9C-8CD3-CF6E4FF96FF9}/XCutting%20PoC%202009.pdf).
18. '2005 World Summit Outcome Document', UN doc., A/60/L.1, 15 Sep. 2005.
19. 'Implementing the Responsibility to Protect', UN doc., A/63/677, 12 Jan. 2009.
20. Referring in particular to comments made by one of Kofi Annan's senior advisers on UN Reform, Stephen Stedman, quoted in Alex J. Bellamy, 'The Responsibility to Protect and the Problem of Military Intervention', *International Affairs*, Vol.84, No.4, 2008, p.616.
21. Ibid., p.624.
22. David Vesel, 'The Lonely Pragmatist: Humanitarian Intervention in an Imperfect World', *Brigham Young University Journal of Public Law*, Vol.18, No.1, 2004, p.52.
23. 'Protection of Civilians in Armed Conflict', UN doc., S/RES/1674, 28 Apr. 2006; 'Darfur Peacekeeping', UN doc., S/RES/1706, 31 Aug. 2006. For additional details on China's position on R2P in the UN, see Sarah Teitt, 'Assessing Polemics, Principles and Practices: China and the Responsibility to Protect', *Global Responsibility to Protect*, Vol.1, No.2, 2009, pp.208–36.
24. Teitt (see n.23 above), pp.212–13, 217–19; 'Peace and Security in Africa', UN doc., S/PV.5749, 25 Sept. 2007, p.13; 'Peace and Security in Africa', UN doc, S/PV.5868, 16 Apr. 2008, p.11.
25. Susan C. Breau, 'The Impact of the Responsibility to Protect on Peacekeeping', *Journal of Conflict and Security Law*, Vol.11, No.3, 2006, p.444. For the link between R2P and POC in PKOs, see also Charles T. Hunt and Alex J. Bellamy, 'Mainstreaming the Responsibility to Protect in Peace Operations', Working Paper No.3, Asia Pacific Centre for the Responsibility to Protect, March 2010; Alex J. Bellamy and Paul D. Williams, 'Protecting Civilians in Uncivil Wars', Working Paper No.1, Program on the Protection of Civilians, Asia Pacific Centre for the Responsibility to Protect, Aug. 2009.
26. 'Cross-Cutting Report' (see n.17 above), p.20.
27. 'Security Council Open Debate on Protection of Civilians in Armed Conflict', UN Doc., S/PV.6354, 7 July 2010, p.28.
28. UN DPKO and Department of Field Support, 'United Nations Peacekeeping Operations: Principles and Guidelines', 2008.
29. For evidence of this omission, see Ministry of Foreign Affairs of the People's Republic of China (see n.15 above), along with China's contributions to UN Security Council debates on peacekeeping and China's remarks on the DPKO's 'New Horizon' (see n.33 below). For example, Ministry of Foreign Affairs of the People's Republic of China, 'Remarks by Vice Foreign Minister He Yafei at the Opening Ceremony of the International Symposium on Peacekeeping Operations', 19 Nov. 2009 (at: www.fmprc.gov.cn/eng/wjdt/zyjh/t631646.htm).

30. 'Protection of Civilians', UN doc., S/RES/1265, 17 Sept. 1999.
31. 'Protection of Civilians', UN doc., S/RES/1296, 19 Apr. 2000.
32. For the most part, these protection mandates have been attached with standard caveats: peace-keeping missions are authorized to protect civilians 'in the areas of deployment', 'within their capabilities' and, importantly in regard to China's support for the task, 'without prejudice to the [host] government' or 'taking into account the responsibilities of the [host] government'.
33. UN DPKO and Department of Field Support, 'A New Partnership Agenda: Charting a New Horizon for UN Peacekeeping', July 2009.
34. Ibid.; Victoria K. Holt, Glyn Taylor and Max Kelly, 'Protecting Civilians in the Context of UN Peacekeeping Operations', UN Independent Study Jointly Commissioned by the Department of Peacekeeping Operations and the Office for the Coordination of Humanitarian Affairs, 2009; 'Protection of Civilians', UN doc., S/RES/1894, 11 Nov. 2009; 'Report of the Special Committee on Peacekeeping Operations: 2010 Substantive Session (22 Feb.–19 Mar. 2010)', UN doc., A/64/19, 2010.
35. William J. Durch and Alison C. Giffen, 'Challenges of Strengthening the Protection of Civilians in Multidimensional Peace Operations', background paper for the third International Forum for the 'Challenges of Peace Operations', 27–9 Apr. 2010, Queenbeyan, 2010, p.7.
36. 'Security Council Open Debate on Peacekeeping Operations', UN doc., S/PV.6178, 5 Aug. 2009, p.23.
37. Permanent Mission of the People's Republic of China to the UN, 'Statement by Ambassador Liu Zhenmin, Deputy Permanent Representative of the Chinese Mission to the United Nations, at the Fourth Committee of the Sixty-Fourth Session of the United Nations General Assembly on Item 33: Comprehensive Review of the Whole Question of Peacekeeping Operations in all their Aspects', 27 Oct. 2009.
38. Ministry of Foreign Affairs of the People's Republic of China (see n.29 above).
39. 'Special Committee Members Commend Performance of United Nations Peacekeepers Faced with Complex Mandates, Lacking Key Capabilities: Delegates Express Views on Early Peace-building, Civilian Protection, "Robust Peacekeeping" as General Debate Concludes', UN doc., GA/PK/204, 23 Feb. 2010.
40. 'Protection of Civilians Monthly Forecast', Security Council Report, Nov. 2009 (at: www.securitycouncilreport.org/site/c.glKWLeMTIsG/b.5566467/k.B551/November_2009brProtection_of_Civilians.htm).
41. 'Security Council Open Debate on Protection of Civilians in Armed Conflict', UN doc., S/PV.5898, 27 May 2008, p.5.
42. Ibid., p.7.
43. 'Security Council Open Debate on Protection of Civilians in Armed Conflict', UN doc., S/PV.5781, 20 Nov. 2007, p.10.
44. 'Draft Resolution on Myanmar',UN doc., S/PV.5619, 12 Jan. 2007.
45. 'Protection of Civilians Monthly Forecast', Security Council Report, Jan. 2009 (at: www.securitycouncilreport.org/site/c.glKWLeMTIsG/b.4838015/k.1FFC/January_2009brProtection_of_Civilians.htm).
46. UN Office for the Coordination of Humanitarian Affairs, Policy Development and Studies Branch, 'Aide Memoire for the Consideration of Issues Pertaining to the Protection of Civilians in Armed Conflict', May 2009.
47. 'Protection of Civilians Monthly Forecast', Security Council Report, July 2010 (at: www.securitycouncilreport.org/site/c.glKWLeMTIsG/b.6115659/k.3FB8/July_2010brProtection_of_Civilians.htm).
48. 'Security Council Open Debate on Protection of Civilians in Armed Conflict Resolution 1296', UN doc., S/PV.4130, 19 Apr. 2000, p.4.
49. 'Security Council Open Debate on Peacekeeping Operations', UN doc., S/PV.6370, 6 Aug. 2010, p.24.
50. 'Special Committee Members Commend Performance of United Nations Peacekeepers Faced with Complex Mandates, Lacking Key Capabilities: Delegates Express Views on Early Peace-building, Civilian Protection, "Robust Peacekeeping" as General Debate Concludes' (see n.39 above).
51. Anne Tang, 'China Donates $700,000 to UN Peacekeeping Missions', Xinhua (Beijing), 2 Dec. 2009 (at: www.reliefweb.int/rw/rwb.nsf/db900sid/JBRN-7YCFEH?OpenDocument).

A Change in Perspective: China's Engagement in the East Timor UN Peacekeeping Operations

MARC LANTEIGNE

To understand China's change in position regarding UN peacekeeping, the country's internal debates and policy towards the UN operations in East Timor from 1999 to 2002 comprise an essential case study. Despite its traditional concerns about the sanctity of state sovereignty, China was willing to support and contribute personnel to East Timor peacekeeping missions. This was a result of its growing confidence in addressing regional strategic issues, its development of the 'New Security Concept', which encourages cooperative solutions to strategic issues, and its desire to remake its regional identity to reflect a more conservative and pragmatic approach to regional peacebuilding. This change in policy not only allowed China to become more at ease with UN peacekeeping participation, but also contributed much to the country's Asia-Pacific diplomacy, which increasingly stressed multilateralism and partnership.

Introduction: How East Timor Changed China's Peacekeeping Perceptions

Since the 1990s, one of the most remarkable changes in China's strategic policy making has been a gradual yet significant shift in policy towards a more willing acceptance of multilateral peacekeeping and peacebuilding initiatives. This is evidenced by China's current views that, aside from the traditional or state-to-state security challenges in the modern international system, several other security issues must not be overlooked. These include civil conflicts and 'non-traditional' threats such as international crime and terrorism which must be addressed and which cannot be solved unilaterally. Therefore, China's position on strategic multilateralism has softened, evolving from suspicion, and at times outright hostility, to support for such initiatives under particular conditions. The main condition is that the UN must assume a leadership role in dealing with non-traditional threats. China has become much more accepting of UN peacekeeping operations (PKOs), even those which skirt matters of state sovereignty. China's views on UN peacekeeping (*lianheguo weiqi heping*, 联合国维持和平) have changed significantly, as the People's Republic of China (PRC) is now the largest troop and personnel provider among the permanent five (P-5) members of the Security Council. China distinguishes what it sees as 'good' and 'bad' approaches to multilateral intervention based on the level of UN involvement. Using this criterion, non-UN missions, including NATO's operations in Kosovo in 1999 and the US-led operations in Iraq and Afghanistan, have been subject to much Chinese criticism.

In understanding the reversal of China's stand on multilateral intervention through the UN, it is helpful to examine the pivotal period in the late 1990s

FIGURE 1

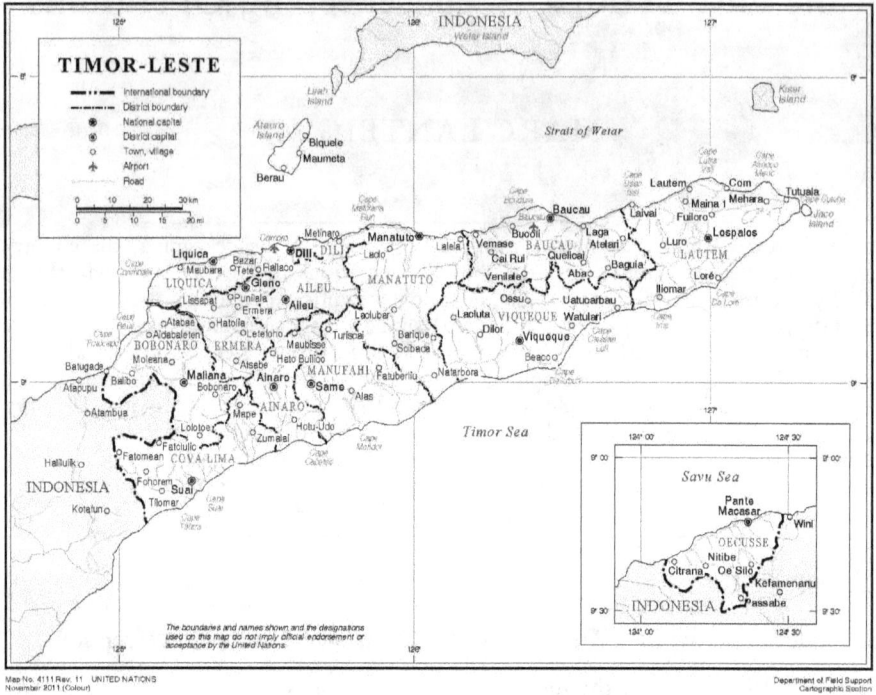

Source: UN Cartographic Section, 'Regions of TIMOR-LESTE', Map No. 4117 Rev.6, Mar. 2007, reproduced with kind permission

and the turn of the century when this new policy began to be translated into perceptible actions. While China had demonstrated various levels of support for UN peacekeeping initiatives earlier in the 1990s, Cambodia being a key example, Chinese policy towards UN operations in what was then East Timor in Southeast Asia between 1999 and 2002 provided the most illustrative example of new thinking on the utility of multilateral peacekeeping operations. These operations culminated in the recognition of East Timor's (now Timor-Leste's) independence from Indonesia and the admission of the new state to the UN as its 191st member in September 2002 (see Figure 1). The structure and operations of the UN Transitional Administration in East Timor (UNTAET, October 1999 to May 2002) included components that on the surface would have been an anathema to China's so-called 'neo-Westphalian' views on the sanctity of borders and the requirement for state sovereignty to be respected. At the same time, China's concerns about the status of Taiwan have made it wary about the development of a precedent for secessionist territories in UN operations. Such wariness had not faded by the late 2000s, as evidenced by China's reluctance to recognize Kosovo as an independent state in 2009.

Yet, despite the considerable parallels to China's own concerns about secessionism, the government supported Security Council Resolution 1264 (1999), which authorized the deployment of UN forces to the territory as well as the temporary transfer of legal and policing authority to the UN before independence.[1] This mission was very much in keeping with the 'activist' UN peacekeeping operations that developed during the 1990s, which combined military and civilian components and involved key legislative powers being assumed by the UN, a process once termed 'painting a country blue'.[2] China not only supported the mission but also provided a contingent for a UN operation for only the second time; the UN Transitional Authority in Cambodia (UNTAC) being the first, when the PRC agreed to send 47 military observers and about 800 hundred engineering troops in 1992–93.[3] Although the Cambodian UN mission was also supported by China and also heavily 'intrusive', as it involved UN actors temporarily assuming control over many state functions, that mission did not involve a modification of borders and thus was less of a challenge to China's traditional views on state sovereignty. China under President Jiang Zemin was also the first country to formally recognize East Timor's independence in 2002.

The reasoning behind Chinese foreign policy decisions about the East Timor mission can be examined on two levels. First, there is the importance of the East Timor case to China's multifaceted efforts during the last decade to build its international reputation as a 'responsible' great power (*fuzeren de daguo*, 负责任的大国). China's effort also led to increased global recognition for its alternative models of strategic cooperation, often termed China's 'New Security Concept' (NSC; *xin anquan guan*, 新安全观). The NSC stresses mutual and equal cooperation to solve security issues rather than unrestrained great power intervention.[4] Second, as discussed below, China's specific strategic interests in Southeast Asia were also served by its support for the UN mission in Timor, suggesting that China had developed much confidence in using international strategic institutions to support its evolving regional policies. Consequently, China's actions in the periods before and during the UN missions to East Timor were pivotal in shaping the country's future policies towards support for, and participation in, subsequent UN peacekeeping missions.

The New Security Concept in China's Strategic Policies in East Timor

China's engagement in East Timor became an important component of its evolving regional and international grand strategy as the country adjusted to the post-Cold-War security milieu. The NSC, introduced in 1992, was a reaction to the rapidly changing global security situation following the dissolution of the Soviet Union, which in numerous cases resulted in 'frozen' or stalemated Cold War conflicts being reignited. Many strategic issues in which the UN was unable to intervene due to superpower interference and use of the Security Council veto could suddenly be openly addressed. This led to considerable debate in the early 1990s over expanding UN peacekeeping initiatives to facilitate the conclusion of civil wars and war-to-peace transitions such as those in Namibia and El Salvador. These cases were referred to as 'orphan conflicts' because they represented leftover wars from the bipolar era in which state governments were unwilling to risk intervention. These cases were therefore 'thrown onto the lap of the United Nations',[5] further contributing to the zeitgeist (or *sichao*, 思潮) of international calls for UN peacekeeping reform. The NSC stressed the needs for ongoing acceptance of state sovereignty, for international cooperation under the guidelines of the UN Charter, and to 'give full play to the leading role of the UN'.[6]

At the same time as peacekeeping faced an expanded agenda, China was in the process of reassessing its views of the peacekeeping process. China had maintained a strongly negative view of peacekeeping from the outset, due in no small part to the People's Republic being one of the initial targets of multilateral UN operations, namely during the 1950–53 intervention in Korea. Following the PRC's exclusion from the UN starting in November 1949, Mao Zedong tended to stress the linkage between any attempts at UN peacekeeping on the part of the UN and thinly disguised superpower imperialism and expansionism. This stance was softened considerably by 1981, when China agreed to extend the peacekeeping mission in Cyprus; it then supported UN diplomacy and the subsequent peacekeeping mission in Cambodia between 1989 and 1993. Between 1990 and 1997, China also agreed to send small detachments of military observers to missions in Kuwait, Liberia and Mozambique, operations well away from the Asia-Pacific region.

There were, however, clear limits to how far China was willing to go in changing its views. The NSC reflected concerns that the UN under Secretary-General Boutros Boutros-Ghali was moving towards a form of UN intervention which was less reliant on consent from local governments and was blurring the line between peacekeeping and peace enforcement. This new stance by the UN was illustrated by Boutros-Ghali's watershed 1992 paper 'An Agenda for Peace', which suggested that 'absolute and exclusive sovereignty' was a concept of the past as the Cold War waned.[7] In discussing the UN's failures in Somalia, a 1994 *Beijing Review* commentary noted that 'peacekeeping must be limited to peacekeeping because the internal affairs of one country can be solved only by the people of that country'.[8] There was also the implied Chinese stance that peacekeepers should only be deployed in cases where at least a tentative settlement between parties was in place and that, once deployed, UN forces should maintain neutrality and use only minimum levels of force.[9] As will be further explained, the East Timor UN missions, despite representing non-traditional peacekeeping, did fulfil those tacit Chinese stipulations.

China's response to both the Boutros-Ghali assessment and the subsequent complications the UN experienced with missions during that decade was to restate its support for a return to a traditional, 'minimalist' approach to intervention. China stressed the need to observe norms of sovereignty and non-interference and to promote peaceful negotiations to end disputes, as well as the need for more pluralist decision-making which should include all states and organizations affected by a given crisis.[10] Foreign Minister Qian Qichen underlined these concerns by noting in a May 2000 speech that 'it is a dangerous tendency to think that attaching importance to human rights means the principle of sovereignty has become obsolete and there is no need to adhere to it'.[11] Nevertheless, despite China's conservative approach, there were strong signs, partially based on the country's policies concerning the East Timor question, that China's views on multilateral intervention by the UN had shifted from a blanket 'no' to a 'yes, but'.

As one study suggested, China's opposition to UN peacekeeping had become more selective by the 1990s, and when opposition was expressed, it was no longer based on ideological reasons but rather on concerns about a potential negative effect on China's own sovereignty or national security.[12] Thus, the East Timor mission was not viewed as a potential strategic risk for China itself. The prime determining factor in gauging China's support for peacekeeping had ceased to be whether it was consistent with Maoist anti-hegemonism, and was now instead the question of actual or potential strategic blowback (*fanzuoyong*, 反作用).

Also prompting a rethinking on China's part was the question of post-Cold-War US power, including in the Asia-Pacific region. With the United States as the remaining superpower, China was growing concerned that the US was seeking to unilaterally address many global security issues while expanding its influence. Consequently, China in the 1990s became an advocate of a 'new international order' (*xin guoji zhixu*, 新国际秩序) to address post-Cold-War uncertainties and promote mutual cooperation rather than the dominance of great powers (i.e. the United States) over smaller ones.[13] The evolution of this new approach to security and cooperation originated from China's evolving views that the end of the Cold War should signal a multilateralist approach to addressing international security. This viewpoint was aptly summarized in a 1997 *Beijing Review* editorial designed to counter a mutual enemy, which described Western alliances, large powers protecting smaller ones and weaker states deferring to stronger ones with as outmoded. Moreover, the work argued that the security of states and state cooperation were traditionally seen as being 'incompatible', since measures taken by one country to better protect itself invariably created insecurities in others – a nod to the Western international relations concept of the 'security dilemma' (*anquan kunju*, 安全困局). However, the piece argued that at the close of the twentieth century state security interests had become interconnected to the degree that it was necessary to approach the ideas of security and cooperation from a different, more conciliatory standpoint.[14]

These views also suggested that China's confidence in its own power capabilities had increased to levels where it was now comfortable addressing the issues and problems of multilateral cooperation without fear of perceived weakness. There is the argument that by the 1990s China's power and confidence had grown enough to allow greater acceptance of a flexible approach to issues of sovereignty, which could now be undertaken without perceived risks to China's own territorial integrity and abilities to withstand outside pressures on its internal affairs.[15] China's positive views on interventionism in East Timor clearly indicated that the Chinese government no longer saw an intractable contradiction between supporting post-Cold-War UN-backed peace missions and maintaining a strong stance towards supporting state sovereignty and non-interference. As well, China was no longer as concerned about a harmful precedent being set in the country's far western regions (Tibet and Xinjiang both of which had experienced separatist movements), which might have been created by supporting an international mission that would result in political secession.

Despite the more favourable stance towards multilateralism expressed in the NSC, the concept borrowed heavily on the Maoist-era Five Principles of Peaceful Coexistence (*heping gongchu wuxiang yuanze*, 和平共处五项原则), which advocated state equality and non-discrimination, mutual trust and benefits, and non-interference in states' sovereign affairs.[16] The Five Principles were dusted off and polished by Chinese policymakers in the early 1990s once it became apparent that the international system was not shifting towards multipolarity as hoped but rather towards US-dominated unipolarity. The NSC had its origins in the middle of that decade and was first noted in a formal setting by Jiang Zemin in 1999 during the UN Conference on Disarmament.[17] Variations of these ideas have been carried into the current century under Hu Jintao, albeit becoming more complex as China began to develop its cross-regional policies, which by necessity prompted a greater Chinese role in security problems further afield from the country's periphery.

As well, after eschewing the post-Cold-War ideas of 'human security' (involving the merging of human rights issues with security initiatives), which had been developed in the West and adapted in parts of Asia, China had begun to examine this branch of security much more closely by the end of the 1990s, albeit under the less politically sensitive term 'non-traditional security' (*fei chuantong anquan*, 非传统安全). Semantics aside, there was a growing consensus in Chinese policy circles that retaining Cold War perceptions of security would result in excessive policy rigidity in the light of changing strategic challenges in the modern international system.[18] Non-traditional security challenges have become embedded in modern Chinese military strategy under Hu Jintao, and have played a part in China's decision since the mid-2000s to pursue the option of engaging in 'long distance manoeuvres' (*changtu yanxi*, 长途演习), meaning strategic operations further away from Chinese borders.[19] Finally, the security crises occurring both during the Cold War and after often started as small, local affairs, only to broaden and have regional and at times global effects. Therefore, China by the 1990s sought to 'plug the small hole before suffering a larger hole' (*xiaodong budu, dadong chiku*, 小洞不堵，大洞吃苦) in its reformed approach to Asian security issues without assuming the role of subaltern to the United States or taking on the role of hegemon-in-waiting. This stance would be illustrated in the conservative and at times tentative policymaking in China towards addressing the East Timor independence crisis.

China's Role in East Timor Operations

The status of the territory of East Timor had been one of the most contentious in Southeast Asia, dating from the time the former Portuguese colony declared independence in 1975 only to be forcibly annexed by Indonesia in December of that year. Indonesian sovereignty over the territory was not formally recognized by the UN, and the organization's General Assembly made periodic calls for Timorese self-determination. The conflict became locked within the greater game of super-power competition in Southeast Asia, as the United States was concerned about an increased communist presence in the region as well as Maoist China's support for the leftist liberation forces of the Frente Revolucionária de Timor-Leste Independente (FRETILIN), which sought to push back the Indonesian army from the territory.[20] Sporadic guerrilla warfare would continue for two decades after the annexation, international actors being unwilling to intervene directly due to Cold War pressures.

It was not until the end of the Cold War and the Asian Financial Crisis in 1997–98 that an opportunity arose to end the conflict. After being powerless to halt Indonesia's rapid economic slide as a result of the regional economic melt-down, President Suharto was forced from office in the wake of mass protests throughout the country under the banner of *reformasi*. He was replaced in May 1998 by Bacharuddin Jusuf (B.J.) Habibie, who was far more open to a negotiated settlement to the conflict than was his predecessor. In January 1999 he made the surprising announcement that a referendum on sovereignty would be held. In May of that year representatives of Indonesia, Portugal and the UN agreed to allow the ballot to be UN supervised with the understanding that if independence was sought it would be the UN that would oversee both the transfer of power and the country's administration during the transitional period.[21] The Habibie government nonetheless attempted to keep East Timor within the country by pro-posing that the breakaway territory be redesignated the 'Special Autonomous Region of East Timor' (SARET) with local government autonomy and Jakarta retaining governance over foreign relations, defence and various legal areas.

To Indonesia's chagrin, the 30 August 1999 referendum resulted in a clear rejection of the SARET proposal and mass support for the option of outright inde-pendence (78.5 per cent to 21 per cent). The politically entrenched leadership of the Indonesian National Armed Forces (TNI, Tentara Nasional Indonesia) rejected the result, and some of its forces linked up with pro-Indonesia irregular militias on the island of Timor to instigate an intense guerrilla campaign known as *Operasi Sapu Jagad* (Operation *Clean Sweep*) to destabilize and reclaim the territory, forcing about 400,000 refugees over the border into West Timor.[22] The Habibie government's hesitation in accepting the vote results until October of that year resulted in an increasingly dangerous political and security vacuum in the interim. Although the Indonesian government denied that it was supporting military intervention in East Timor, there was much international condemnation of Habibie's lack of control over the TNI. In response, the UN sought to expand the parameters of the Timor mission to include both the pacification of the terri-tory and prepare it for potential full independence.

China's involvement in the East Timor mission came only months after Sino-US relations soured over NATO's military operations in Serbia/Kosovo (May–June 1999). China was highly critical of the lack of UN involvement, especially after the May bombing of its embassy in Belgrade during a US attack on the Serbian capital. China reacted with suspicion to US claims that the bombing, which resulted in the deaths of three Chinese journalists, was accidental due to faulty maps.[23] China's reactions to the Serbian and the East Timorese conflicts suggested that it was drawing distinctions between the various means by which multilateral intervention should be undertaken. Specifically, the UN should be involved and consent from as many parties as possible should be sought. However, as Allen Carlson notes, Indonesia's 'consent' to the peacekeeping mission was at best lukewarm and no doubt influenced by implacable Western pressure. Yet China opted to overlook those circumstances, he added, as well as the fact that Australia rather than the UN was acting as the main broker with tacit UN backing, when the conditions for undertaking peacekeeping operations were established.[24]

The economic leaders' meeting of the Asia Pacific Economic Cooperation (APEC) forum in Auckland in September 1999 became another test of the commitment of regional governments to address the security crisis in East Timor. Habibie did not attend the summit, but sent his Minister of the Economy, Ginandjar Kartasamita, as Indonesian representative. Kartasamita became the focal point for a great deal of scrutiny over Jakarta's stance regarding an international solution to the Timor crisis. Adding to the urgency of the situation, José Ramos-Horta, representing FRETLIN, stridently called for joint APEC action to stop the fighting.[25] Although APEC meetings traditionally focus strictly on trade and economic issues, East Timor was too pressing an issue to be ignored. Australian Prime Minister John Howard and US President Bill Clinton led the call for an international intervention to halt the violence, and Habibie buckled by agreeing in principle to a multinational force. Much debate about the structure and logistics of such a force took place on the fringes of the summit.[26] Although China, as an attendee, was in a position to question other governments' policies on how to address the Timor question, representatives from Beijing were uncomfortable with the idea of APEC serving as a platform for non-economic matters, especially on an issue of this sensitivity.

Jiang Zemin released a speech he had given during the summit, stating that APEC should adhere to its original mandate, the negotiation of liberalized trade in the Asia-Pacific region. He added that deviating from this mandate would 'inevitably result in difficulties and setbacks' for the APEC forum. Nevertheless, despite this reluctance, as well as lingering tensions with the United States as a result of the Belgrade bombing, China was represented in the side-meetings on East Timor and negotiations over a potential intervention policy.[27] Yet, following the summit, China maintained that APEC should remain dedicated to economic issues. A meeting specifically to address East Timor was hastily arranged by the New Zealand Ministry of Foreign Affairs, attended by all of the delegations present at APEC, though not considered an APEC event *per se*, and by the UK Foreign Minister Robin Cook.[28] Immediately after the summit, China stood with the other permanent Security Council members in passing Resolution 1264, which authorized the creation of an International Force for East Timor (INTERFET) under UN auspices with Australia taking the lead in logistics and organization. Crucially, the new operation would be given the right to use force in the name of stabilizing the territory and providing needed humanitarian assistance.[29] INTERFET would act as a strictly provisional force until formal peacekeepers could be deployed.

As the prospect of a UN peacekeeping mission to Timor began to solidify in the autumn of 1999, China was in the difficult position of wanting to contribute support but being wary of doing so without approval from Indonesia for the overall mission itself. China, having veto power in the Security Council, could also have scuttled the mission unilaterally if it were dissatisfied with the local conditions. Therefore, other actors were concerned about how China would respond to the potential operation, particularly as China did not send personnel to assist INTERFET. The Chinese government's sensitivity towards Indonesian sovereignty was exemplified by guarded comments made by the PRC's permanent representative to the UN, Qin Huasun, that while China was 'gravely concerned' about the violence in East Timor, a peacekeeping force should only be deployed under the aegis of the Security Council and at Indonesia's formal request.[30] As well, China publicly disagreed with the opinion of the Clinton administration in Washington that Indonesia should not be allowed to participate in the development of the peacekeeping mission, insisting that any mission should only be undertaken with Indonesian consent.[31]

This response suggested that China was not only overcoming its initial opposition to multilateral intervention in general but also more willing to adopt a flexible approach to formally authorizing participation in such missions. While NATO's operations in Serbia/Kosovo were widely denigrated in China as 'interference' or 'meddling' (*ganshe*, 干涉), such a label was not applied to the developing international operations in East Timor. In fact, it was noted that in contrast to the often vitriolic responses in the former case, Chinese responses to the developing East Timor operations under UNTAET were on the whole mild, supportive and succinct.[32] This transpired despite the fact that the East Timor mission was authorized under Chapter VII of the Charter, which allows for direct military intervention when a case can be made for a threat to international peace.[33] China was, and still is, periodically sensitive to the UN's authorization of Chapter VII activities in civil conflicts or crises, out of concerns about state sovereignty and the setting of precedents. Also of note was China's willingness to put aside its equally wary approach to UN missions that involve the, even temporary, usurpation of local governmental powers in order to create a more congenial milieu for peacekeeping operations. In the case of East Timor, and Cambodia before it, China was willing to accept this component despite the interventionist, or 'paternalistic', attributes of the missions.[34]

China's delicate approach to involvement in East Timor was also influenced by the welfare of the overseas Chinese population in Indonesia, which the Chinese government did not want subjected to reprisals. The Chinese minority had been a politically sensitive subject since Indonesian independence, and there had been incidents of ethnic Chinese being subject to violence in the 1950s and 1960s as well as during the 1998 May Revolution which unseated the Suharto government. At the same time, the Maoist government had not been reticent in its hopes of spreading communist ideology via the Indonesian Communist Party (Partai Komunis Indonesia, PKI), which was outlawed in 1965 after Suharto's rise to power and the new president's alignment with the United States.[35] Indonesian protestors also targeted Chinese minorities and businesses during the 1998 May Revolution which culminated in the fall of the Suharto regime. The scale and brutality of the attacks resulted in both an exodus of Chinese nationals and considerable pressure on China to respond. However, the Jiang government opted to take a measured and restrained approach that preserved diplomatic and economic ties between the two states while expressing China's concerns using quiet diplomacy.[36] Indonesia was also unwilling to allow the incident to derail the gradually warming relations with China. For example, the 'New Order' (*Orde Baru*) policies under Suharto had included the controversial suppression of Chinese language and culture (in place since the 1970s), and these were rapidly repealed after the change of government.[37] Suharto's removal and the solidifying of the successor reformist Habibie government, therefore, offered the possibility for China to take a measured approach to engaging with the Timor crisis. Once the blessing for UNTAET was given by Indonesia, Portugal and the UN itself, China was politically unshackled to begin planning its specific response to the call for peacekeeping forces.[38]

The UNTAET force was groundbreaking in peacekeeping history mainly due to the fact that for the first time UN forces were not overseen in conjunction with another authority, state or otherwise. In October 1999, Portugal, which had been seen as a legal stakeholder in East Timor even during the years of Indonesian occupation, confirmed its renunciation of all claims to the territory and that UNTAET was the legitimate, recognized successor.[39] The large number of states contributing to UNTAET, including Australia, Brazil, France, Japan, New Zealand, the Philippines, South Korea and the UK, further bolstered China's stance that its own aim was multilateral cooperation in the name of pacifying the region rather than unilateral interference. In other words, China could effectively downplay its presence in the crowd under these conditions (see Miwa Hirono's article in this issue). Shen Guofang, Deputy Permanent Representative to the UN, encapsulated this idea when he noted on the eve of UNTAET's deployment that the people of East Timor were the 'main actors' and that their 'wishes and choices' should be made paramount.[40] An interpretation can be held that China's role in the mission was not to interfere but rather to assist with the process of self-determination; in other words, building sovereignty rather than tearing it down.

Despite the degree of scrutiny China faced, its decision to delay taking a public position until all relevant parties had given their permission for the force to proceed is consistent with the hypothesis provided by one analyst that China's support for a given multilateral peace mission increases as more of the stakeholders involved agree on the means and ends of a mission.[41] The lack of a strong overt US presence in the development of the East Timor operations, despite US activism in Auckland, was also a contributing factor in China's decision to participate in UNTAET – which could not be viewed as a proxy operation on behalf of the US, Australia or Western interests. These concerns would be further mollified with the appointment of Lt Gen. Jaime de Los Santos of the Philippines as Force Commander in January 2000 and Lt Gen. Boonsrang Niumpradit of Thailand as de Los Santos's successor in July,[42] confirming the regional character of the peacekeeping operation.

The Chinese government came under considerable pressure to clarify its stance on East Timor. During the period of ambiguity over East Timor's eventual status, China was concerned that Taiwan would attempt to use its 'chequebook diplomacy' practices (*zhipiaobu waijiao*, 支票簿外交) to entice the potential new state to recognize Taiwan, creating a potentially valuable diplomatic outpost for the Taiwanese government in Southeast Asia. The South Pacific had already become an arena for competition as China and Taiwan wooed governments with economic incentives to choose between them.[43] The 1990s had also seen an overall acceleration of diplomatic manoeuvres between the two which at times spilled over into the Security Council.[44] Concerns about Taiwan's influence on East Timor were addressed in early 2000 when the Chinese Foreign Minister Tang Jiaxuan met Xanana Gusmao, head of FRETILIN, in Beijing, and received assurances that an independent East Timor would follow the 'one China' policy (*yige Zhongguo zhengce*, 一个中国政策) and recognize the PRC, thus stopping any Taiwanese diplomatic push in its tracks. Moreover, Tang authorized what would be the first of many economic deals by offering the territory a 50 million yuan (about US$6 million) aid package to assist in post-war reconstruction.[45] This deal was one of the first signs that the PRC was willing to use its own growing economic power to provide incentives to encourage developing and newly independent states to refrain from recognizing Taiwan. Gusmao retained and enhanced Chinese ties upon taking office as East Timor's first president in May 2002, while Taiwan announced in the same month that it would not attempt to seek diplomatic relations with East Timor.[46]

The initial 15 Chinese civilian police officers, drawn from the country's People's Armed Police (PAP), were selected for deployment in January 2000, and UNTAET officially took over from INTERFET a month later. The PAP-personnel-turned-blue-helmets, the first time Chinese police were deployed outside China under international auspices, were deployed in remote parts of the territory and on occasion came under fire from Indonesian guerrilla forces while on patrol.[47] By the time the Chinese government published its 2002 'White Paper on China's National Defence', the number of Chinese police who had served in East Timor had risen to 198.[48] There were no Chinese casualties among UNTAET participants and China's involvement in the mission was judged to be successful by both the Chinese and other states, setting a standard for future Chinese participation in UN peace operations. One Chinese police officer was even promoted during the operations to the rank of deputy police commissioner for UNTAET, which was the highest rank a Chinese national had attained in a peacekeeping mission.[49] There was, however, one side-effect of China's soft and cautious approach to personnel deployment. Although there was support in the Chinese People's Liberation Army (PLA) for including military observers as part of the Chinese contingent, prolonged debate within the central government resulted in official approval being delayed until after all military observer positions had been filled.[50] Thus, China's participation in UNTAET was exclusively civilian in nature.

In addition to policing and establishing governmental agencies in preparation for East Timorese independence, UNTAET also supervised the return of more than 150,000 refugees who had fled to West Timor as a result of the violence during the first half of 2000. The UN authority also organized elections for the new country's parliament, the Constituent Assembly, which took office after balloting took place in August 2001.[51] UNTAET ceased operations when East Timor became independent in May 2002 and the force was replaced by a much smaller international contingent charged with a mandate to improve the security of the new nation and assist with civilian law enforcement. The UN Mission of Support for East Timor (UNMISET) operated from May 2002 to May 2005 and, once again, China contributed police forces. Between January 2000 and July 2006 a total of 207 Chinese police were assigned to the East Timor UN missions.[52] UNMISET was subsequently replaced in August 2006 with the current UN Integrated Mission in Timor-Leste (UNMIT), which was designed to further consolidate political and security institutions in the country. China provided both police and military liaison officials for this mission, which was scheduled to be in operation until February 2011. In May 2010, a 24-person detachment which included specialists in criminal investigation, public security and traffic maintenance was deployed to Timor-Leste under UNMIT.[53] Assuming UNMIT is completed on schedule, China will have had the distinction of being involved in this complex peacekeeping process right from its inception.

Conclusions: East Timor as a Test and a Beginning

The enhancement of cooperation in China's bilateral and regional relations, not only in terms of depth but also in variety, has been a cornerstone of China's expanded diplomacy since the reform era. China's about-face in its views of UN peacekeeping, and more importantly its growing flexibility in its approach and its support of different types of multilateral intervention by the UN, have brought it added prestige and diplomatic power. In examining this phenomenon, the East Timor case study offers a clear understanding of how these changes came about. Despite appearing to conclude that UNTAET and its support operations contained too many 'negative' components, including intervention in a sovereign state and managed secession, China was willing to put aside its previous reservations about UN operations of this type and not only support the East Timor process but also provide integral assistance in guiding it to its conclusion.

Since the East Timor operations and subsequent peacekeeping missions, China has demonstrated much greater confidence and has become more willing to deploy its forces as blue berets overseas. China is now commonly seen as filling the gap created by the other permanent members of the UN Security Council, which have become less willing to offer their forces for peacekeeping missions. As well, China has been able to build increased 'soft power' internationally by pointing to its achievements in UN peacekeeping as further proof that China is developing as a responsible great power.[54] At the same time, China has been able to use its growing power both in the abstract and within the UN to push for what it regards as 'correct' methods of UN multilateral intervention, which incorporate the consent of parties, minimum force, neutrality and clear mandates and strategies. Under Hu Jintao, the Chinese government has made more frequent references to the need for greater 'democratization' in international relations (*guoji guanxi minzhuhua*, 国际关系民主化), which has been interpreted as greater respect for laws and norms on the international level as opposed to the predominance of power politics.[55] Support for UN peace operations has provided a ready mechanism for China to illustrate this commitment in a non-confrontational way.

East Timor provided a timely opportunity for China to bring forward these views to the international audience while demonstrating that it no longer intended to be obstructionist during the process of creating new UN peacekeeping objectives. The mission coincidentally came about at a time when China was reassessing its views on peacekeeping and seeking ways to demonstrate its evolving goodwill towards multilateral intervention under specific conditions. The timing was also beneficial for China to transform its views on the NSC from abstraction to a working policy that would be acknowledged and taken seriously by a large global audience through its reactions to the developing East Timor mission. The security situation in East Timor before the deployment of UNTAET was considered by China to be dangerous enough to have a significant impact on Asian strategic affairs, while at the same time China viewed UN intervention as lacking the potential to create a significant level of harm to China's own security and regional policy. Accordingly, China has benefited on several fronts from its activities in East Timor both locally and internationally.

NOTES

1. UN doc. S/RES/1264 (1999).
2. Marrack Goulding, 'The Evolution of United Nations Peacekeeping', *International Affairs*, Vol.69, No.3, 1993, p.459.
3. Bates Gill and James Reilly, 'Sovereignty, Intervention and Peacekeeping: The View from Beijing', *Survival*, Vol.42, No.3, 2000, p.44.
4. David M. Lampton, 'China's Rise in Asia Need Not Be at America's Expense', in David Shambaugh (ed.), *Power Shift: China and Asia's New Dynamics*, Berkeley and Los Angeles: University of California Press, 2005, pp.314–15.
5. Saadia Touval, 'Why the UN Fails', *Foreign Affairs*, Vol.73, No.5, 2004, p.46.
6. 'China's Position Paper on the New Security Concept', Ministry of Foreign Affairs of the People's Republic of China, 31 July 2002 (at: www.mfa.gov.cn/eng/wjb/zzjg/gjs/gjzzyhy/2612/2614/t15319.htm).
7. Boutros Boutros-Ghali, 'An Agenda for Peace: Preventive Diplomacy, Peacemaking and Peacekeeping', UN doc. A/47/277-S/24111, 17 Jun. 1992, p.17.
8. He Hongze, 'New Role for UN', *Beijing Review*, Vol.37, No.2, 1994, p.23.
9. Gill and Reilly (see n.3 above).
10. Samuel S. Kim, 'China and the United Nations', in Elizabeth Economy and Michel Oksenberg (eds), *China Joins the World: Progress and Prospects*, New York: Council on Foreign Relations Press, 1999, pp.52–3.
11. Qian Qichen, *Ten Episodes in Chinese Diplomacy*, New York: HarperCollins, 2005, p. 297.
12. Taylor M. Fravel, 'China's Attitude toward UN Peacekeeping Operations since 1989', *Asian Survey*, Vol.36, No.11 1996, p.1109.
13. Mel Gurtov and Byong-Moo Hwang, *China's Security: The New Roles of the Military*, Boulder, CO: Lynne Rienner, 1998, pp.66–7.
14. A. Ying, 'New Security Mechanism Needed for Asian-Pacific Region', *Beijing Review*, 18–24 Aug. 1997, pp.6–7.
15. Joel Wuthnow, 'China and the Processes of Cooperation in UN Security Council Deliberations', *Chinese Journal of International Politics*, Vol.3, No.1, 2010, p.65.

16. 'Some Thoughts on Establishing a New Regional Security Order', Statement by Ambassador Sha Zukang at the East–West Center's Senior Policy Seminar, 7 Aug. 2000, Honolulu, Ministry of Foreign Affairs for the People's Republic of China, Aug. 2000 (at: www.fmprc.gov.cn/eng/wjdt/zyjh/t24961.htm).

17. Russell Ong, *China's Security in the 21st Century*, London: Routledge, 2007, p.13.

18. Paul M. Evans, 'Human Security in East Asia: In the Beginning', *Journal of East Asian Studies*, No.4, 2004, p.275.

19. Jonathan Holslag, 'Embracing Chinese Global Security Ambitions', *Washington Quarterly*, Vol.32, No.3, 2009, p.109.

20. Jani Purnawanty, 'Various Perspectives on Understanding the East Timor Crisis', *Temple International and Comparative Law Journal*, No.72, 2000, p.65.

21. Michael G. Smith with Maureen Dee, *East Timor's Journey to Freedom*, Boulder, CO: Lynne Rienner, 2003, pp.42–3.

22. Kristen E. Schulze, 'The East Timor Referendum Crisis and Its Impact on Indonesian Politics', *Studies in Conflict and Terrorism*, Vol.24, No.1, 2001, pp.77–8.

23. Peter Hayes Gries, 'Tears of Rage: Chinese Nationalist Reactions to the Belgrade Embassy Bombing', *China Journal*, No.46, 2001, pp.25–43.

24. Allen Carlson, 'More Than Just Saying No: China's Evolving Approach to Sovereignty and Intervention since Tiananmen', in Alastair Iain Johnson and Robert S. Ross (eds), *New Directions in the Study of Chinese Foreign Policy*, Stanford, CA: Stanford University Press, 2006, pp.227–8.

25. Charles Hutzler, 'Clinton, APEC Leaders Offer Help for East Timor Peacekeeping', Associated Press, 13 Sept. 1999; 'Ramos-Horta Calls for APEC Action on Timor', Reuters, 10 Sept. 1999.

26. 'APEC Leaders to Confer on East Timor as Jakarta Bows before Pressure', Agence France Presse, 12 Sept. 1999.

27. David Barber, 'Auckland Summit Gives APEC a World-Beating Reputation', *National Business Review* (Auckland), 17 Nov. 1999, p.1.

28. Interview with former New Zealand Foreign Affairs official, Aug. 2010.

29. Jackson Nyamuya Maogoto, 'From Congo to East Timor in Forty Years: The UN Finally Crossing the Rubicon between Peace-Keeping and Peace-Making?', *Newcastle Law Review*, No.2, 2000, pp.61–2; David Dickens, 'Can East Timor Be a Blueprint for Burden-Sharing?', *Washington Quarterly*, Vol.25, No.3, 2002, pp.29–40; UN doc., 'Resolution 1264 (1999) Adopted by the Security Council at its 4045th Meeting on 15 September 1999' (at: www.un.org/peace/etimor99/9926481E.htm).

30. 'China Urges Halt to Violence in East Timor', *Xinhua News Agency*, 11 Sept. 1999.

31. Matthew Brockett, 'China Backs Indonesian Role in Peacekeeping', *The Dominion* (Wellington), 15 Sept. 1999, p.2.

32. Gill and Reilly (see n.3 above), p.50.

33. Matthias Ruffert, 'The Administration of Kosovo and East Timor by the International Community', *International and Comparative Law Quarterly*, Vol. 50, No.3, 2001, pp.619–20.

34. Shogo Suzuki, 'Chinese Soft Power, Insecurity Studies, Myopia and Fantasy', *Third World Quarterly*, Vol.30, No.4, 2009, p.780.

35. David M. Lampton, *The Three Faces of Chinese Power: Might, Money and Minds*, Berkeley and Los Angeles: University of California Press, 2008, pp.185–6.

36. See Zha Daojiong, 'China and the May 1998 Riots of Indonesia: Exploring the Issues', *Pacific Review*, Vol.13, No.4, 2000, pp.557–75.

37. Ignatius Wibowo, 'China's Soft Power and Neoliberal Agenda in Southeast Asia', in Mingjiang Li (ed.), *Soft Power: China's Emerging Strategy in International Politics*, Lexington, MA: Lexington Books, 2009, pp.214–15.

38. 'China Waiting on UN Call to Send Police to East Timor', *Kyodo News/Japan Economic Newswire*, 19 Oct. 1999.

39. Jarat Chopra, 'Building State Failure in East Timor', *Development and Change*, Vol.33, No.5, 2002, p.984.

40. 'China on Establishing UNTAET in East Timor', *Xinhua*, 25 Oct. 1999.

41. Wuthnow (see n.15 above), p.11.

42. 'Annan Appoints New Force Commander for UNTAET', *Xinhua*, 12 July 2000.

43. Joel Atkinson, 'China–Taiwan Diplomatic Competition and the Pacific Islands', *Pacific Review*, Vol. 23, No.4, 2010, pp.407–27.

44. Jing Chen, 'Explaining the Change in China's Attitude toward UN Peacekeeping: A Norm Change Perspective', *Journal of Contemporary China*, Vol.18, No.58, 2009, p.168.

45. Matt Pottinger, 'Gusmao Seeks East Timorese Ties with China', Reuters, 28 Jan. 2000.

46. 'Taiwan Activists "Encouraged" by East Timor, But No Diplomatic Ties Planned', Agence France Presse, 20 May 2002.
47. 'How Chinese Police in East Timor Won Respect from Locals and Colleagues', *South China Morning Post* (Singapore), 19 Dec. 2008, p.8; 'Chinese Police Will Head to East Timor to Join UN Force', *Dow Jones International News*, 11 Jan. 2000.
48. 'Full Text of China's Defence White Paper in 2002', *Xinhua*, 9 Dec. 2002.
49. Yin He, 'China's Changing Policy on UN Peacekeeping Operations', Institute for Security and Development Policy Asia Paper, July 2007, p.31.
50. Bates Gill, *Rising Star: China's New Security Diplomacy*, Washington, DC: Brookings, 2007, p.124.
51. 'East Timor – UNTAET Background', United Nations Department of Public Information, 2002 (at: www.un.org/en/peacekeeping/missions/past/etimor/UntaetB.htm).
52. 'China's Participation in UN Peacekeeping Operations 2009/01/21', Permanent Mission of the People's Republic of China to the United Nations, 21 Jan. 2009 (at: www.china-un.org/eng/zt/wh/t534321.htm).
53. 'Chinese Peacekeeping Squad Leaves for East Timor', *Xinhua*, 11 May 2010.
54. Bonnie Ling, 'China's Peacekeeping Diplomacy', *China Rights Forum*, No.1, 2007, pp.47–9.
55. Pan Zhongying, 'China's Changing Attitude to UN Peacekeeping', *International Peacekeeping*, Vol.12, No.1, 2005, p.99.

China's Charm Offensive and Peacekeeping: The Lessons of Cambodia – What Now for Sudan?

MIWA HIRONO

China's participation in UN peacekeeping is often viewed as a part of a global 'charm offensive' aimed at enhancing China's image in host countries. However, when viewed in the light of its support for dictatorial regimes in those host countries, do Chinese peacekeeping efforts improve the perceptions local populations have of China? This article examines changes in Cambodian perceptions of China during the UN Transitional Authority in Cambodia (UNTAC) from 1992 to 1993. It argues that China's peacekeeping contribution to UNTAC helped to overcome negative perceptions of that country rooted in its support of the Khmer Rouge before 1992. The key to overcoming current negative perceptions is to project an image of Chinese neutrality with respect to all parties in a civil war. This article concludes by discussing the implication of this argument with regard to China's peacekeeping in Sudan from 2006 to the present, and suggesting that China will need to be more attentive to the needs of other warring factions in the north–south and Darfur conflicts.

Introduction: China's Peacekeeping from Local Perspectives

The politics of image have been important to China for at least the last two decades. In the 1990s, the People's Republic of China (PRC) engaged in 'peripheral diplomacy' (*zhoubian waijiao*, 周边外交), seeking a favourable image in Southeast and East Asia, thereby securing its borders and enabling it to rapidly develop economically. As China's rise continued to increase its reach globally in the 2000s, the government made cautious efforts to project the idea that it does not threaten the world. These efforts are demonstrated by such policy discourses in China as 'peaceful development', 'harmonious world', 'soft power' and 'responsible power'. Chinese officials and analysts see peacekeeping as an important component of its 'charm offensive' aimed at enhancing its image in host countries.[1]

However, reports indicate that there are problems of distrust between the Chinese and local populations in several host countries, including Sudan. A representative example is the kidnapping of Chinese oil workers in Sudan in October 2008.[2] This was a consequence of China's close relations with the regime in Khartoum. In Sudan, China has provided the Khartoum government in the north with political, security and economic support, including arms used in the north–south and Darfur conflicts.[3] The conflict between the northern and southern regions persisted over two decades from 1983 to 2005, and resulted in an estimated two million deaths, four million internally displaced people, and about half a million refugees.[4] In Darfur, the Sudanese government and its Janjaweed militia have conducted mass killings and ethnic cleansing since 2003, resulting in the deaths or disappearances of as many as 200,000 people.[5] China's close relations with a genocidal regime was not unprecedented. In Cambodia, the Chinese government provided the Khmer Rouge with political, economic and military support.[6] For three years and nine months (April 1975 to January 1979), the Khmer Rouge carried out the massacre that led to the death of more than 1.5 million people, no less than a fifth of the Cambodian population, and the regime forced many others into hard labour.[7]

When local populations perceive that China is aiding a genocidal regime, how do they then perceive China's peacekeeping? Does it help to wipe out negative impressions and help local peoples to reconstruct a more favourable image of China? In other words, does China's 'charm offensive' work in complex conflicts? This article addresses these questions by examining how local Cambodian perceptions of China changed as a result of the Chinese peacekeeping contribution to the UN Transitional Administration in Cambodia (UNTAC) from 1992 to 1993. The term 'charm offensive' began to appear in the literature in the early 2000s and may not apply directly to the 1992–93 period. However, the fact that Cambodia was a crucial part of China's peripheral diplomacy in the early 1990s, which aimed to gain China a favourable image among local populations (the same diplomatic objective as China's 'charm offensive' in a global context in the 2000s), implies that China's Cambodia policy can be understood as a precursor to the 'charm offensive'. The Cambodian case is chosen because the country has experienced one of the worst genocides in history, and local populations saw China as a supporter of the dictatorial regime. Local Cambodian suspicion of the PRC as a prelude to the UNTAC operation resembles the current case in Sudan, where the Chinese face the problem of local distrust in southern Sudan and Darfur. Therefore, it is useful to examine China's peacekeeping in Cambodia and to consider what that experience can offer about ways in which the PRC could address the issue of local distrust in southern Sudan and Darfur.

The article argues that, as a result of the peacekeeping operation, China's 'charm offensive' in Cambodia was successful in transforming negative local perceptions of China's past into more positive ones. This argument comes with an important caveat. The reason local Cambodians changed their perceptions in favour of China is *not just that* the PRC provided infrastructure to facilitate local Cambodian state-building and economic development – the reason often assumed in discussion of the 'hearts and minds' strategy of peace operation, as mentioned below. In fact, the more important factor is that China had engaged in diplomacy with multiple actors prior to the peacekeeping period – it had close relations with the Khmer Rouge, but simultaneously also with the King Father Sihanouk, who was a widely respected and still is a popular figure in Cambodia. The approach taken in Cambodia has significant policy implications for China's peacekeeping in Sudan in the 2000s onwards. To gain local trust in areas substantially governed by factions other than the Khartoum government, China's diplomacy with Sudan needs to be more neutral, and attentive to the needs of other warring factions, such as the southern Sudan autonomous government, the Justice and Equality Movement (JEM) and the Sudan Liberation Army in Darfur.

The following section begins by briefly discussing the theoretical literature on local perspectives in peace operations. This is followed by an examination of the changes in local perceptions of China and of its peacekeeping efforts. The focal point of the analysis is how local Cambodians perceived China's apparently Janus-faced attitude towards their country – supporting a genocidal regime on the one hand, and contributing to keeping peace on the other. To investigate local attitudes and perceptions, research was undertaken in Cambodia from August to September 2009. This consisted of two parts: first, semi-structured interviews with Cambodian intellectuals, former UNTAC personnel and government officials in Phnom Penh (a total of 27), and six local village leaders on National Road No.6, which Chinese peacekeepers repaired during part of their mission (from April 1992 to September 1993); and, second, a questionnaire survey with Cambodian students at the Royal Cambodian Armed Forces' College of Social Sciences and Languages. This was chosen because it was expected that Cambodian military officers would have specialized knowledge of the country's international military ties, including of the Chinese military contribution to UNTAC. As revealed in more detail later, China's activities during UNTAC are not necessarily well known among local Cambodians because China chose to keep a low profile. However, the images of China among those who *did* have the chance to come into contact with Chinese peacekeepers generate some interesting implications regarding the later discussion of China's 'charm offensive' project in the context of Sudan in the 2000s. The author carried out a questionnaire survey among those who were expected to have a better knowledge of China's contribution. The questionnaire was structured and its questions formulated on the basis of general Cambodian perceptions of China gathered from the semi-structured interviews.

Local Perspectives

The peacekeeping literature suggests that local perspectives should be considered of foremost importance because they relate closely to the legitimacy of peacekeeping operations.[8] For example, the *United Nations Peacekeeping Operations: Principles and Guidelines* states that

> [t]he manner in which a United Nations peacekeeping operation conducts itself may have a profound impact on its *perceived legitimacy on the ground*. The firmness and fairness with which a United Nations peacekeeping operation exercises its mandate, the circumspection with which it uses force, the discipline it imposes upon its personnel, the respect it shows to local customs, institutions and laws, and the decency with which it treats the local people all have a direct effect upon *perceptions of its legitimacy*.[9]

The tendency to pay more attention to local perspectives has increased since the problematic interventions in Iraq and Afghanistan.[10] The International

Security Assistance Force (ISAF) in Afghanistan attracts much criticism because of its increasing involvement in counter-insurgency, which has led to significant civilian casualties and 'has greatly reduced local support for ISAF – and with it perceptions of the operation's legitimacy, both locally and internationally'.[11]

In this context, military provision of aid and infrastructure is often understood as a means to win the 'hearts and minds' of local people, thereby raising the legitimacy of a peacekeeping operation and leading to mission success. For example, Merriam Mashatt, Maj.-Gen. Daniel Long and James Crum mention that 'infrastructure adds "arms and legs" to strategies aimed at winning "hearts and minds." Infrastructure is fundamental to moving popular support away from prewar or during-conflict loyalties and to moving spoilers in favor of postwar political objectives'.[12] The majority of China's peacekeepers are military engineers, and its main peacekeeping contribution can be seen as the building of infrastructure. Theoretically, therefore, Chinese peacekeeping should be popular among local populations in operational areas.[13]

However, as the examples of Iraq and Afghanistan clearly suggest, the provision of aid and infrastructure does not directly translate into gaining local trust. Instead, as is often claimed by NGO workers in conflict zones, whether outside forces can gain local trust depends on how 'neutral' local people perceive them.[14] NGOs assert that the 'shield' on which they rely to enable them to operate safely in conflict areas is the neutrality of the organizations and their independence in a civil war. This raises significant concerns with regard to China's peacekeeping because China was seen as having close relations with dictatorial regimes – for example, the Pol Pot regime in Cambodia and the Omar al-Bashir government in Sudan.[15] For whatever reasons the PRC has supported these regimes,[16] what matters when the PRC attempts to enhance local perceptions of China through its peacekeeping activity is the question of how local populations perceive China's relationship to the dictatorial regime, and how its peacekeeping affects such perceptions.

Indeed, the importance of local perceptions informs the pluralist approach to the study of peace. In part, 'a crisis of legitimacy' of the liberal paradigm has led the study of peacekeeping and peacebuilding to pay more attention to local agency.[17] Oliver Richmond also contends that the 'universal and hegemonic discourse' of liberal peace has produced peacebuilding failures, and that peace needs to be 'contextualised more subtly, geographically, culturally, in terms of identity, and the evolution of the previous socio-economic polity'.[18] In this context, 'peace' needs to be researched in terms not only of *how* it is achieved, but also, more fundamentally, of *what* it means (or what 'they' mean if one takes the pluralist notion of 'peaces') and *whose* peace needs more attention.[19] Interdisciplinary perspectives that draw upon sociology, anthropology, human geography and cultural studies enable one to examine the sources of legitimacy of peace operation from local perspectives.[20]

This article is informed by these theoretical studies and complements them by offering an explanation of why the Cambodians changed their perceptions of China after the latter's peacekeeping efforts. As will be discussed below,

Cambodian perceptions shifted not just because of infrastructures built by Chinese peacekeepers. More importantly, the shift occurred because of China's dual political support in Cambodia. Before I discuss this in more detail, the following section will briefly set the broader political context of China–Cambodia relations prior to the UNTAC operation in 1992.

China's Dual Political Support in Cambodia

The PRC has been one of the key actors in Cambodia's international and domestic political scene since well before the end of the Cold War. At the time of the Vietnam conflict (1955–75), Sihanouk was under pressure from China and North Vietnam to assist their communist forces, and had ceded the northeast of Cambodia to North Vietnam. The PRC also waged a limited and ineffective war in early 1979 against Vietnam, which had invaded Cambodia the previous year, installed a new communist government in Phnom Penh and ousted the Khmer Rouge from the capital.[21]

China maintained close relations with two different warring factions in Cambodia simultaneously, one represented by the Khmer Rouge and the other by Sihanouk. To the Khmer Rouge, China sent political, economic and military support for nearly two decades from the early 1970s to the end of the 1980s, including the period in which this faction committed genocide.[22] At the same time, China twice allowed Sihanouk to form a government in exile in Beijing, and once to seek refuge there.[23] Chinese backing of the Khmer Rouge in Phnom Penh and Sihanouk in Beijing from April 1976 to December 1978 is particularly interesting, because the two factions opposed each other. When the Khmer Rouge forced Sihanouk out of office, China gave assistance to the prince and provided him refuge in China, while supporting the Khmer Rouge and continuing to be 'its only link to the outside world'.[24]

China's dual political support for both sides continued until 1993, although military assistance to the Khmer Rouge was severed in 1990. During the peace process (1988–92) and the UNTAC period (1992–93), China attempted to sustain Khmer Rouge involvement in the transitional Cambodian government. It did so despite the Khmer Rouge's uncooperative attitude to the peace process and failure to fulfil its commitment to a ceasefire. Most states attempted to exclude the Khmer Rouge from a national election but China consistently maintained that the Khmer Rouge should be included. For example, the UN Security Council resolution 783 on 30 November 1992 stipulated sanctions against the Khmer Rouge and an election in which all parties but the Khmer Rouge would take part. China was the only country among the Security Council's 15 members that abstained. The Ambassador to the UN, Li Daoyu, commented in 1992 that sanctions and three-party elections 'will further increase differences and sharpen contradictions and could consequently lead to new, complicated problems in the Cambodian situation'.[25] However, by May 1993 China had completely severed relations with the Khmer Rouge. This is demonstrated by the fact that the Khmer Rouge offered no apology to China when it unintentionally killed two Chinese peacekeepers and injured four in the Chinese camp at Skun village in Kompong Cham province on 21 May 1993.[26]

Cambodian Perspectives on China

Since China had supported the Khmer Rouge, the Cambodian people had formed very negative perceptions of China before UNTAC. These perceptions were reinforced particularly by a smear campaign against China undertaken by the Vietnamese-installed government in the 1980s. It disseminated a pamphlet, *Crime of Beijing Chinese Hegemony Enlargement and Servants Pol Pot, Eang Sary, Khieu Samphan during 1975–1978* [*sic*], arguing that China had been supporting the Khmer Rouge during the period of genocide. This pamphlet resulted in the Cambodian population believing that China was actually behind the genocide.[27] Against this background, how did Cambodians perceive China during and after the period of UNTAC?

As far as Cambodian perceptions are concerned, China's objective of enhancing its image was met to a limited extent only. Of 27 interviewees in Phnom Penh, nine were not even aware of the Chinese contribution to UNTAC, even though most of them were working for, or closely with, UNTAC. The questionnaire survey at the Royal Cambodian Armed Forces' College of Social Sciences and Languages also indicates that only 14 out of 48 respondents (29.2 per cent) were aware that China had contributed military personnel to the UNTAC mission, despite the author's initial expectation that military college students would know more about military-to-military ties with China.

The level of knowledge about China's participation was very different from, for example, knowledge about Japan's participation, though the type and scale of their respective contributions were similar. Both countries sent engineer units: two battalions of 400 troops totalling 800 from China, and two battalions of 600 troops totalling 1,200 from Japan.[28] All of the interviewees knew that the Japanese had made a significant contribution to the UNTAC operation, but more than half of the interviewees were completely unaware of the role the Chinese had played in the operation. The other half knew of a Chinese presence, but many had only vague memories of where the Chinese contingent had worked and what they had done. Likewise, the loss of two Japanese (UN volunteer Nakata Atsushi and superintendent Takada Haruyuki) in April and May 1993, respectively, is well known among Cambodians. However, the loss of two Chinese (Chen Zhiguo and Yu Shili, both from engineering battalions) in May 1993 is less well known.

The high profile of the Japanese forces, in large part, was derived from having Akashi Yasushi as Special Representative of the UN Secretary-General for Cambodia. Moreover, Japanese foreign policy at that time aimed to make a *visible* international contribution.[29] In contrast, China's involvement was invisible because it did not greatly endeavour to gain publicity about its military presence in Cambodia. This may relate first to a concern that China's military presence might have reminded the Cambodians of the support China had given to the Khmer Rouge. In fact, 'keep a low profile' (*tao guang yang hui*, 韬光养晦) was one of China's broader foreign policy stances in the decade after 1989. This policy was formulated by Deng Xiaoping when the West tried to establish a new world order at the end of the Cold War and China needed to focus on its domestic economic development while avoiding any perception that it was a challenger in the new order.[30] Its peacekeeping contribution to UNTAC was consistent with this policy, and was literally obscured 'beneath blue berets'.

However, the author's interviews with Cambodian intellectuals and government officials who had been directly engaged with the Chinese peacekeepers, or were aware of the Chinese contribution, reveal a different story. The views expressed in those interviews have important implications with regard to the later discussion of Sudan in this article because, by contrast, China in the 2000s wants to be seen globally. It is embarking on a global 'charm offensive' to try to reassure the view that China's rise is benign in nature.

Those Cambodians with a knowledge of Chinese peacekeepers were favourably disposed towards them, owing mainly to the peacekeepers' diligent work ethic.[31] Furthermore, the Chinese engineering contribution to UNTAC was invaluable to the overall operation, given that they contributed approximately 19 per cent of UNTAC's entire engineering troop complement.[32] As correctly suggested by the above-mentioned theoretical literature on the importance of building infrastructure in peacekeeping, local villagers who lived alongside national roads repaired by the Chinese peacekeepers also praised them because they 'fixed the road very well and I could go to the nearby town more quickly'; 'they worked effectively and diligently'; 'they were very friendly and smiling at us'; and 'they had good discipline'.[33] Some villagers shared favourable stories of their encounters with the Chinese soldiers. Villagers appreciated their help, so they would for instance bring them local produce. On another occasion, Chinese peacekeepers, bored one evening, visited a villager's house to watch TV with them. Not all the UN troops were able to create such a popular reputation as the Chinese peacekeepers. The Bulgarians, for example, were cited as major offenders, as some of them were reportedly very rude towards local Cambodians.[34]

Furthermore, several interviews with villagers along National Road No.6, which Chinese engineering battalions renovated, revealed more specific examples of cooperation between the Chinese and local people. This road goes through Khompon Thom Province, where the Khmer Rouge was still engaging in attacks against the local population and the police force during the UNTAC period. The Chinese peacekeepers needed force protection against the Khmer Rouge, but the UNTAC mandate allowed peacekeepers to use weapons only in self-defence. Therefore, armed local police and a group of armed villagers gathered to protect the engineers. In interviews villagers expressed their trust in the Chinese.[35] One villager commented that 'it was great that the Chinese did not bring weapons other than those to be used for self-defence. If they had done, that would have created a sense of doubt towards them'.[36]

Despite the fact that China had supported the Khmer Rouge historically, 24 (out of 33) Cambodian interviewees who knew about the Chinese peacekeepers tended to be very positive. They were asked how they had developed such positive views even though they had experienced the terror of the Khmer Rouge's reign and had known that China had earlier supported the Khmer Rouge. Several villagers suggested that it was because China had close relations with Sihanouk. The questionnaire survey also reveals the importance of the PRC's relations with Sihanouk. Based on the perspectives commonly given by the interviewees, the questionnaire suggested the following six possible reasons for the PRC to have contributed its troops to UNTAC: (1) an altruistic view of Cambodia's development and stability; (2) to make amends or apologies for what it had done to Cambodia in the past; (3) to use the opportunity to make economic inroads into Cambodia; (4) because of close relations with the King Father Sihanouk; (5) because of Western pressure after Tiananmen Square in June 1989; and (6) some other reason. Respondents could choose multiple answers. As Figure 1 indicates, the overwhelming majority (91.3 per cent) chose option 4, the Sihanouk factor, as the reason for China's contribution to UNTAC. From the perspective of those who survived the genocide, Chinese support for the figure whom they respected highly was seen as an important prerequisite to China's ability to build a relationship with the new Cambodia.

In addition to the Sihanouk factor, another prominent and common view related to 'forgiveness', which ten out of 33 interviewees explained as being a part of Cambodian culture or religion. They repeatedly stated that Chinese support for the Khmer Rouge 'is a story of the past', and 'Cambodia is a Buddhist country. We can forgive others'.[37] Such sentiments may have been declaratory rather than genuine belief, but the theme of forgiveness was consistently expressed in interviews. Some interviewees even considered that one of the reasons China sent its peacekeepers to Cambodia was to make amends or apologize for what it had done in the past. In the questionnaire survey, also, more than a quarter of respondents chose the option, 'China wanted to make amends or apologize for what it had done to Cambodia in the past' (28.3 per cent). This

FIGURE 1
CAMBODIAN PERCEPTIONS OF CHINA'S MOTIVES FOR UNTAC PARTICIPATION

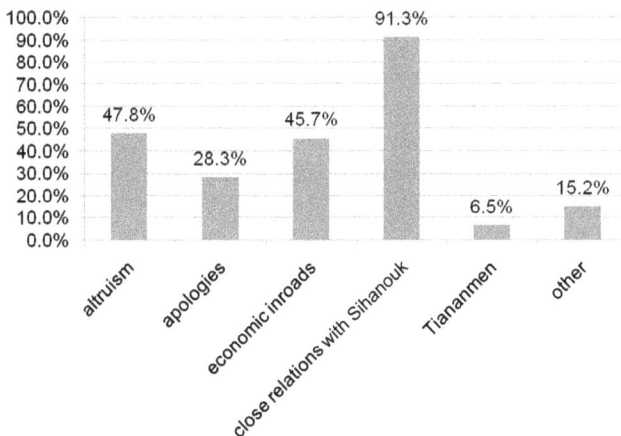

Source: Author's questionnaire survey conducted at the Royal Cambodian Armed Forces' College of Social Sciences and Languages, 2009.

93

contrasts with general theoretical observations on the importance of providing infrastructure for gaining local trust, which ignore local agency and assumes that local populations are content simply with material benefits. The interviews and questionnaire survey suggest that an anthropological perspective allows an exploration of the nature of interactions between local community members and outsiders, when considering issues around the local distrust of peacekeepers.[38]

Another finding from the questionnaire survey is divergence between Cambodian and certain international perceptions of Tiananmen Square as the reason for China's deployment of peacekeepers. Some analysts have posited that the most plausible explanation for China's participation in UNTAC is that the country sought to improve its international reputation, which had been severely damaged by the violent suppression of the demonstrations in Tiananmen Square.[39] However, only 6.5 per cent of respondents chose this as a reason.

In short, important factors that led to the improvement of China's image are: first, the PRC's enduring support for Sihanouk, Cambodia's legitimate figurehead; second, the Cambodian interpretation that China came to make amends or apologize for its past deeds in providing support to the Khmer Rouge, which Cambodians could forgive; and third (relevant only to those who interacted with Chinese peacekeepers), Chinese peacekeepers' diligent work ethic. These three factors were essential in improving China's image among Cambodian local populations.

Implications with Regard to China's Peacekeeping in Sudan

Approximately two decades have passed since UNTAC operated in Cambodia. Various changes have taken place in both international and Chinese policies and practices. Together with increased use of Chapter VII mandates, peacekeeping practices have become more robust and complex. China's peacekeeping policy has changed from advocating mere participation in traditional peacekeeping to engaging in a range of UN peace operations, by taking a more flexible stance in relation to the notion of sovereignty.[40] These operations include peace enforcement in United Nations Operation in Somalia II (UNOSOM II) from 1993 to 1995, and peace support operations in Liberia, Côte d'Ivoire and the Democratic Republic of Congo among others in the 2000s.[41] Chinese diplomacy has also changed. As mentioned earlier, China's diplomacy is much more visible, and its 'charm offensive' is attracting much more attention in the global politics of the new century.

However, some important aspects of China's peacekeeping practices remain similar to those of the China of 20 years ago. Among these is the practice of preferring host government consent. No matter how local populations and/or other states view particularly illegitimate governments, China insists on obtaining host government consent as a prerequisite for UN Security Council approval of a peacekeeping operation.[42] Therefore, for example, China viewed as necessary the gaining of endorsement from such dictatorial regimes as the Khmer Rouge and al-Bashir before it decided to contribute to UN peacekeeping operations in

Cambodia and Sudan. Those local populations that were victims of these dictatorial regimes retain deeply ingrained negative impressions of China's support for these regimes. China's peacekeeping operations in Cambodia and Sudan are thus similar in this sense. But a countervailing factor is that, throughout China's 20-year involvement in UN peacekeeping, not a single Chinese peacekeeper has been charged with misconduct, and the Chinese work ethic has been praised by many policymakers and analysts.[43] Based on the above analysis of Cambodian attitudes towards China, how could the Chinese government and its peacekeepers gain the trust of local populations in Sudan, and thereby successfully carry out a 'charm offensive' there?

In Sudan, China is seen as a part of the problem behind two civil wars: one between Arab northern Sudan and Christian southern Sudan (1983–2005); and the other between northern Sudan and Darfur (2003 to the present).[44] The restriction of oil exports to Western states since the 1980s has led the Sudanese government to forge closer relations with China.[45] People in southern Sudan regard China as being too closely linked to the al-Bashir government. China is seen as focused on obtaining access to oil, and by extension on supporting the Khartoum government. For that reason, a UN peacekeeper suggested, the Chinese were 'not perceived as neutral by some of the population, primarily those of the pro-Sudanese People's Liberation Army' (SPLA).[46]

However, the situation has changed in southern Sudan since 2008. China has been developing closer relations with the semi-autonomous government in southern Sudan. As the 2005 Comprehensive Peace Agreement sets out, a referendum in southern Sudan was undertaken in January 2011 to decide whether it would secede from the north to form an independent nation. There are also abundant oil resources in the southern region, and discussion is already underway between China and Kenya on building a pipeline to Kenyan ports.[47] Oil will not have to go through the Port of Sudan in the north, and this has led China to reconsider its position in relation to the north–south conflict. In September 2008, China established the Chinese Consulate-General in Juba, the capital of the southern Sudan region. The Consulate-General has delivered aid directly to southern Sudan.[48] Consul-General Zhang Qingyang met with Riek Machar, Deputy Chairman of the Sudan People's Liberation Movement (SPLM) and Vice-President of the semi-autonomous government of southern Sudan in November 2009 and September 2010, exchanging views on such issues as strengthening cooperation between the two parties.[49] Until 2008, the Chinese government had regarded the SPLM as a 'rebel group', and had not sought to form any meaningful relationship with it. China has, however, changed its diplomatic stance on southern Sudan in order 'to navigate Sudan's uncertain political future'.[50]

With regard to Darfur, according to a peacekeeper who was stationed at Nyala in Darfur province in late 2007, the Chinese were particularly concerned about being targeted by 'rebels' in acts of retribution against the Sudanese government. Chinese oil investment supported the Khartoum government, and therefore striking at the Chinese contingent could have been a way of attacking the government. Although there has been no such attack, it appears that there is a continuing and deep concern among the Chinese peacekeepers that one could occur.[51] Unlike in the case of China's dual diplomacy in Cambodia and in the north–south conflict in Sudan, there has been no interaction between Chinese peacekeepers and 'rebel groups' in and around Darfur, such as the JEM and the Sudan Liberation Army. In October 2007, the JEM attacked the facilities of a Chinese-led business consortium, the Greater Nile Petroleum Operating Company, in the Defra oilfields in the Kordofan region, and demanded that China withdraw support from the Sudanese government.[52] As Jonathan Holslag states, China's 'pure state-centric approach fails to consider other important actors in the region of Darfur. A peace mission will need to deal as much with private militias and rebel movements as with regular forces, and neglecting this will constrain its impact'.[53]

Can China's peacekeeping presence change perceptions of China as the 'friend of a dictatorial regime', as held by a Darfurian? The Cambodian case suggests that the answer to this question depends on whether the PRC can maintain its political neutrality by supporting multiple actors, including a figure who is seen as legitimate by local populations, and whether local cultures will facilitate reconciliation or forgiveness. Establishing and maintaining relations with more than one actor does not necessarily mean that China will need to move away from the principle of sovereignty. It is possible to establish and maintain relationships with other actors in a civil war without contradicting that principle. China managed to maintain relations with both the Khmer Rouge and Sihanouk in Cambodia while adhering to the principle of sovereignty by recognizing only one government at a time. After all, the maintaining of relationships can take a variety of forms. China has been doing this in the southern Sudan, but not in Darfur. Taking the lessons learned from Cambodia, China could orchestrate engagement with more than one actor in Darfur, such as the JEM and the Sudanese Liberation Army. To do so, China would need to reconsider its policy regarding the trade of arms and oil with the Sudanese government in the north. Once this issue has been addressed, China could address the issue of reconciliation. How it does so without losing face will need to be considered deliberately, but as a starting point, for example, it is meaningful for China to utilize a track two approach (such as discussions among academics, officials in non-government capacities, and civil society groups) to make an anthropological enquiry into the ways Sudanese local communities view the issue of reconciliation with outsiders.

Conclusion

This article has demonstrated that China's 'charm offensive' was successful in that its peacekeeping helped change negative local Cambodian perceptions of China to more positive ones. The impact of the 'charm offensive' *vis-à-vis* Cambodian populations was limited due to China's *tao guang yang hui* policy at the end of the Cold War. However, with the change in China's diplomacy that has an increasingly high profile, the impact of a Chinese 'charm offensive' on Sudanese local populations has significantly increased.

Observers might expect that Chinese peacekeepers could have gained favour among local peoples because the peacekeepers consisted mainly of engineering units, and because the engineers built social infrastructure such as roads and bridges – something visible and of direct benefit to the local populations. Contrary to such expectation, however, local Cambodian perceptions of China emerged as positive because the PRC had consistently supported the influential figure of Sihanouk over time, and because Cambodians had come to 'forgive' past Chinese policy apparently because of their socio-cultural background. If China had supported the Khmer Rouge only, it would have been difficult for Chinese peacekeepers to win local trust quickly, and to complete their peacekeeping contribution successfully. A Cambodian political culture also appeared to have helped overcome people's negative views towards China and led to forgiveness.

What do the lessons from Cambodia say about how China might consider policy changes to ensure the success of its peacekeeping operations in Sudan? First, China's image as a friend of the al-Bashir government needs to be addressed in the context of attempting to gain the trust of the local southern Sudanese and Darfurian people. China's peacekeeping contribution in Sudan cannot easily be reconciled with its provision of oil revenue and its arms sales to the Khartoum government. These are detrimental to the local perceptions of China, and reinforce the view that China is a friend of the Khartoum government and an opponent of the local people of southern Sudan and Darfur. The key to winning local trust is to be neutral in a broader political context and attentive to the needs of the various actors in the civil war. Local perceptions of China as a neutral actor in a broader political context have improved in southern Sudan since 2008. However, more effort is needed to improve local Darfurian perspectives of China's neutrality, by balancing between Khartoum and other actors in the civil war, such as the JEM and the Sudanese Liberation Army. Once this point is addressed, Chinese scholars and civil society groups could engage in discussion of the issue of reconciliation from a socio-anthropological perspective.

This discussion has important implications with regard to China's government-oriented diplomacy based on the principle of sovereignty. While UN peacekeeping is useful for China's increasingly global 'charm offensive', it requires China to take a sophisticated approach to the principle of sovereignty of host states that are engaged in civil wars. Being a high-profile power in the twenty-first century, China can no longer afford to stick simply to the rigid interpretation of sovereignty. As discussed above in the case of Sudan, doing so inevitably leads to the local perception that China is a friend of the 'government', which antagonizes other warring factions that do not recognize the government's legitimacy. The sophisticated approach that China can take relates to how flexible the country can be in applying the principle of sovereignty to individual cases, by addressing the needs of other warring factions and maintaining neutrality in a broader political context.

ACKNOWLEDGEMENTS

I express sincere appreciation to the Cambodian Institute for Cooperation and Peace for its wonderful support during my research visit to Cambodia. I am especially grateful to H.R.H. Norodom

Sirivudh, Chheang Vannarith and Neth Naro for their gracious help. I am also indebted to the members of the Royal Cambodian Armed Forces' College of Social Sciences and Languages, particularly Maj.-Gen. Dok Sopha and Col. Sok Pito for their kind support. I also thank Benny Widyono, Doung Viroth, and all the anonymous and non-anonymous interviewees who shared their valuable insights and so helped me prepare this article. My thanks also go to the University of Nottingham for the Fellows Recruitment Fund that enabled me to undertake field research in Cambodia and Australia, and to Catherine Gegout, Marc Lanteigne, Michael Pugh, Shogo Suzuki, Rod Thornton and Peter Trebilco for their helpful comments on earlier drafts of the article.

NOTES

1. Joshua Kurlantzick, 'Charm Offensive: How China's Soft Power Is Transforming the World', New Haven, CT: Yale University Press, 2007; Shogo Suzuki, 'Chinese Soft Power, Insecurity Studies, Myopia and Fantasy', *Third World Quarterly*, Vol.30, No.4, pp.779–93.
2. 'Chinese Oil Workers Kidnapped in Sudan's Kordofan', *Sudan Tribune* (Roubaix), 19 Oct. 2008 (at: www.sudantribune.com/spip.php?article28979); David Shinn, 'Chinese Involvement in African Conflict Zones', *China Brief*, Vol.9, No.7, 2009, pp.7–10.
3. David Keen, *Complex Emergence*, Cambridge: Polity Press, pp.48,208; Human Rights Watch, *Sudan, Oil, and Human Rights*, Brussels, 2003, pp.456–69; SaveDarfur, 'Briefing Paper: China in Sudan: Having It Both Ways', 18 Oct. 2007 (at: www.savedarfur.org/pages/policy_paper/briefing_paper_china_in_sudan_having_it_both_ways/).
4. Daniel Large, 'China's Sudan Engagement: Changing Northern and Southern Political Trajectories in Peace and War', *China Quarterly*, 2009, p.614; US Holocaust Memorial Museum, 'Overview: Sudan' (at: www.ushmm.org/genocide/take_action/atrisk/region/sudan).
5. For surveys that indicate different figures, see Alex J. Bellamy, 'Responsibility to Protect or Trojan Horse?: The Crisis in Darfur and Humanitarian Intervention after Iraq', *Ethics and International Affairs*, Vol.19, No.2, 2006, p.31.
6. Ben Kiernan, *The Pol Pot Regime: Race, Power and Genocide in Cambodia under the Khmer Rouge, 1975–79*, 3rd edn, New Haven, CT: Yale University Press, 2008; Sophie Richardson, *China, Cambodia, and the Five Principles of Peaceful Coexistence*, New York: Columbia University Press, 2010.
7. Friedrich-Ebert-Stiftung, *Cambodia 1975-2005 Journey through the Night*, Bonn: Friedrich-Ebert-Stiftung, 2006, p.1.
8. See, e.g., Robert A. Rubinstein, 'Intervention and Culture: An Anthropological Approach to Peace Operations', *Security Dialogue*, Vol.36, No.4, 2005, pp.527–44; Stockholm International Peace Research Institute (SIPRI), *SIPRI Yearbook 2009: Armaments, Disarmaments and International Security*, Stockholm, 2009, p.105.
9. UN Department of Peacekeeping Operations, *United Nations Peacekeeping Operations: Principles and Guidelines*, 2008, p.36 (emphasis added).
10. George R. Lucas, 'The Morality of "Military Anthropology"', *Journal of Military Ethics*, Vol.7, No.3, 2008, pp.165–87; Roberto J. Gonzalez, 'Towards Mercenary Anthropology? The New US Army Counterinsurgency Manual *FM 3–24* and the Military–Anthropology Complex', *Anthropology Today*, Vol.23, No.3, 2007, pp.14–19.
11. SIPRI (see n.8 above), p.105.
12. Merriam Mashatt, Maj.-Gen. Daniel Long and James Crum, 'Conflict-Sensitive Approach to Infrastructure Development', Special Report No.197, US Institute of Peace, Jan. 2008 (at: www.usip.org/files/resources/sr197.pdf), p.12.
13. David Alexander Robinson, 'Hearts, Minds and Wallets: Lessons from China's Growing Relationship with Africa', *Journal of Alternative Perspectives in the Social Sciences*, 2009, Vol.1, No.3, p.863; interview with UK military personnel (location anonymized), 4 Aug. 2009, and telephone interviews with two peacekeepers for the African Union/UN Hybrid Operation in Darfur (UNAMID) (place anonymized), 16 Apr. 2009.
14. Many NGOs, whose strength lies in their neutrality, attempt to dissociate themselves from the military in humanitarian intervention, largely because local populations perceive the military as lacking neutrality. Daniel Byman, 'Uncertain Partners: NGO and the Military', *Survival*, Vol.43, No.2, 2001, pp.97–114; Fiona Terry, *Condemned to Repeat?: The Paradox of Humanitarian Action*, Ithaca, NY: Cornell University Press, 2002; Jacinta O'Hagan and

Katherine Morton (eds), *Humanitarianism and Civil–Military Relations in a Post-9/11 World*, Canberra: Department of International Relations, Australian National University, 2009.

15. Stephanie Kleine-Ahlbrandt and Andres Small, 'China's New Dictatorship Diplomacy', *Foreign Affairs*, Vol.87, No.1, 2008, pp.38–56.

16. David Zweig suggests that China's policy on dictatorial regimes should be understood as 'amoral', rather than 'immoral': '"Resource Diplomacy" Under Hegemony: The Sources of Sino-American Competition in the 21st Century?', Working Paper No.18, Center on China's Transnational Relations, Hong Kong University of Science and Technology, n.d. (at: www.cctr.ust.hk/materials/working_papers/WorkingPaper18_DavidZweig.pdf).

17. Neil Cooper, 'Review Article: On the Crisis of the Liberal Peace', *Conflict, Security & Development*, Vol.7, No.4, 2007, pp.605–16; Michael Pugh, 'Accountability and Credibility: Assessing Host Population Perceptions and Expectations', in Cedric de Coning, Andreas Stensland and Thierry Tardy (eds), *Beyond the New Horizon*, Oslo: Norwegian Institute of International Affairs, 2010, pp.56–65.

18. Oliver P. Richmond, *Peace in International Relations*, London: Routledge, 2008, p.17.

19. Ibid., pp.21–2.

20. Paul Higate and Marsha Henry, 'Space, Performance and Everyday Security in the Peacekeeping Context', *International Peacekeeping*, Vol.17, No.1, 2010, pp.32–48; Béatrice Pouligny, *Peace Operations Seen from Below: UN Missions and Local People*, London: Hurst, 2006.

21. Stephen J. Morris, *Why Vietnam Invaded Cambodia: Political Culture and the Causes of War*, Stanford, CA: Stanford University Press, 1999.

22. For detailed discussions of the reasons why China supported both factions, see Kiernan (n.6 above) and Richardson (n.6 above), pp.89–106.

23. The first government in exile was formed after Gen. Lon Nol's coup d'état in 1970. Sihanouk formed a government in exile in Beijing, embracing the Khmer Rouge as one of the dominant forces in the exiled government as well as at the frontline of the civil war in Cambodia. The second government in exile was formed after Vietnam ousted the Khmer Rouge in December 1978, and Cambodia entered a period of civil war between the Vietnamese-installed Heng Samrin government and the Coalition Government of Democratic Kampuchea (CGDK) – consisting of the Funcinpec Party led by Prince Sihanouk, the Khmer Rouge led by Khieu Samphan and the Khmer People's National Liberation Front, a conservative group led by Son Sann. The CGDK exile government was established at the Friendship Hotel in Beijing.

24. Richardson (see n.6 above), p.144.

25. 'Provisional Verbatim Record of the Three Thousand One Hundred and Forty-Third Meeting', UN doc., S/PV.3143, 30 Nov. 1992, p.4.

26. Interview with the Chief of the Department of Chheng Prey District, Kampong Cham Province, Cambodia, 11 Sept. 2009.

27. The People's Republic of Cambodia, *Crime of Beijing Chinese Hegemony Enlargement and Servants Pol Pot, Eang Sary, Khieu Samphan during 1975–1978*; Sophie Richardson and Brantly Womack, 'China, Cambodia, and the Five Principles of Peaceful Coexistnce', East–West Center, Honolulu,18 June 1010 (at: www.eastwestcenter.org/ewc-in-washington/events/previous-events-2010/june-18-dr-sophie-richardson-and-dr-brantly-womack/); interview with Youk Chhang, Documentation Centre of Cambodia Director, Phnom Penh, 7 Sept. 2009.

28. There was a sense of competition between China and Japan on the level of military contribution to UNTAC. Miwa Hirono, 'The Road to Recovery: The Spill-Over Effects of Multilateralism in Cambodia on Sino–Japanese Relations', in Victor Teo and Peng Er Lam (eds), *Southeast Asia Between China and Japan*, Newcastle Upon Tyne: Cambridge Scholars, Forthcoming.

29. This was because Japan had been criticized by domestic and international policymakers and analysts about merely contributing financial assistance to international security at the time of the First Iraq War. Therefore, more 'physical' – rather than merely financial – contributions were advocated among the Japanese.

30. Chien-Peng Chung, 'The "Good Neighbour Policy" in the Context of China's Foreign Relations', *China*, Vol.7, No.1, 2009, pp.109–10.

31. Interviews with: Lt Gen. John Sanderson, Force Commander UNTAC, Canberra, 31 Mar. 2009; Cambodian military personnel, Phnom Penh, 31 Aug. 2009; Cambodian goverment personnel, Phnom Penh, 31 Aug. 2009.

32. As of 16 Oct. 1992, China contributed 399, Japan 600, France 155, Poland 227 and Thailand 700. UNTAC Spokesman's Office, unpublished material, 1992.

33. Interviews with three village chiefs, Kompong Cham Province, Cambodia, 11 Sept. 2010.

34. Sandra Whitworth, 'Gender, Race and the Politics of Peacekeeping', in Edward Moxon-Browne (ed.), *A Future for Peacekeeping?*, London: Macmillan, 1998, p.180.
35. Interviews with three village chiefs (see n.33 above). This is also confirmed by Lt Gen. John Sanderson (see n.31 above).
36. Interview with a village head, Kompong Cham Province, Cambodia, 11 Sept. 2009. Reports on humanitarian intervention suggest that the level of local trust and the kind of arms held by outsiders are correlated. For example, in the context of intervention in Afghanistan, the UK Ministry of Defence claims that 'winning the trust of the Afghan population is a key element in the battle against Taliban' and therefore 'we use foot patrols to make them feel less intimidated so we can make friends with them'. 'RAF Gunners Continue Protecting Cam Bastion', *Defence News*, 22 Feb. 2010 (at: www.mod.uk/DefenceInternet/DefenceNews/MilitaryOperations/RafGunnersContinueProtectingCampBastion.htm).
37. Interviews with two civil society activists, Phnom Penh, 28 and 31 Aug. 2009; and a former UNTAC official, Phnom Penh, 4 Sept. 2009.
38. On the anthropological analytical framework for the interaction between local communities and outsiders, see Miwa Hirono, *Civilizing Missions: International Religious Agencies in China*, New York: Palgrave Macmillan, 2008, pp.36–40.
39. M. Taylor Fravel, 'China's Attitude toward U.N. Peacekeeping Operations since 1989', *Asian Survey*, Vol.36, No.11, 1996, pp.1102–21.
40. On China's flexible stance on the notion of sovereignty, see Stefan Stähle, 'China's Shifting Attitude towards United Nations Peacekeeping Operations', *China Quarterly* Vol.195, 2008, pp.631–55; Pang Zhongying, 'China's Non-intervention Question', *Global Responsibility to Protect*,Vol.1, No.2, 2009, pp.237–52; Allen Carlson, 'Helping to Keep the Peace (Albeit Reluctantly): China's Recent Stance on Sovereignty and Multilateral Intervention', *Pacific Affairs*, Vol.77, No.1, 2004, pp.9–27; Shogo Suzuki (see n.1 above); International Crisis Group (ICG), 'China's Growing Role in UN Peacekeeping', *Asia Report*, No.166, 2009.
41. On the distinction between traditional peacekeeping, peace enforcement and peace support operations, see Alex Bellamy, 'The Responsibility to Protect and the Problem of Military Intervention', *International Affairs*, Vol.84, No.4, 2008, pp.615–40. See Stähle (n.40 above, pp. 640–42) for China's votes on relevant UN Security Council resolutions authorizing a variety of UN peace operations from 1992 to 2007.
42. However, it is important to note that 'consent' is not always given under the condition of perfect freedom. 'Consent' can be coerced or induced. Nicholas J. Wheeler, 'Operationalising the Responsibility to Protect: The Continuing Debate over Where Authority Should Be Located for the Use of Force', Report No.3, Responsibility to Protect, Norwegian Institute of International Affairs, 2008; David Roberts, 'A Dangerous Game: Managing Consent in the Cambodian UN Peacekeeping Operations', *Studies in Conflict and Terrorism*, Vol.21, No.1, 1998, pp.29–57.
43. Bates Gill and Chin-Hao Huang, *China's Expanding Role in Peacekeeping: Prospects and Policy Implications*, Stockholm: Stockholm International Peace Research Institute, 2009, pp.25–6; telephone interviews with UNAMID peacekeepers (see n.13 above).
44. Keen (see n.3 above), pp.48,208.
45. Mark Duffield, 'Foreword', in Michael Pugh, Neil Cooper and Mandy Turner, *Whose Peace? Critical Perspectives on the Political Economy of Peacebuilding*, Basingstoke: Palgrave Macmillan, 2011.
46. Email correspondence with a peacekeeper for UNAMID (location anonymized), 18 Sept. 2010.
47. 'China, Kenya Discuss New Corridor for Southern Sudan Oil', *Sudan Tribune*, 16 Oct. 2009 (at: www.sudantribune.com/spip.php?article32803); Barney Jopson, 'China and Kenya in Infrastructure Talks', *Financial Times*, 14 Oct. 2009 (at: fcaea.org/aid=287.phtml).
48. Ministry of Foreign Affairs of the People's Republic of China, 'Hand-over Ceremony of Anti-malaria Medicines to Southern Sudan Held in Chinese Consulate General in Juba', 11 Aug. 2010 (at: www.fmprc.gov.cn/eng/wjb/zwjg/zwbd/t723295.htm).
49. 'China Should Prepare for Possible South Sudan Independence – Machar', *Sudan Tribune*, 19 Sept. 2010 (at: www.sudantribune.com/spip.php?page=imprimable&id_article=36295); 'China's Zhou Yongkang hails China–Sudan relations', *BBC Monitoring Asia Pacific*, 18 Nov. 2009.
50. Daniel Large, 'China's Sudan Engagement: Changing Northern and Southern Political Trajectories in Peace and War', *China Quarterly*, Vol.199, 2009, p.610.

51. Email correspondence with a peacekeeper for UNAMID (see n.46 above).
52. 'Rebels Tell China "Leave Sudan"', *BBC News*, 25 Oct. 2007 (at: news.bbc.co.uk/1/hi/ 7061066.stm).
53. Jonathan Holslag, 'China's Diplomatic Manoeuvring on the Question of Darfur', *Journal of Contemporary China*, Vol.17, No.54, 2008, p.84.

Two Pillars of China's Global Peace Engagement Strategy: UN Peacekeeping and International Peacebuilding

ZHAO LEI

Building a harmonious world featuring sustained peace and common prosperity has become a lynchpin of China's international strategy. In order to implement it, the government has developed a series of key operational sub-strategies, including a global peace engagement strategy. The main theme of this approach is that China will strive for peace and promote development by means of peace missions mainly consisting of UN peacekeeping operations (PKOs) and international peacebuilding operations (IPBOs). The article argues that this strategy is based on two cornerstones, peace and development. In practice, China takes different stances towards PKOs and IPBOs: it is a far more cautious contributor in IPBOs, because China's understanding of peacebuilding pays particular attention to development, and Western states are suspicious of China's growing power and intention.

China's enhanced national strength derived from continuous economic successes and accumulated experience have provided the country with resources, confidence and enthusiasm for fulfilling its global peace engagement strategy, which is an integral part of China's grand strategy.[1] Its grand strategy can be conceived as part of a triangle in which domestic, regional and global policies interact in the pursuit of three overarching interests and demands: first and foremost, economic development to enhance domestic stability and legitimacy; second, promotion of a peaceful external environment free of threats to Chinese sovereignty and territorial integrity in Asia; and, third, cultivation of China's status and influence as a responsible great power in global politics.[2] To this end, the global peace engagement strategy aims to maintain a peaceful external environment to sustain China's peaceful development and portray a civilized and peace-loving country.[3]

UN peacekeeping operations (PKOs) and international peacebuilding operations (IPBOs) are two major kinds of peace missions within the global peace engagement strategy. Whereas peacekeeping is UN led and/or mandated to monitor ceasefires and/or to support the implementation of comprehensive peace agreements, peacebuilding is a much broader concept, extending the peace function to a wide range of political, developmental, humanitarian and human rights programmes and mechanisms conducted by the UN and other national or non-national actors, in order to address both the immediate consequences and root causes of a conflict.[4]

China's White Paper, 'China's Peaceful Development Road', of 22 December 2005 systematically clarified for the first time the connection between the peaceful development road and the harmonious world idea:

> building a harmonious world of sustained peace and common prosperity is the lofty goal of China in taking the road of peaceful development ... China persists in its pursuit of harmony and development internally while pursuing peace and development externally.[5]

It guides China's peacekeeping and peacebuilding practices, enabling a smooth integration into international institutions and assuring the world of China's goodwill and intention to become a responsible power.

This article examines the nature of China's global peace engagement strategy, and discusses the Chinese characteristics of peacekeeping. It reveals the results of a questionnaire survey of the Chinese public and peacekeepers' perceptions of peacekeeping, which the author conducted in January 2009. A total of 389 respondents took part in the survey, comprising 59 peacekeepers and 330 undergraduate and postgraduate students of Peking University, Tsinghua University, China Foreign Affairs University, University of International Relations, Beijing Language and Culture University and Beijing Foreign Studies University, among others. The survey consisted of multiple-choice questions, allowing respondents to select only one answer from several choices; and to select three answers from seven choices. This questionnaire was the first of its kind, and has increased understanding of the perception that the Chinese public have of their country's global peace engagement strategy.

The article is divided into three sections. The first and second sections detail China's different stances on UN peacekeeping and international peacebuilding, respectively. The third section highlights the developmental priorities in China's global peace engagement strategy.

China's Stance on PKOs: A Firm and Confident Supporter

The twentieth anniversary of the participation of the Chinese People's Liberation Army (PLA) in PKOs and the tenth anniversary of the participation of Chinese police forces in such operations was marked in 2010. As a permanent member of the UN Security Council, China is currently contributing much-needed personnel, financial support and political momentum for peacekeeping. These 20 years can be divided into two phases: in the 1990s, the PLA participated in PKOs at a time when Western states were heatedly debating the 'End of History' and the 'China threat'. In the 2000s, Chinese police forces joined the PLA in taking part in operations, and international policymakers and analysts spiritedly discussed 'China's responsibility' and the 'China opportunity'. From the perspective of 'image politics', China participated in UN peacekeeping to tackle the 'China threat' thesis in the 1990s, and to promote China's 'responsible great power' image in the twenty first century. On 26 April 2010, the PLA issued a special report to commemorate the 20-year contribution:

> Up to the end of March 2010, the PLA has contributed peacekeepers over 15,000 persons/times to 18 UN peacekeeping missions worldwide ... The Chinese peacekeeping troops have built and maintained over 8,000 kilometres of road, constructed 230-odd bridges and given medical treatment to patients for 60,000 persons/times in the UN peacekeeping mission areas, playing a positive role in promoting the peaceful settlement of disputes, maintaining the regional safety and stability, and facilitating the economical and social development in some countries.[6]

According to a 2010 report from China's Ministry of Public Security, from January 2000 to January 2010 the contribution of Chinese police officers is as follows:

> China sent 1,569 police officers to carry out peacekeeping missions in Afghanistan, Bosnia and Herzegovina, Kosovo, Liberia, Sudan and Haiti. They have had no casualties, no discipline violations and never left in the middle of a mission (8 Chinese peacekeepers died in the Haiti earthquake on 13 January 2010) ... They have made a great contribution to regional peace and stability, as well as people's lives and safety.[7]

Concurrent with the sharp increase in China's contributions since the end of the Cold War, Western powers have been largely withdrawing or reducing their commitments to UN peacekeeping, and their role has been increasingly assumed by less wealthy countries. In the context of this change, playing a significant role in PKOs is perceived by China's leaders as a rare opportunity to display 'China's charm'. In 2006, the Ambassador to the UN, Wang Guangya, stated, 'China felt it is the right time for us to fill this vacuum [of personnel contribution left by the West]. We want to play our role'.[8] To a certain extent, China's growing contribution is meeting the demands of increasingly complex and challenging modern peacekeeping activities. As of June 2010, China was the fifteenth-largest contributor to UN missions, providing more troops, police and military observers than any other permanent member of the Security Council (P-5), including France.[9]

China's Interests and Motivations in PKOs

China has reiterated its official commitment to PKOs in its White Papers for National Defence since 2004. It has consistently supported and actively participated in peacekeeping operations consistent with the spirit of the UN Charter.[10] China's peacekeeping behaviour is motivated by diverse interests, of which three are highlighted here.

First, participation in PKOs has served to raise China's international profile. Acutely aware of, and sensitive to, its global image and reputation, China sees PKOs as an effective way to project a more benign and positive image to the world. By contributing, China cannot so readily be labelled a 'dissatisfied' or 'irresponsible' power. As the questionnaire survey below reveals, the Chinese people hope that their country's current foreign policy can be equated with that of a 'responsible power' with a peace-loving culture, and they endeavour to avoid giving an impression that their country is an egotistical 'giant' as it continues to grow in international strength.

According to the questionnaire survey, when asked about what are the national interests that China achieves in peacekeeping engagement, the top three answers were: 'setting up an image of a great responsible power', 'improving China's capacity of global governance' and 'building a harmonious world'; while 'ensuring the energy supply' was ranked third-to-last, as shown in Figure 1.

Second, participation in PKOs has served to bolster China's relations with the United States and other Western governments. On 30 June 2008, former US Secretary of Defense William Perry met Xu Caihou, Vice-Chairman of China's Central Military Commission, and proposed that 'the two armed forces should enhance cooperation on humanitarian operations and peacekeeping missions'.[11] On 28 January 2010, Chinese peacekeeping police and US troops carried out their first joint patrol in Haiti. As part of the UN Stabilization Mission in Haiti (MINUSTAH), a tactical team of ten Chinese riot police and two squads from the American 82nd Airborne Division conducted a 90-minute patrol in Port-au-Prince.[12] This joint effort has special symbolic significance: the most powerful developed Western country and the largest developing country have common interests in the maintenance of world peace. Moreover, increasing military contacts in peace missions promote military transparency and political mutual trust, which are of great benefit to reducing the possibility of accidental confrontations. There is a huge potential for closer peacekeeping cooperation between China and other major Western countries, and China is currently

FIGURE 1
WHAT ARE THE NATIONAL INTERESTS THAT CHINA ACHIEVES IN PKOS? (SELECTING THREE ANSWERS)

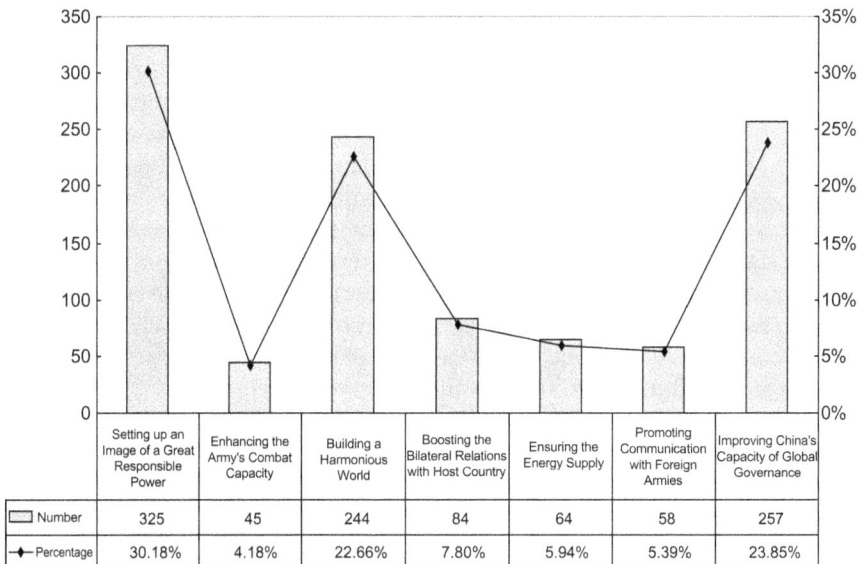

	Setting up an Image of a Great Responsible Power	Enhancing the Army's Combat Capacity	Building a Harmonious World	Boosting the Bilateral Relations with Host Country	Ensuring the Energy Supply	Promoting Communication with Foreign Armies	Improving China's Capacity of Global Governance
Number	325	45	244	84	64	58	257
Percentage	30.18%	4.18%	22.66%	7.80%	5.94%	5.39%	23.85%

Source: Analysis of 359 valid questionnaires.

exploring prospects for working with the United States and the EU to help build Africa's indigenous peacekeeping capacity.[13]

Third, participation in PKOs has served to protect Chinese interests abroad. With the growing globalization of its interests, public and private, China needs stable overseas markets to secure its sustainable economic development. As Jerker Hellström notes, 'China is in increasing need for natural resources in order to sustain its role as the workshop of the world and requires stable markets where it can afford its products'.[14] On a similar note, Michael J. Green states that 'instability in ... energy producing parts of Africa and the Middle East is clearly not in China's interests'.[15] However, while peacekeeping operations complement China's economic interests, the argument that its involvement is solely intended to promote these, especially resources in Africa, is too simplistic. While China has indeed sent peacekeepers to countries with resources of interest, such as Liberia (timber), the Democratic Republic of Congo (minerals) and Sudan (oil), it has also sent peacekeepers to areas with few or no natural resources, such as the Western Sahara United Nations Mission for the Referendum in Western Sahara [MINURSO].[16]

Chinese peacekeepers have witnessed remarkable strides in China's 'Going Abroad' strategy (*zouchuqu zhanlue*, "走出去"战略) since the 1990s. Chinese organizations, enterprises and citizens have been increasingly going abroad, and some have been harassed, attacked or kidnapped by 'terrorists' and criminals in foreign countries. In the country of residence, Chinese peacekeepers collaborate with Chinese institutions and organizations to protect the interests of Chinese people and enterprises. For example, in Liberia, Chinese peacekeepers took the initiative to rescue Chinese fishermen accosted by pirates. In East Timor, Chinese peacekeepers rescued wounded and dying Chinese businessmen attacked by mobs, and donated blood for them.[17] In the early days of Kosovo's independence, Chinese-owned shops and offices were repeatedly looted and burned down. Since the People's Republic of China (PRC) has no diplomatic relations with Kosovo, Chinese peacekeeping police stationed there assumed responsibility to ensure the safety of Chinese nationals. They cooperated with the Chinese embassy in Serbia to collect and update personal information of Chinese entrepreneurs in Kosovo, then reported to the embassy daily.[18] In short, Chinese peacekeepers have also been guardians of China's overseas national interests.

China stands to gain much from its peacekeeping contribution, and that in turn encourages it to contribute further. In November 2009, Alain Le Roy, UN Undersecretary-General for Peacekeeping Operations, stated, '[w]e would like China to continue its extremely constructive attitude toward peacekeeping by increasing steadily but firmly and continuously its participation, Chinese peacekeepers are well trained, well disciplined, and able to live in hard conditions while willing to interact with local people'.[19] International Peacekeepers Day and International Peacekeepers Week, on 29 May 2010, was launched at the UN Pavilion in Shanghai, which highlighted the importance of China's contribution and the increasing commitment of the Chinese government. In response to such positive recognition and appreciation, China is deploying increasing numbers of peacekeepers. In 2001 and 2002, only about a hundred Chinese peacekeepers served in UN missions, significantly less than other P-5 states. However, from March 2004 to August 2006, China was for the first time the largest contributor. Since September 2006, China and France have ranked as the biggest contributors of personnel to PKOs, leaving the other three P-5 countries far behind (see Figure 2).

China's commitment to PKOs is also supported by its domestic audience. This is partly because the Chinese state media have cultivated a public perception in favour of China's contribution, and China has partially and gradually adjusted its perception of the three Hammarskjöld principles of PKOs (impartiality, neutrality and host consent). In order to spread public knowledge of China's peacekeeping policy, the Ministry of Public Security filmed a television series, *Chinese Peacekeeping Police*, reflecting their work and lives in host countries in 2009; the Ministry of National Defence also filmed a full-length television documentary, *China Peacekeeping Force*, revealing the hardships of Chinese peacekeeping soldiers and China's growing contribution to PKOs in 2009. The author's survey reveals that the public not only support China's contributions but also prefer a more proactive stance towards peacekeeping, 45.5 per cent of respondents believing that 'before conflict' is the best time to deploy peacekeeping operations and indicating that they prefer conflict prevention, rather than traditional peacekeeping (see Figure 3). Furthermore, in terms of the three principles, 43.19 per cent of respondents supported the notion that peacekeeping

FIGURE 2
RANKING OF P-5 MILITARY AND POLICE CONTRIBUTIONS TO PKOS (JANUARY 2006 TO MARCH 2009)

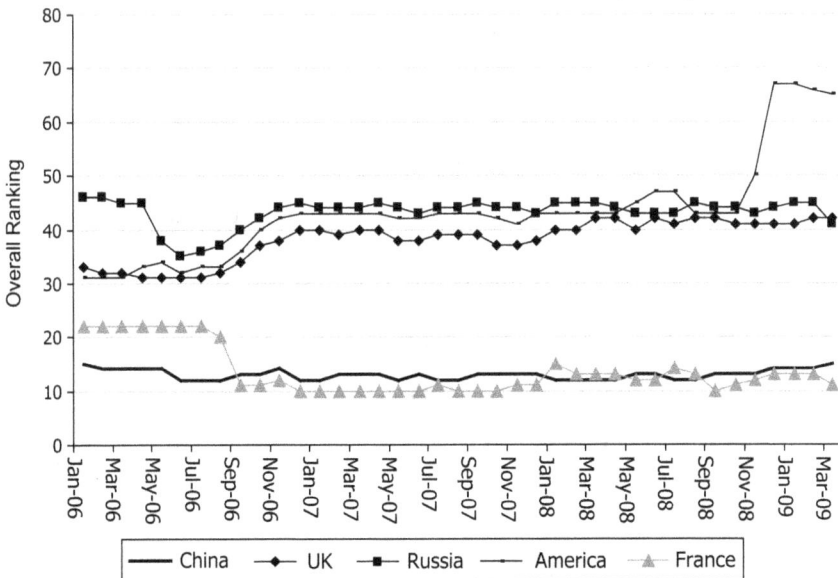

Source: Adapted from UN Department of Peacekeeping Operations, 'Ranking of Military and Police Contributions to UN Operations', from January 2006 to March 2009 (at: www.un.org/en/peacekeeping/contributors).

FIGURE 3
WHEN IS THE BEST TIME TO DEPLOY PEACEKEEPING OPERATIONS? (SELECTING ONE
ANSWER)

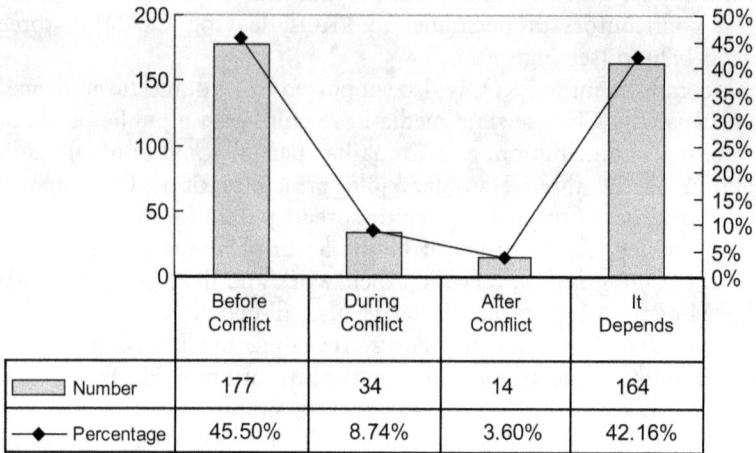

	Before Conflict	During Conflict	After Conflict	It Depends
Number	177	34	14	164
Percentage	45.50%	8.74%	3.60%	42.16%

Source: Analysis of 389 valid questionnaires.

can be deployed without the consent of the parties (see Table 1). Nevertheless, China still maintains that Security Council authorization is a vital precondition to deploy any peacekeeping operation.[20]

However, the survey reveals some contradiction, because 25 per cent of respondents consider that the biggest advantage of Chinese peacekeepers is that they adhere to the principle of non-interference in the internal affairs of host countries (see Figure 4). The inconsistency may arise because the general public does not understand the issue very well. Nonetheless, it suggests that China's non-interference policy enjoys wide public support.

China's Stance on IPBOs: A Cautious Participant

China spent almost 40 years seeking to understand, accept and trust the UN and its peacekeeping operations, to China the rapid changes and sensitive nature of

TABLE 1
ATTITUDES TOWARDS THE THREE PRINCIPLES OF PEACEKEEPING OPERATIONS
(SELECTING ONE ANSWER)

Choices	Should PKOs always adhere to the consent principle?		Should PKOs always adhere to the neutrality principle?		Should PKOs always adhere to the non-use of force principle?	
	Number	Percentage	Number	Percentage	Number	Percentage
Yes	139	35.73	293	75.32	186	47.81
No	168	43.19	44	11.31	155	39.85
Uncertain	82	21.08	52	13.37	48	12.34

Source: Analysis of 389 valid questionnaires.

FIGURE 4
WHAT ARE THE ADVANTAGES OF CHINESE PEACEKEEPERS (SELECTING THREE ANSWERS)

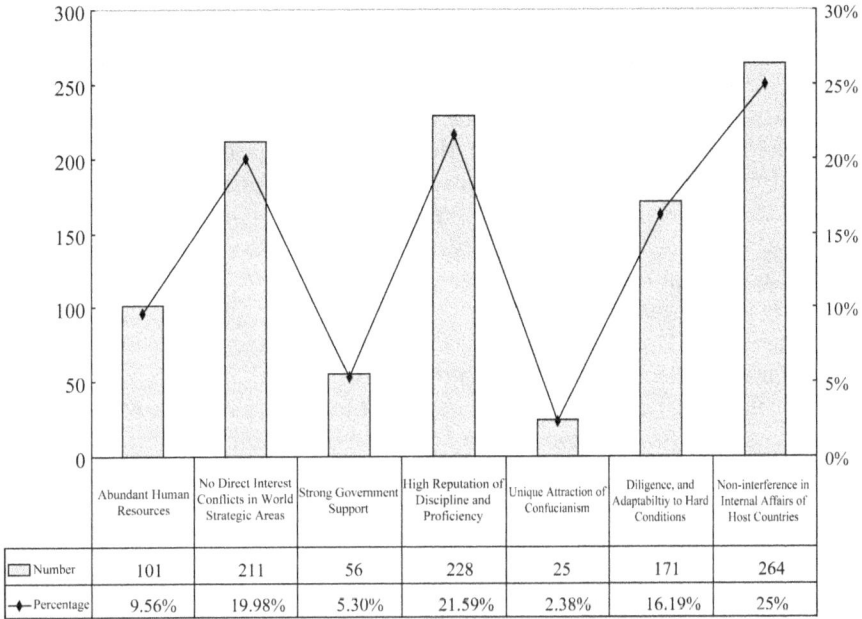

	Abundant Human Resources	No Direct Interest Conflicts in World Strategic Areas	Strong Government Support	High Reputation of Discipline and Proficiency	Unique Attraction of Confucianism	Diligence, and Adaptabiltiy to Hard Conditions	Non-interference in Internal Affairs of Host Countries
Number	101	211	56	228	25	171	264
Percentage	9.56%	19.98%	5.30%	21.59%	2.38%	16.19%	25%

Source: Analysis of 352 valid questionnaires.

peacebuilding exceeded its acceptance level, which inevitably resulted in China's cautious attitudes towards peacebuilding. Yet along with the wide acceptance of peacebuilding by many states, China is beginning to embrace it as a stakeholder. Chinese policymakers recognize that peacebuilding is more complex than peacekeeping, but is favourable to the establishment and enlargement of IPBOs that seek to consolidate peace and prevent a recurrence of armed confrontation. IPBOs has become the other crucial pillar of the architecture of global peace engagement strategy. There are two major dynamics behind China's support of peacebuilding.

The first is a subtle but significant shift in Chinese strategic culture from passively following international norms to actively making them (see Miwa Hirono and Marc Lanteigne, this issue). Chinese-made material products are sold all over the world, but Chinese-made 'normative products' are very rare. Thus, Chinese leaders have begun to focus on China's institutional contribution, placing an emphasis on 'discourse power' and the principle that a great power should constructively set agendas, not just follow the rules set by others.[21] China is not in favour of peacebuilding conflated with military action, humanitarian intervention or regime change, and vigorously opposes any state-building operations. The Chinese government asserts that 'state-building may not always automatically lead to peacebuilding, and due to state-building's inherently political nature, it may in fact spark further conflict'.[22] China accepts that in IPBOs there is a need to help a country carry out political and economic restructuring, and understands that the UN needs to carry out certain administrative functions on behalf of its government. Yet China consistently stresses the following points: respect for the right of the country concerned to make its own decisions is fundamental to post-conflict peacebuilding; the primary task of peacebuilding is to restore the administrative functions of state organs of the country; and international assistance should take into full consideration the development priorities identified independently by the country.[23] So 'good government', 'administrative efficiency' and especially 'development priority' are all regarded as focal points of peacebuilding. China endeavours to curb a perceived Western interventionist trend by participating in agenda-setting for peacebuilding. On the other hand, as the only 'developing' country among the P-5, China tends to counterbalance Western influence and to implement peacebuilding policies that benefit China's and non-Western countries' interests (see Hirono and Lanteigne, this issue).

The second dynamic behind China's support for IPBOs relates to the fact that such support benefits the promotion of 'soft power'. Globalization has greatly influenced not only the dynamics of power on the world stage but also the very meaning of national power.[24] To many Chinese peacekeepers, the rise of a country means the rise of its comprehensive power, amidst which soft power stands equal to hard power.[25] China's peacebuilding contribution centres on developing countries as well as regional and global multilateral institutions. From this perspective, IPBOs are a multilateral and effective way to enhance China's soft power by means of, or in the form of, its military (hard) power. Through these efforts, China's image as an aid donor, peace contributor, conflict mediator, emergency rescuer and even initiator of new institutions, coupled with the attractiveness of its development model, allows China to accelerate the pace of its 'peaceful rise'.

The uniqueness of China's role in IPBOs is that China can behave as a developing country that, like many such countries, can contribute personnel to IPBOs. However, China also has the power to set agendas. Therefore, in IPBOs and on the Security Council, China can act as a conduit between developed and developing countries. More importantly, China's growing participation grants further political credibility and legitimacy to peacebuilding missions, and tempers the host governments' suspicions that the missions are really dominated by Western countries.

Obstacles to China's Peacebuilding Participation

China's different understanding of peacebuilding contrasted with Western developed countries. First, the key obstacle to China's contribution is its understanding of peacebuilding. While peacekeeping aims to realize 'negative' peace, meaning no armed conflicts between or within countries, peacebuilding is about creating or restoring stable political, economic and social conditions for long-lasting peace (that is, 'positive' peace). The coexistence of these two missions reflects the shifts in peace missions: the changing nature of the operational environment, with a more complex link between diplomacy, military action and humanitarian intervention; the changing status of national government in global governance from leadership to co-partnership; and the changing understanding of the concept of security from state security to civilian security. In relation to these shifts, however, China and Western developed countries have different perspectives on the implications for peacebuilding, as illustrated in Table 2.

In practice, Western countries adhere to the 'liberal peace' agenda: a simultaneous pursuit of economic and political reform placed alongside the measures to resolve the conflict, and peace is supposedly ensured by liberal democracy and a market economy.[26] By contrast, China maintains that liberal democracy is not a panacea, and that a one-size-fits-all model will not work. Security and development are intrinsically linked, and peacebuilding would be impossible without achievement on the development front. Therefore, as explained by Shen Guofang, Deputy Permanent Representative to the UN, China believes that

> Poverty leads to social instability, which will in turn be a threat to peace and security at the national and even regional levels ... In order to uproot the causes of conflicts, we must help developing countries, especially the least-developed countries, to seek economic development, eradicate poverty, curb diseases, improve the environment and fight against social injustice ... The early realization of the disarmament, demobilization and reintegration of ex-combatants and the promotion of the repatriation, resettlement and the economic recovery of refugees and displaced persons constitute the short-term objectives of peacebuilding. The long-term objectives, however, are the eradication of poverty, development of economy as well as a peaceful and rewarding life for people in the post-conflict countries and regions.[27]

However, the trend of the dominance of 'liberal peace' in IPBOs challenges China's position on state sovereignty and non-intervention. Although China shows some degree of flexibility in these principles, it cannot go too far. Specifically, the principle of sovereignty is enshrined by China as the crucial foundation

TABLE 2
PERSPECTIVES ON THE IMPLICATIONS OF PEACEBUILDING

	Western perspective	China's perspective
Objective	Liberal democracy priority	Development priority
Focus	Good governance	Good government
Principle	Democracy promotion	Assistance orientation
	Necessary intervention	Non-intervention
Strategic culture	Pre-emptive	Reactive
Method	Top-down and bottom-up management: establish new constitution; hold national election; build multiparty system; strengthen civil society, etc.	Top-down management: strengthen state capacity; enhance national identification and national reconciliation; promote economic recovery, etc.
Defect	Challenge local ownership	Lack of public participation

for maintaining international peace as well as a fair and rational international order.[28]

Second, China faces a dilemma of cooperation. Due to its socialist ideology and status as a rising power, being inactive on the world stage is defined as 'irresponsible', but being too active is also regarded as 'irresponsible' because some analysts are wary of China's intentions and are unfamiliar with China's growing contribution to peacebuilding. Western states value China's contribution to peacebuilding and hope it will take more responsibility, but simultaneously they also have suspicions about China's growing power and intentions. Policymakers and pundits remain largely unaware of the scale and scope of China's participation.[29] In many cases, therefore, China has no choice but to keep a low profile and avoid being a world leader. As a result, selectively cautious participation becomes a wise option – to avoid being either marginalized or demonized.

The dilemma of cooperation formulates China's distinct mode of diplomatic behaviour, which is to 'choose the lesser of two evils' rather than 'choose the better of two goods'. Although China has the incentive to play a great role in international affairs with distinctive characteristics, a distrustful stance by Western states would adversely affect its peacekeeping aspirations. The Chinese government also worries that proactive statements and responses to peacebuilding will set a precedent for Western states to intervene in Chinese internal affairs.[30] That is why China's diplomacy is often regarded as 'hesitant and not confident, inward-looking not outward-looking, parochial and not sophisticated, reactive not proactive, and composed more of words than deeds'.[31]

Finally, China's peacebuilding policy is government-centric. China prefers to provide assistance on a government-to-government level, ignoring the importance of grassroots initiatives. The role of civil society in peacebuilding has gained wide recognition in China, and the emergence of civil society in China (with 431,000 civil society organizations at the end of 2009)[32] has created new opportunities for citizen participation in peacebuilding.[33] So far, however, they are not effective actors in China's political life and foreign-policymaking, because of the government's restrictive policies on civil society and because of Chinese Confucian culture that has emphasized loyalty to the emperor in ancient China and to central authority in contemporary China.[34] Further, due to the difficulties in interacting with grassroots actors and a lack of supervision by civil society, China's assistance to recipient governments in some cases, such as in Sudan and other African countries, has resulted in corruption and irresponsible arms sales.

There are widespread demands among the Chinese for enhancing non-governmental efforts and building a stronger relationship between China and the recipient country's local actors, including civil society agencies. For example, in April 2010, a 'Workshop on Capacity Building for Sudanese NGOs for Poverty Alleviation' hosted by the China Foundation for Poverty Alleviation and the International Poverty Reduction Centre in China was held in Beijing. The purpose was to share with Sudanese NGOs China's experience in poverty alleviation and social development, and to deepen cooperation between Chinese NGOs and their Sudanese counterparts.[35] Decision-makers in Beijing

are expected to take societal factors into consideration when making peacebuilding policy. The growth of civil society in China will most likely lead to a
more dynamic and sustainable peacebuilding policy. Although the interaction
with local civil society adds complexity to the efficiency of China's assistance,
it is conducive to the legitimacy of China's peace engagement strategy.

Development Priority in China's Global Peace Engagement Strategy

China has greatly contributed to poverty reduction and economic development,
highlighting the priority of development in its global peace engagement strategy.
This preference derives from China's multifaceted national identities. China has
developed its own definition of dual national identity: as a rising power and the
largest developing country. The two seemingly conflicting identities are not irre-
concilable and they have been widely recognized by the people. The survey
revealed that up to 64 per cent of respondents believed that China had
'global responsibility' (see Figure 5), but as high as 47 per cent of respondents
recognized 'the largest developing country' as China's primary national identity,
and 31 per cent of respondents regarded China as 'a responsible great power' (see
Figure 6). The duality determines that China perceives self-development and
common development as its main international responsibility and contribution
to world peace.

Although peacekeeping and peacebuilding are different operations, they are
interrelated and mutually reinforcing. In PKOs, Chinese peacekeepers are
mostly engaged in engineering, transport and medical work, which places great
emphasis on infrastructure development projects as a pivotal means to tackle conflicts. However, China noted that it would consider the possibility of sending
combat units if the UN requested them.[36] Yet China still maintains that 'the
areas currently in need of peacekeeping are suffering from turmoil at the local
level without any serious conflict involved. Even if China sends combat troops,
it won't be of much use, because engineering and medical aid are what the
locals need most'.[37] Consequently, in dangerous mission areas, Chinese peacekeepers prefer to take on work, such as basic but necessary infrastructure, that
benefits the facilitation of trade and communication, accelerating economic

FIGURE 5
DOES THE CHINESE GOVERNMENT HAVE 'GLOBAL RESPONSIBILITY'? (SELECTING
ONE ANSWER)

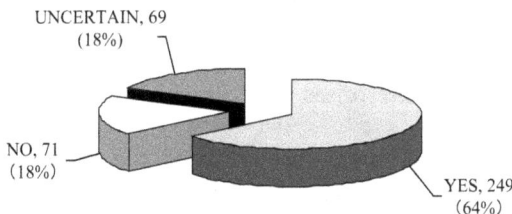

UNCERTAIN, 69
(18%)

NO, 71
(18%)

YES, 249
(64%)

Source: Analysis of 389 valid questionnaires.

FIGURE 6
WHAT IS CHINA'S PRIMARY NATIONAL IDENTITY? (SELECTING ONE ANSWER)

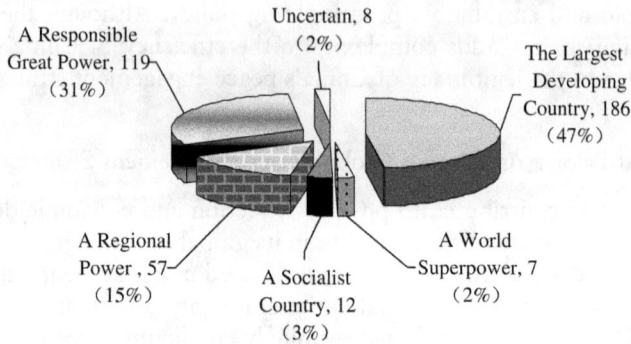

A Responsible Great Power, 119 (31%)

Uncertain, 8 (2%)

The Largest Developing Country, 186 (47%)

A Regional Power, 57 (15%)

A Socialist Country, 12 (3%)

A World Superpower, 7 (2%)

Source: Analysis of 389 valid questionnaires.

recovery and foreign investment as well as helping to improve local people's confidence in the future.

Several peacekeeping operations have included, to varying degrees, tasks of post-conflict peacebuilding.[38] Therefore China has been increasing the number of peacebuilding tasks in its operations. In acknowledgement of the needs of civilian populations marginalized from access to healthcare and the fact that the origin of conflicts is usually intimately linked to under-development,[39] Chinese peacekeepers focus on providing critical logistical services, such as rebuilding roads and bridges and providing essential healthcare services to UN staff and local populations, which open up the possibility for local people to contribute to their own development and lay a solid foundation for peacebuilding. For example, the UN Mission in Liberia (UNMIL) currently depends entirely on a Chinese transport unit to move personnel, fuel, water and other essential goods around the country. The unit has proven reliable even though it frequently has to travel through dangerous areas and is only lightly armed and despite the country having only 1000 km of paved roads.[40] China has also deployed well-drilling platoons to Africa. In December 2009, after more than 20 days of drilling operations, the third contingent of the Chinese engineering cohort in Darfur finally drilled clean water wells.[41] So far, six wells have been successfully drilled, contributing notably to the alleviation of water shortages in the region.[42]

In addition, in order to cooperate with its peacekeepers in disarmament, demobilization and reintegration, the Chinese government encourages its enterprises to hire and train local people, including ex-combatants, to solve the problem of local unemployment and accelerate their reintegration. As of the end of 2009, Chinese enterprises had directly hired 300,000 and trained 54,000 locals.[43]

In 2004, President Hu Jintao promulgated the 'New Historic Missions', which ordered the PLA to develop the capabilities necessary to protect China's interests at home and abroad. This parallels the PLA's growing interest in expanding its military operations other than war (MOOTW), such as counter-piracy, disaster response and humanitarian relief, both in China and abroad.[44] The first Disaster Prevention and Reduction Day was celebrated in China on 12 May 2009. The General Staff Headquarters of the PLA announced that the PLA had established an 'armed force system' for MOOTW, consisting of five specialized forces: flood and disaster relief force; post-earthquake emergency rescue force; emergency rescue force for nuclear, chemical and biological disasters; emergency relief force for transportation facilities; and international peacekeeping force.[45] These forces formulate the main functional arrangements of China's IPBOs.

Since the civilian contribution within IPBOs has expanded, China is strengthening its civilian deployment capacity with requisite expertise in health, education and economic development to directly help improve livelihoods. Developing countries suffer the greatest impact of conflict. To date, under its foreign assistance, China has also built over 150 schools, nearly 100 hospitals, more than 70 drinking water facilities and over 60 stadiums for other developing countries. China has sent a total of more than 20,000 medical personnel to nearly 70 countries, offering treatment to hundreds of millions of patients. China has built more than 200 agricultural cooperation projects in developing countries and has sent a large number of agro-technology experts. Premier Wen Jiabao stated at the 2010 UN High-Level Plenary Meeting on the Millennium Development Goals that,

> In the coming five years, China will take the following steps in support of better livelihood for people in other developing countries: build 200 schools; dispatch 3,000 medical experts, train 5,000 local medical personnel and provide medical equipment and medicines to 100 hospitals, giving priority to women's and children's health and the prevention and treatment of malaria, tuberculosis and HIV/AIDS. China will dispatch 3,000 agricultural experts and technical staff, provide 5,000 agriculture-related training opportunities in China.[46]

China's counter-piracy involvement off the Horn of Africa is also a part of IPBOs. Piracy emerged off Somalia as a consequence of its civil war, poverty and mass unemployment. In 2009, Somali pirates carried out 217 attacks and 47 vessels were hijacked and 867 crew members were taken hostage. Pirates held captive 30 ships with 450 crew members aboard in the first seven months of 2010.[47] Under these circumstances, China has expanded its patrol zone in piracy-hazardous waters off Somalia. In January 2010, the Shared Awareness and Deconfliction (SHADE) meeting in Bahrain approved China to lead the coordination of international anti-piracy patrols, meaning that China will need to send more than the three ships it keeps deployed off the Horn of Africa to protect vital trade routes linking Asia to Europe.[48] China also advocates global maritime governance and maintaining law and order at sea through cooperation rather than competition.

Finally, participation in disaster prevention and reduction is another significant aspect of China's IPBOs. Natural disasters pose a common challenge to all the countries in the world, and China suffers the most natural disasters of all countries. The country lists disaster prevention and reduction in its economic and social development plan as an important guarantee of sustainable development. China's White Paper 'China's Actions for Disaster Prevention and Reduction' of March 2009 specifically highlights its international contribution in this field.[49] In 2009 the China International Search and Rescue Team (CISAR) successfully passed the International Search and Rescue Advisory Group External Classification of heavy rescue teams, becoming the twelfth such team in the world and the second in Asia. CISAR is expanding and will be increased to 480 members with new equipment in 2011. The development of CISAR will contribute greatly to China's crisis response and management as well as to its international humanitarian relief.

Conclusions

Peace missions based on PKOs and IPBOs are the main channels to achieving the objectives of China's global peace engagement strategy. The evolution of the strategy has been greatly influenced by changes in China's international strategy and the recognition of its national identity. China's contribution to PKOs is likely to grow as it feels more comfortable with such activity. In IPBOs, China is undergoing another process of 'socialization', but, besides adaptation and learning as well as making concrete contributions, China feels it has the accountability and ability to set agendas to influence the focus of IPBOs to make stability and development the priority.

For sustainable contribution to PKOs and IPBOs, China and other contributing countries should learn from each other. Western states and China should take steps to trust each other in managing the cooperation dilemma. The encouragement of responsible Chinese international engagement offers a patently preferable policy to either antagonistic containment or short-sighted disregard of China.[50] If Western governments hope that China will assume greater responsibility in peace missions, they should respect China and avoid challenging its core national interests in order to overcome its reluctance to collaborate further.

After the 2010 Haiti earthquake, ensuring the safety of peacekeepers in mission areas was a priority for Chinese citizens. The failure of many previous peacekeeping operations often stemmed from the fact that casualties far exceeded the limits tolerable to the contributing countries. After 20 years, China has paid a heavy price in the cause of world peace: the lives of eight military officers and eight police officers sacrificed for PKOs (see Figure 7).[51] Affording to the survey, 29.57 per cent of respondents agreed that what China should treasure the most is the 'safety of peacekeepers' (see Figure 8). To some degree, due to the complexity as well as lack of self-defence equipment, peacebuilding is much more dangerous than peacekeeping, hence China's extreme caution regarding IPBOs.

In sum, China's confidence in PKOs and its cautiousness in IPBOs reflect the complex implementation environment of China's global peace engagement strategy. Despite the challenges, the two kinds of peace mission offer opportunities to augment China's national interests and further extend its influence overseas.

FIGURE 7
CAUSES OF DEATH OF CHINESE PEACEKEEPERS

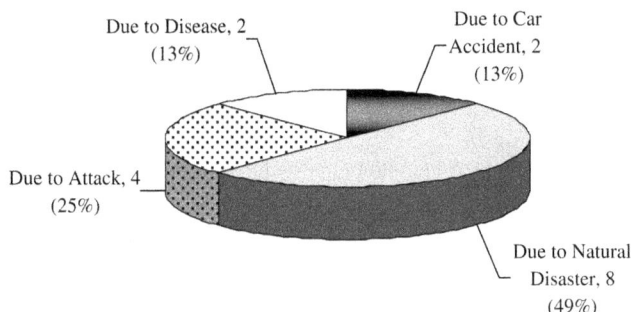

Due to Disease, 2
(13%)

Due to Car
Accident, 2
(13%)

Due to Attack, 4
(25%)

Due to Natural
Disaster, 8
(49%)

FIGURE 8
WHAT SHOULD CHINA CHERISH MOST IN PKOS? (SELECTING THREE ANSWERS)

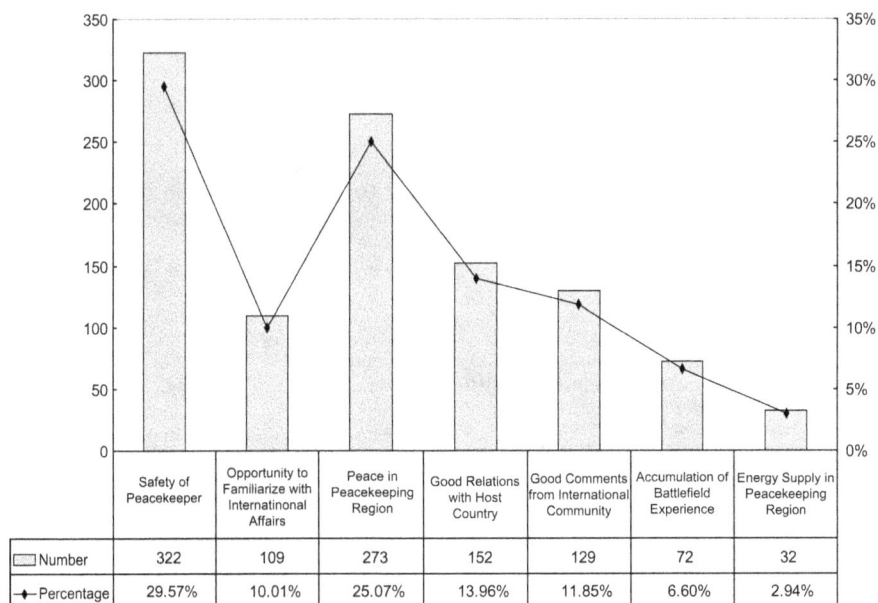

	Safety of Peacekeeper	Opportunity to Familiarize with Internatinonal Affairs	Peace in Peacekeeping Region	Good Relations with Host Country	Good Comments from International Community	Accumulation of Battlefield Experience	Energy Supply in Peacekeeping Region
Number	322	109	273	152	129	72	32
Percentage	29.57%	10.01%	25.07%	13.96%	11.85%	6.60%	2.94%

Source: Analysis of 363 valid questionnaires

ACKNOWLEDGEMENTS

I received useful feedback from Marc Lanteigne and Miwa Hirono. The author would like to thank Michael Pugh and anonymous reviewers for their comments, and also thank China Peacekeeping Civilian Police (CIVPOL) Training Centre in Beijing for its support in the questionnaire survey.

NOTES

1. The author invented the term 'China's global peace engagement strategy' to describe China's contribution to world peace and China's security cooperation policies. See Zhao Lei [赵磊], 'Zhongguo de guoji heping canyu zhanlue' [中国的国际和平参与战略] (China's international engagement strategy for world peace), *Guoji Guanxi Xueyuan Xuebao* [国际关系学院学报] (Journal of University of International Relations), Vol.114, No.3, 2010, pp.47–54.
2. Samuel S. Kim, 'China and Globalization: Confronting Myriad Challenges and Opportunities', *Asian Perspective*, Vol.33, No.3, 2009, p.53.
3. 'Hold High the Great Banner of Socialism with Chinese Characteristics and Strive for New Victories in Building a Moderately Prosperous Society in All Respects', Hu Jintao's Report to the 17th National Congress of the Communist Party of China, 15 Oct. 2007 (at: www.china.org.cn/english/congress/229611.htm).
4. See Hanna Ojanen (ed.), 'Peacekeeping-Peacebuilding: Preparing for the Future', Report of Finnish Institute of International Affairs, 2006 (at: www.upi-fiia.fi/assets/publications/-var-www-html-customers-wwwupi-fiiafi-doc-UPI_raportti_14.pdf); UN Department of Peacekeeping Operations, 'United Nations Peacekeeping Operations: Principles and Guidelines', 2008 (at: www.peacekeepingbestpractices.unlb.org/Pbps/Library/Capstone_Doctrine_ENG.pdf); Research Centre for Arms Control and Disarmament of China International Institute for Strategic Society [中国国际战略学会军控与裁军研究中心], *Dangdai guoji weihe xingdong* [当代国际维和行动] (Contemporary International Peacekeeping Operations), Beijing: Junshiyiwen Press, 2006, pp.50–55.
5. Information Office of the State Council of the People's Republic of China, 'White Paper on China's Peaceful Development Road', 12 Dec. 2005 (at: www.china.org.cn/english/features/book/152684.htm).
6. 'PLA Contributes a Lot to UN Peacekeeping Operations', *PLA Daily* (Beijing), 26 Apr. 2010.
7. 'A Decade of China's Peacekeeping Mission', 18 Jan. 2010 (at: www.china.org.cn/world/haitiquake/2010-01/18/content_19262239.htm).
8. Colum Lynch, 'China Filling Void Left by West in UN Peacekeeping', *Washington Post*, 24 Nov. 2006 (at: www.washingtonpost.com/wp-dyn/content/article/2006/11/23/AR2006112301007.html).
9. China committed 2,012 military and police individuals in PKOs; France 1,701; the Russia Federation 364; the United Kingdom 281; and the United States only 89. See the UN Department of Peacekeeping Operations, 'Ranking of Military and Police Contributions to UN Operations' (Monthly Report), 30 June 2010 (at: www.un.org/en/peacekeeping/contributors/2010/june10_2.pdf).
10. Information Office of the State Council of the People's Republic of China, 'White Paper on China's National Defence in 2004', Dec. 2004 (at: www.china.org.cn/e-white/20041227/index.htm).
11. 'China, US Armed Forces Vow to Enhance Cooperation', *China Daily* (Beijing), 1 July 2008 (at: www.china.org.cn/international/photos/2008-07/01/content_15912319.htm).
12. 'China, US Peacekeepers Conduct Joint Patrol in Haiti', *China Daily*, 29 Jan. 2010 (at: www.chinadaily.com.cn/china/2010-01/29/content_9400965.htm).
13. Interview with senior official, Ministry of Foreign Affairs of the People's Republic of China, Beijing, 17 Apr. 2010.
14. Jerker Hellström, 'Blue Berets under the Red Flag: China in the UN Peacekeeping System', Swedish Defence Research Agency, Report No.FOI-R-2772-SE, June 2009, p.34 (at: www2.foi.se/rapp/foir2772.pdf).
15. Michael J. Green, 'Democracy and the Balance of Power in Asia', *American Interest*, Vol.2, No.1, 2006, p.101.
16. International Crisis Group, 'China's Growing Role in UN Peacekeeping', 17 Apr. 2009, p.15.
17. Zhao Lei, 'China Is a Responsible Power in PKOs Arena', *China Report*, Vol.72, No.2, 2010, p.41.
18. Interview with Counsellor, Embassy of the People's Republic of China in Kosovo, Pristina, 10 Mar. 2010.
19. 'China to Enhance Support for UN Peacekeeping', *Beijing Review*, 23 Nov. 2009, p.25.
20. Chinese officials have consistently maintained that two preconditions are necessary to gain Chinese support for initiating a peacekeeping operation: host nation acquiescence and Security Council approval. See Bates Gill and James Reilly, 'Sovereignty, Intervention and Peacekeeping: The View from Beijing', *Survival*, Vol.42, No.3, 2000, p.44.
21. Zheng Yongnian [郑永年], 'Queli zhongguo waijiao zhengce de guoji huayuquan' [确立中国外交政策的国际话语权] (Enlarging the discourse power of China's foreign policy), *Gonggong waijiao* [公共外交] (Public Diplomacy Quarterly), Vol.1, No.1, 2010, pp.11–15.

22. Gabriel Almond, 'The Return to the State', *American Political Science Review*, Vol.82, No.3, 1988, pp.853–74.
23. Permanent Mission of the People's Republic of China to the United Nations, 'Statement by Ambassador Liu Zhenmin at Security Council Open Debate on Post-conflict Peacebuilding', 22 July 2009 (at: www.china-un.org/eng/hyyfy/t575181.htm).
24. Samuel S. Kim, 'China's Path to Great Power Status in the Globalization Era', *Asian Perspective*, Vol.27, No.1, 2003, pp.35–75.
25. Zhang Xiaomin [张效民] and Luo Jianbo [罗建波], 'Zhongguo ruanshili de pinggu yu fazhan lujing' [中国软实力的评估与发展路径] (Evaluation of China's soft power and roadmap of its development), *Guoji luntan* [国际论坛] (International Forum), Vol.10, No.5, 2008, pp.24–9.
26. Oliver P. Richmond, *The Transformation of Peace*, Basingstoke: Palgrave Macmillan, 2005.
27. Permanent Mission of the People's Republic of China to the United Nations, 'Statement by Ambassador Shen Guofang, Deputy Permanent Representative of China to UN at the Security Council on the Topic of "Peace-Building: Towards a Comprehensive Approach"', 5 Feb. 2001 (at: www.china-un.org/eng/chinaandun/securitycouncil/thematicissues/peacekeeping/t29428.htm).
28. Ian Taylor, 'The Future of China's Overseas Peacekeeping Operations', *China Brief*, Vol.8, No.6, 2008, pp.8–9. In 1974, at the special General Assembly, Deng Xiaoping said that China stood for establishing a new international political and economic order that was fair and rational, indicating that China was the challenger of the current international order. After issuing the 'harmonious world' concept, however, China amended its stance. At the 2007 Seventeenth National Congress of the Communist Party of China, Hu Jintao stated that China would work to make the international order fairer and more equitable, which emphasizes that China is a defender of the existing international order.
29. Bates Gill and Chin-Hao Huang, 'China's Expanding Role in Peacekeeping: Prospects and Policy Implication', Stockholm International Peace Research Institute, 2009, p.3.
30. Zhao Lei [赵磊], *Jiangou heping: zhongguo dui lianheguo waijiaoxingwei de yanjin* [建构和平: 中国对联合国外交行为的演进] (Significant Practice of Building a Harmonious World: Research on China's Participation in UN Peacekeeping Operations), Beijing: Central Party School Press, 2010, p.503.
31. David Shambaugh, 'Reforming China's Diplomacy', discussion paper, Asia Research Centre of Copenhagen Business School, 31 Jan. 2010, p.1 (at: openarchive.cbs.dk/bitstream/handle/10398/8013/Hele_discussion_paper.pdf?sequence = 1).
32. Ministry of Civil Affairs of the People's Republic of China, 'Report on the Development of China Civil Affairs in 2009', 10 June 2010 (at: www.mca.gov.cn/article/zwgk/mzyw/201006/20100600080798.shtml?2).
33. Wang Yizhou [王逸舟], 'Shimin shehui yu zhongguo waijiao' [市民社会与中国外交] (Civil society and Chinese diplomacy), *Zhongguo Shehui Kexue* [中国社会科学] (Social Sciences in China), No.3, 2000, pp.28–38; Li Qingsi [李庆四], 'Shehui zuzhi de waijiao gongneng: jiyu zhongxi hudong de kaocha' [社会组织的外交功能: 基于中西互动的考察] (The diplomatic functions of social organizations: an observation based on China–West interaction), *Shijie jingji yu zhengzhi* [世界经济与政治] (World Economics and Politics), No.6, 2009, pp.70–72.
34. Yu Keping [俞可平], 'Zhongguo gongmin shehui: gainian fenlei yu zhidu huanjing' [中国公民社会: 概念、分类与制度环境] (Civil society in China: concepts, classification and institutional environment), *Zhongguo shehui kexue* [中国社会科学] (Social Sciences in China), No.1, 2006, pp.109–22; Zhang Hongqing [张宏卿], 'Shilun chuantong wenhua yu gongmin shehui de yangcheng' [试论传统文化与公民社会的养成] (On the traditional culture and formation of the civic society), *Jiangxi caijing daxue xuebao* [江西财经大学学报] (Journal of Jiangxi University of Finance and Economics), Vol.67, No.1, 2009, pp.94–8.
35. Forum on China–Africa Cooperation, 'China Carries out Poverty Alleviation Cooperation with Sudanese NGOs', 27 Apr. 2010 (at: www.facac.org/eng/zxxx/t687712.htm).
36. 'China Will Consider Sending Combat Units under the Request of the United Nations', *Xinhua*, 20 Nov. 2009 (at: news.xinhuanet.com/mil/2009-11/20/content_12511405.htm).
37. 'Chinese Combat Troops "Can Join UN Peacekeeping"', *China Daily*, 7 July 2010.
38. Permanent Mission of the People's Republic of China to the United Nations, 'Statement by Ambassador Shen Guofang, Deputy Permanent Representative of China to UN at the Security Council on the Topic of "Peace-Building: Towards a Comprehensive Approach"', 5 Feb. 2001 (at: www.china-un.org/eng/chinaandun/securitycouncil/thematicissues/peacekeeping/t29428.htm).
39. 'China Stresses Role of Development in Peacebuilding', *People's Daily*, 8 Feb. 2001.
40. Gill and Huang (see n.29 above), p.26.
41. 'Chinese Peacekeepers to Darfur Drill Two Drinking Water Wells', *PLA Daily*, 17 Dec. 2009.

42. 'Chinese Soldiers Hone Skills on Frontlines of Peace', *Global Times* (Beijing), 10 May 2010.
43. Ministry of Commerce of the People's Republic of China, 'Tenth Anniversary of China–Africa Cooperation Forum', 9 Oct. 2010 (at: www.gov.cn/gzdt/2010-10/09/content_1718314.htm).
44. Gill and Huang (see n.29 above), p.15.
45. 'PLA Constructs MOOTW Arms Force System', *PLA Daily*, 14 May 2009.
46. Permanent Mission of the People's Republic of China to the United Nations, 'Statement by Wen Jiabao Premier of the State Council of the People's Republic of China at the UN High-Level Plenary Meeting on the Millennium Development Goals', 22 Sept. 2010 (at: www.china-un.org/eng/zt/wjb65ga/P020100929408860967466.pdf).
47. 'Eradicating Pirates by Means of Safeguarding the Stability of Somali Government', *People's Daily*, 29 Sept. 2010.
48. By committing to providing an 'enduring' presence on the trade route, China will be eligible to lead in conformity with a new rotating chairmanship. See 'China to Lead Anti-piracy Patrols off Somali Coast', *Global Times*, 28 Jan. 2010.
49. Information Office of the State Council of the People's Republic of China, 'China's Actions for Disaster Prevention and Reduction', 11 Mar. 2009 (at: www.china.org.cn/archive/2009-05/11/content_17753558_8.htm).
50. Bates Gill and James Reilly, 'Sovereignty, Intervention and Peacekeeping: The View from Beijing', *Survival*, Vol.42, No.3, 2000, p.42.
51. '16 Chinese Peacekeepers Sacrificed Their Lives in the Missions', *China Report*, Vol.72, No.2, 2010, pp.46–7.

Bibliography

Acharya, Amitav (2004) 'How Ideas Spread: Whose Norms Matter? Norm Localization and Institutional Change in Asian Regionalism', *International Organization*, 58(2): 239–75.

Adas, Michael (1989) *Machines as the Measure of Men: Science, Technology, and the Ideologies of Western Dominance*, Ithaca, NY: Cornell University Press.

Agence France Presse (1999) 'APEC Leaders to Confer on East Timor as Jakarta Bows Before Pressure', 12 September.

——(2002) 'Taiwan Activists "Encouraged" by East Timor, But No Diplomatic Ties Planned', 20 May.

Atkinson, Joel (2010) 'China-Taiwan Diplomatic Competition and the Pacific Islands', *The Pacific Review*, 23(4): 407–27.

Bain, William (2003) *Between Anarchy and Society: Trusteeship and the Obligations of Power*, Oxford: Oxford University Press.

Banerjee, Dipankar (2005) 'Current Trends in UN Peacekeeping: A Perspective from Asia', *International Peacekeeping*, 12(1): 18–33.

Barabantseva, Elena (2011) *Overseas Chinese, Ethnic Minorities and Nationalism: Decentering China*, London: Routledge.

Barber, David (1999) 'Auckland Summit Gives APEC a World-Beating Reputation', *National Business Review* (New Zealand), 17 November: 1.

Barnett, Doak A. (1985) *The Making of Foreign Policy in China: Structure and Process*, Boulder, CO: Westview Press.

Baylies, Carolyn (1995) '"Political Conditionality" and Democratization', *Review of African Political Economy*, 22(65): 321–37.

BBC Monitoring Asia Pacific (2009) 'China's Zhou Yongkang Hails China-Sudan Relations', 18 November.

BBC News (2006) 'China Ups Lebanon Force to 1,000' (at: news.bbc.co.uk/2/hi/asia-pacific/5355128.stm).

——(2007) 'Rebels Tell China "Leave Sudan"', 25 October 2007 (at: news.bbc.co.uk/1/hi/7061066.stm).

Bellamy, Alex J. (2006) 'Responsibility to Protect or Trojan Horse?: The Crisis in Darfur and Humanitarian Intervention after Iraq', *Ethics and International Affairs*, 19(2): 31–53.

——(2006) 'Whither the Responsibility to Protect?: Humanitarian Intervention and the 2005 World Summit', *Ethics and International Affairs*, 20(2): 143–69.

——(2008) 'The Responsibility to Protect and the Problem of Military Intervention', *International Affairs*, 84(4): 615–40.

——(2009) *Responsibility to Protect: The Global Effort to End Mass Atrocities*, Cambridge: Polity.

Bellamy, Alex J. and Paul D. Williams (2009) 'Protecting Civilians in Uncivil Wars', *Working Paper No.1*, Program on the Protection of Civilians, Brisbane: Asia Pacific Centre for the Responsibility to Protect, August.

——(2009) 'The West and Contemporary Peace Operations', *Journal of Peace Research*, 46(1): 39–57.

Bellamy, Alex J., Paul Williams and Stuart Griffin (2010) *Understanding Peacekeeping* (2nd edn), Cambridge: Polity.

Bertran, Eva (1995) 'Reinventing Governments: The Promise and Perils of United Nations Peace Building', *Journal of Conflict Resolution*, 39(3): 387–418.

Boutros-Ghali, Boutros (1992) 'An Agenda for Peace: Preventive Diplomacy, Peacemaking and Peacekeeping', UN Document, A/47/277-S/24111, 17 June.

Brautigam, Deborah (2009) *The Dragon's Gift: The Real Story of China in Africa*, Oxford: Oxford University Press.

Breau, Susan C. (2006) 'The Impact of the Responsibility to Protect on Peacekeeping', *Journal of Conflict and Security Law*, 11(3): 429–64.

Breslin, Shaun (2009) 'Understanding China's Regional Rise: Interpretations, Identities and Implications', *International Affairs*, 85(4): 817–35.

Brockett, Matthew (1999) 'China Backs Indonesian Role in Peacekeeping', *The Dominion* (New Zealand), 15 September.

Bull, Hedley (1995) *The Anarchical Society: A Study of Order in World Politics*, London: Macmillan.

Bull, Hedley and Adam Watson (1984) 'Introduction' in Hedley Bull and Adam Watson (eds), *The Expansion of International Society*, Oxford: Clarendon Press: 1–9.

Byman, Daniel (2001) 'Uncertain Partners: NGO and the Military', *Survival*, 43(2): 97–114.

Capie, David and Paul Evans (2007) 'Middle Power', *The Asia-Pacific Security Lexicon* (2nd edn), Singapore: Institute of Southeast Asian Studies: 155–8.

Carlson, Allen (2004) 'Helping to Keep the Peace (Albeit Reluctantly): China's Recent Stance on Sovereignty and Multilateral Intervention', *Pacific Affairs*, 77(1): 9–27.

——(2005) *Unifying China, Integrating with the World: Securing Chinese Sovereignty in the Reform Era*, Stanford, CA: Stanford University Press.

——(2006) 'More Than Just Saying No: China's Evolving Approach to Sovereignty and Intervention since Tiananmen', in Alastair Iain Johnson and Robert S. Ross (eds), *New Directions in the Study of Chinese Foreign Policy*, Stanford, CA: Stanford University Press: 217–41.

Central People's Government of the People's Republic of China (2010) '*Texie: musong haidi dizhen yunan zhongguo weihe jingcha huijia*' [特写：目送海地地震遇难中国维和警察回家] (Feature Article: The Sending Home of the Chinese Policemen Who Died in the Haiti Earthquake)', 18 January (at: www.gov.cn/jrzg/2010-01/19/content_1514397.htm).

Chapnick, Adam (1999) 'The Middle Power', *Canadian Foreign Policy*, 7(2): 73–82.

Chase, Michael S. and Kristen Gunness (2010) 'The PLA's Multiple Military Tasks: Prioritizing Combat Operations and Developing MOOTW Capabilities', *China Brief*, 10(2): 5–7.

Checkel, Jeffrey T. (1999) 'Norms, Institutions and National Identity in Contemporary Europe', *International Studies Quarterly*, 43(1): 83–114.

Chen, Gerald (1999) *Chinese Perspectives on International Relations: A Framework for Analysis*, New York: St. Martin's Press.

Chen, Jing (2009) 'Explaining the Change in China's Attitude toward UN Peacekeeping: A Norm Change Perspective', *Journal of Contemporary China*, 18(58): 157–73.

Chen, Xiaomei (1992) 'Occidentalism as Counterdiscourse: "He Shang" in Post-Mao China', *Critical Inquiry*, 18(4): 686–712.

Cheng, Guangjin (2010) 'Chinese Combat Troops "Can Join UN Peacekeeping" ', *China Daily*, 7 July (at: www.fmprc.gov.cn/eng/xwfw/s2510/t522607.htm).

Cheng Shuaihua [成帅华] (2000) '*Guojia zhuquan yu guoji renquan de ruogan wenti*' [国家主权与国际人权的若干问题] (Issues Involving International State Sovereignty and International Human Rights), *Ouzhou* [欧洲] (*Europe*), 1: 32–35.

China Daily (2005) 'China's Position Paper on UN Reforms', 8 June (at: www.chinadaily.com.cn/china/2005-06/08/content_536124.htm).

China Institute for International Strategic Studies [中国国际战略学会] (2003) *Guoji weihe xingdong xinshijiao* [国际维和行动新视角] (New Perspectives on International Peacekeeping Operations), Beijing: *Junshi yiwen chubanshe*.

Chinese Government (2006) 'China's African Policy', 20 September (at: www.gov.cn/misc/2006-01/12/content_156490.htm).

Chinese Ministry of Foreign Affairs (2008) 'Foreign Ministry Spokesperson Qin Gang's Remarks on the So-Called Issue of China Contributing Troops to ISAF in Afghanistan', 18 November (at: www.fmprc.gov.cn/eng/xwfw/s2510/t522607.htm).

Choedon, Yeshi (1990), *China and the United Nations*, New Delhi: South Asian Publishers.

Chopra, Jarat (2002) 'Building State Failure in East Timor', *Development and Change*, 33(5): 979–1000.

Chung, Chien-Peng (2009) 'The "Good Neighbour Policy" in the Context of China's Foreign Relations', *China: An International Journal*, 7(1): 107–23.

Cooper, Neil (2007) 'Review Article: On the Crisis of the Liberal Peace', *Conflict, Security & Development*, 7(4): 605–16.

Copper, John Franklin (1986) *China's Global Role: An Analysis of Peking's National Power Capabilities in the Context of an Evolving International System*, Stanford, CA: Hoover Institution Press.

Crawford, Neta C. (1996) 'Imag(in)ing Africa', *Harvard International Journal of Press/Politics*, 1(2): 30–44.

Darby, Phillip (2009) 'Rolling Back the Frontiers of Empire: Practising the Postcolonial', *International Peacekeeping*, 16(5): 699–716.

de Guevara, Berit Bliesemann and Florian P. Kühn (2011) '"The International Community Needs to Act": Loose Use and Empty Signalling of a Hackneyed Concept', *International Peacekeeping*, 18(2): 135–51.

Defence News (2010) 'RAF Gunners Continue Protecting Cam Bastion', 22 February (at: www.mod.uk/DefenceInternet/DefenceNews/MilitaryOperations/RafGunnersContinue ProtectingCampBastion.htm).

Deng, Francis (1995) 'Frontiers of Sovereignty', *Leiden Journal of International Law*, 8(2): 249–86.

——(1995) 'Reconciling Sovereignty with Responsibility: A Basis for International Humanitarian Action', in John Harbeson and Donald Rothchild (eds), *Africa in World Politics: Post-Cold War Challenges*, Boulder, CO: Westview Press: 295–310.

Deng, Francis, Sadikiel Kimaro, Terrence Lyons, Donald Rothchild and I. William Zartman (1996) *Sovereignty as Responsibility: Conflict Management in Africa*, Washington, DC: Brookings Institution.

Deng, Yong and Feiling Wang (1999) *In the Eyes of the Dragon: China Views the World*, Lanham, MD: Rowman & Littlefield.

Department of Policy Planning of the Ministry of Foreign Affairs of the People's Republic of China (2005) *China's Foreign Affairs 2005*, Beijing: World Affairs Press.

Dickens, David (2002) 'Can East Timor be a Blueprint for Burden-Sharing?', *The Washington Quarterly*, 25(3): 29–40.

Dikötter, Frank (1992) *The Discourse of Race in Modern China*, Stanford, CA: Stanford University Press.

Ding, Sheng (2008) 'To Build a "Harmonious World": China's Soft Power Wielding in the Global South', *Journal of Chinese Political Science*, 13(2): 193–213.

Dow Jones International News (2000) 'Chinese Police Will Head to East Timor to Join UN Force', 11 January.

Duffield, Mark (2011) 'Foreword', in Michael Pugh, Neil Cooper and Mandy Turner (eds), *Whose Peace? Critical Perspectives on the Political Economy of Peacebuilding*, Basingstoke: Palgrave Macmillan: xviii–xxi.

Durch, William J. and Alison C. Giffen (2010) 'Challenges of Strengthening the Protection of Civilians in Multidimensional Peace Operations', Background Paper for the Third International Forum for the 'Challenges of Peace Operations', 27–29 April, Queenbeyan, Australia.

Economy, Elizabeth and Michel Oksenberg (1999) *China Joins the World: Progress and Prosperity*, New York: Council on Foreign Relations.

EFE News Service /Factiva (1999) 'China-East Timor: China Open to Peacekeeping Force for East Timor', 9 September.

Eisenman, Joshua (2007) 'China's Post-Cold War Strategy in Africa: Examining Beijing's Methods and Objectives', in Joshua Eisenman, Eric Heginbotham and Derek Mitchell (eds) *China and the Developing World: Beijing's Strategy for the Twenty-First Century*, Armonk, NY: M. E. Sharpe: 29–59.

Ericksson, Andrew and Gabe Collins (2010) 'Looking after China's Own: Pressure to Protect PRC Citizens Working Overseas Likely to Rise', *China Signpost*, 2, 17 August (at: www.andrewerickson.com/2010/08/china-signpost%C2%A9-%E6%B4%9E%E5%AF%9F%E4%B8%AD%E5%9B%BD-looking-after-china%E2%80%99s-own-pressure-to-protect-prc-citizens-working-overseas-likely-to-rise/).

Evans, Paul M. (2004) 'Human Security in East Asia: In the Beginning', *Journal of East Asian Studies*, 4: 263–84.

Fetherston, A. B. (1994) *Towards a Theory of United Nations Peacekeeping*, New York: St. Martin's Press.

Finnemore, Martha (1996) *National Interests in International Society*, Ithaca, NY: Cornel University Press.

Fiorenza, Nicholas (2007) 'China Bolsters Peacekeeping Commitment', *Jane's Defense Weekly*, 14 February.

Foot, Rosemary (2001) 'Chinese Power and the Idea of a Responsible State', *China Journal*, 45: 1–19.

Forum on China and Africa Cooperation (2009) 'FOCAC Sharm el Sheikh Action Plan 2010-2012' (at: www.focac.org/eng/dsjbzjhy/hywj/t626387.htm).

——(2010) 'China's Role in Africa', Speech by Du Xiaocong of the Chinese Permanent Mission to the UN (at: www.focac.org/eng/zfgx/dfzc/t689653.htm).

Fravel, M. Taylor (1996) 'China's Attitude toward UN Peacekeeping Operations since 1989', *Asian Survey*, 36(11): 1102–21.

Friedrich-Ebert-Stiftung (2006) *Cambodia 1975–2005 Journey through the Night*, Bonn: Friedrich-Ebert-Stiftung.

Frost, Ellen L. (2007) 'China's Commercial Diplomacy in Asia: Promise or Threat?', in William W. Keller and Thomas G. Rawski (eds), *China's Rise and the Balance of Influence in Asia*, Pittsburgh, IL: University of Pittsburgh Press: 97–117.

Gill, Bates (2007) *Rising Star: China's New Security Diplomacy*, Washington, DC: Brookings Institution.

——(2010) 'New Directions in Chinese Security Policy', Paper at Conference on 'Chinese and American Approaches to Non-Traditional Security Challenges: Implications for the Maritime Domain', 4 May, Newport, Rhode Island.

Gill, Bates and Chin-Hao Huang (2009) 'China's Expanding Presence in UN Peacekeeping Operations and Implications for the United States', in Roy Kamphausen, David Lai and Andrew Scobell (eds), *Beyond the Strait: PLA Missions other than Taiwan*, Philadelphia, PA: Strategic Studies Institute: 99–126.

——(2009) 'China's Expanding Role in Peacekeeping: Prospects and Policy Implications', *Policy Paper 25*, Stockholm: Stockholm International Peace Research Institute, November (at: books.sipri.org/files/PP/SIPRIPP25.pdf).

Gill, Bates and James Reilly (2000) 'Sovereignty, Intervention and Peacekeeping: The View from Beijing', *Survival*, 42(3): 41–60.

Gill, Bates, Chin-Hao Huang and Stephen Morrison (2007) 'Assessing China's Growing Role in Africa', *China Security*, 3(3): 3–21.

Glaser, Bonnie S. and Evan S. Medeiros (2007) 'The Changing Ecology of Foreign Policy-Making in China: The Ascension and Demise of the Theory of "Peaceful Rise" ', *China Quarterly*, 190: 291–310.

Glaser, Bonnie S. and Philip C. Saunders (2002) 'Chinese Civilian Foreign Policy Research Institutes: Evolving Roles and Increasing Influence', *China Quarterly*, 171: 597–616.

Global Coalition (2010) 'Renewing the Pledge: Re-Engaging the Guarantors to the Sudanese Comprehensive Peace Agreement', 14 July (at: www.globalwitness.org/media_library_detail.php/1025/en/renewing_the_pledge_re_engaging_the_guarantors_to_the_sudanese_comprehensive_peace_agreement).

Goldstein, Avery (2005) *Rising to the Challenge: China's Grand Strategy and International Security*, Stanford, CA: Stanford University Press.

Gordon, Ruth E. (1995) 'Some Legal Problems with Trusteeship', *Cornell International Law Journal*, 28(2): 301–47.

Goulding, Marrack (1993) 'The Evolution of United Nations Peacekeeping', *International Affairs*, 69(3): 451–64.

Gries, Peter Hays (2001) 'Tears of Rage: Chinese Nationalist Reactions to the Belgrade Embassy Bombing', *China Journal*, 46: 25–43.

Gros, Jean-Germain (1996) 'Towards a Taxonomy of Failed States in the New World Order: Decaying Somalia, Liberia, Rwanda and Haiti', *Third World Quarterly*, 17(3): 455–71.

Gurtov, Mel and Byong-Moo Hwang (1998) *China's Security: The New Roles of the Military*, Boulder, CO, and London: Lynne Rienner.

Halper, Stefan (2010) *The Beijing Consensus: How China's Authoritarian Model will Dominate the Twenty-First Century*, New York: Basic Books.

He, Hongze (1994) 'New Role for UN', *Beijing Review*, 37(2): 23.

He, Yin (2007) 'China's Changing Policy on UN Peacekeeping Operations', Asia Paper, Stockholm: Institute for Security and Development Policy, July.

Higate, Paul and Marsha Henry (2010) 'Space, Performance and Everyday Security in the Peacekeeping Context', *International Peacekeeping*, 17(1): 32–48.

Higgins, Andrew (2009) 'China Showcasing its Softer Side: Growing Role in UN Peacekeeping Signals Desire to Project Image of Benign Power', *Washington Post*, 2 December (at:www.washingtonpost.com/wp-dyn/content/article/2009/12/01/ AR2009120104060.html).

Hill, John (2003) 'China Takes on Major Peacekeeping Role', *Jane's Intelligence Review*, 1 November.

Hirono, Miwa (2008) *Civilizing Missions: International Religious Agencies in China*, New York: Palgrave Macmillan.

——(2011) 'The Road to Recovery: The Spill-Over Effects of Multilateralism in Cambodia on Sino–Japanese Relations', in Victor E. Teo and Lam Peng Er (eds), *Southeast Asia between China and Japan*, Newcastle upon Tyne: Cambridge Scholars Publishing: 295–313.

Holslag, Jonathan (2008) 'China's Diplomatic Manoeuvring on the Question of Darfur', *Journal of Contemporary China*, 17(54): 71–84.

——(2009) 'Embracing Chinese Global Security Ambitions', *The Washington Quarterly*, 32(3): 105–18.

Holt, Victoria K., Glyn Taylor and Max Kelly (2009) 'Protecting Civilians in the Context of UN Peacekeeping Operations', UN Independent Study Jointly Commissioned by the Department of Peacekeeping Operations and the Office for the Coordination of Humanitarian Affairs.

Hu, Yumin (2009) 'China Plays its Peacekeeping Role', *China Daily*, 29 June (at: www.chinadaily.com.cn/cndy/2009-06/29/content_8331296.htm).

Huang, Chin-Hao (2008) 'US–China Relations and Darfur', *Fordham International Law Journal*, 31(4): 827–42.

Huang, Shan (2010) 'A Decade of China's Peacekeeping Missions', www.China.org, 18 January (at: www.china.org.cn/world/haitiquake/2010–01/18/content_19262239.htm).

Human Rights Watch (2003) *Sudan, Oil, and Human Rights*, Brussels: Human Rights Watch.

Hunt, Charles T. and Alex J. Bellamy (2010) 'Mainstreaming the Responsibility to Protect in Peace Operations', *Working Paper No.3*, Brisbane: Asia Pacific Centre for the Responsibility to Protect, March.

Hutzler, Charles (1999) 'Clinton, APEC Leaders Offer Help for East Timor Peacekeeping', Associated Press, 13 September.

Ikenberry, G. John and Charles Kupchan (1990) 'Socialization and Hegemonic Power', *International Organization*, 44(3): 283–315.

Information Office of the State Council of the People's Republic of China (2009) 'China's National Defence in 2008', 20 January (at: www.china.org.cn/government/whitepaper/node_7060059.htm).

International Commission on Intervention and State Sovereignty (2001) *The Responsibility to Protect: Report of the International Commission on Intervention and State Sovereignty*, Ottawa: International Development Research Centre.

International Committee of the Red Cross (ICRC) (2010) 'Annual Report 2009', Geneva: ICRC.

International Crisis Group (2009) 'China's Growing Role in UN Peacekeeping'. Asia Report 166, 17 April.

Jakobson, Linda and Dean Knox (2010) 'New Foreign Policy Actors in China', *Policy Paper 26*, Stockholm: Stockholm International Peace Research Institute.

Jepperson, Ronald, Alexander Wendt and Peter Katzenstein (1996) 'Norms, Identity and Culture in National Security', in Peter Katzenstein (ed.), *The Culture of National Security*, New York: Columbia University Press: 33–75.

Jiefangjun Bao (2008) 'The Deterrence Function of Launching Military Training Exercises', 29 April.

——(2009) 'PLA Constructs MOOTW Arms Force System', 26 June.

Johnston, Alastair Iain (1998) 'International Structures and Chinese Foreign Policy', in Samuel S. Kim (ed.), *China and the World: Chinese Foreign Policy Faces the New Millennium*, Boulder, CO: Westview: 55–90.

——(2008) *Social States: China in International Institutions, 1980–2000*, Princeton, NJ: Princeton University Press.

Johnston, Alastair Iain and Robert Ross (eds) (2006) *New Directions in the Study of China's Foreign Policy*, Stanford, CA: Stanford University Press.

Jones, Bruce and Feryal Cherif (2003) *Evolving Models of Peacekeeping Policy Implications and Responses: Report to the DPKO*, New York: Center on International Cooperation.

Jones, Bruce, Carlos Pascual and Stephen John Stedman (2009) 'Building on Brahimi: Peacekeeping in an Era of Strategic Uncertainty' (at: www.peacekeepingbestpractices.unlb.org/PBPS/Library/CIC%20New%20Horizon%20Think%20Piece.pdf).

——(2009) *Power & Responsibility: Building International Order in an Era of Transnational Threats*, Washington, DC: Brookings Institution.

Jopson, Barney (2009) 'China and Kenya in Infrastructure Talks', *Financial Times*, 14 October (at: fcaea.org/aid=287.phtml).

Jordaan, Eduard (2003) 'The Concept of a Middle Power in International Relations: Distinguishing between Emerging and Traditional Middle Powers', *Politikon: South African Journal of Political Studies*, 30(2): 165–81.

Keen, David (2003) *Complex Emergencies*, Cambridge: Polity.

Kent, Ann (1999) *China, the United Nations and Human Rights: The Limits of Compliance*, Philadelphia, PA: University of Pennsylvania Press.

——(2007) *Beyond Compliance: China, International Organizations and Global Security*, Stanford, CA: Stanford University Press.

Kiernan, Ben (2008) *The Pol Pot Regime: Race, Power and Genocide in Cambodia under the Khmer Rouge, 1975–79* (3rd edn), New Haven, CT: Yale University Press.

Kim, Samuel S. (1979) *China, the United Nations, and World Order*, Princeton, NJ: Princeton University Press.

——(1991) *China In and Out of the Changing World Order*, Princeton, NJ: Princeton University Press.

——(1995) 'China's International Organization Behavior', in Thomas Robinson and David Shambaugh (eds), *Chinese Foreign Policy: Theory and Practice*, Oxford: Oxford University Press: 401–34.

——(1999) 'China and the United Nations', in Elizabeth Economy and Michel Oksenberg (eds), *China Joins the World: Progress and Prospects*, New York: Council on Foreign Relations Press: 42–89.

——(2003) 'China's Path to Great Power Status in the Globalization Era', *Asian Perspective*, 27(1): 35–75.

——(2009) 'China and Globalization: Confronting Myriad Challenges and Opportunities', *Asian Perspective*, 33(3): 41–80.

Kleine-Ahlbrandt, Stephanie and Andres Small (2008) 'China's New Dictatorship Diplomacy', *Foreign Affairs*, 87(1): 38–56.

Knight, Nick (2007) 'Thinking about Globalisation, Thinking about Japan: Dichotomies in China's Construction of the Modern World', in Michael Heazle and Nick Knight (eds), *China–Japan Relations in the Twenty-first Century: Creating a Future Past?*, Cheltenham: Edward Elgar: 54–73.

Kurlantzick, Joshua (2007) *Charm Offensive: How China's Soft Power is Transforming the World*, New Haven, CT: Yale University Press.

Kyodo News (1999) 'China Waiting on UN Call to Send Police to East Timor', 19 October.

Lampton, David M. (2005) 'China's Rise in Asia Need Not Be at America's Expense', in David Shambaugh (ed.), *Power Shift: China and Asia's New Dynamics*, Berkeley, Los Angeles and London: University of California Press: 306–28.

——(2008) *The Three Faces of Chinese Power: Might, Money and Minds*, Berkeley, Los Angeles and London: University of California Press.

Lanteigne, Marc (2005) *China and International Institutions: Alternate Paths to Global Power*, London: Routledge.

——(2010) 'Security, Strategy and the Former USSR: China and the Shanghai Cooperation Organization', in Shaun Breslin (ed.), *A Handbook of Chinese International Relations*, London: Routledge: 166–76.

Large, Daniel (2009) 'China's Sudan Engagement: Changing Northern and Southern Political Trajectories in Peace and War', *China Quarterly*, 199: 610–26.

Leftwich, Adrian (1993) 'Governance, Democracy and Development in the Third World', *Third World Quarterly*, 14(3): 605–24.

Li Anshan [李安山] (2008) '*Wei zhongguo zhengming: zhongguo de feizhou zhanlüe yu guojia xingxiang*' [为中国正名：中国的非洲战略与国家形象] (Establishing a Name for China: China's Africa Strategy and National Image), *Shijie zhengzhi* [世界政治] (*World Politics*), 4: 6–15

Li Buyun [李步云] (1999) '*Renquan de liangge lilun wenti*' [人权的两个理论问题] (Two Theoretical Human Rights Issues), *Zhongguo Faxue* [中国法学] (*Chinese Legal Studies*), 3: 38–42.

Li Mu (2010) 'China Holds High-Level UN Peacekeeping Training Class', People's Daily Online, 21 September (at: english.peopledaily.com.cn/90001/90776/90786/ 7147474.html).

Li Tiecheng [李铁城] and Qian Wenrong [钱文荣] (2006) *Lianheguo kuangjiaxia de zhongmei guanxi* [联合国框架下的中美关系] (*The Sino-US Relations Within the UN Framework*), Beijing: *Renmin chubanshe*.

Liaowang (2005) 'PRC's "New Diplomacy" Stresses on More Active International Role', 11 July.

Lieberthal, Kenneth and Michel Oksenberg (1988), *Policy Making in China: Leaders, Structures, and Processes*, Princeton, NJ: Princeton University Press.

Lin-Greenberg, Erik (2009) 'Blue-Helmeted Dragons: Explaining China's Participation in United Nations Peace Operations', unpublished Master's thesis, Massachusetts Institute of Technology.

Ling, Bonny (2007) 'China's Peacekeeping Diplomacy', *China Rights Forum*, 1: 47–49.

Lucas, George R. (2008) 'The Morality of "Military Anthropology"', *Journal of Military Ethics*, 7(3): 165–87.

Luo Jianbo [罗建波] (2007) '*Ruhe lijie zhongfei xinxing zhanlüe huoban guanxi*' [如何理解中非新型战略伙伴关系] (How Should China and Africa's New Strategic Partnership be Understood), *Guoji luntan* [国际论坛] (*International Forum*), 9(5): 31–36.

——(2007) '*Ruhe youhua zhongguo heping jueqi de guojia xingxiang*' [如何优化中国和平崛起的国家形象] (How Should China's Image of Peaceful Rise be Optimized?), in Men Honghua [门洪华] (ed.), *Zhongguo: ruanshili fanglüe* [中国：软实力方略] (*China: Soft Power Strategy*), Hangzhou: *Zhejiang renmin chubanshe*: 241–63.

Maogoto, Jackson Nyamuya (2000) 'From Congo to East Timor in Forty Years: The UN Finally Crossing the Rubicon between Peace-keeping and Peace-making?', *Newcastle Law Review*, 2: 45–73.

Mashatt, Merriam, Maj-Gen. Daniel Long and James Crum (2008) 'Conflict-Sensitive Approach to Infrastructure Development', Special Report No.197, US Institute of Peace, January (at: www.usip.org/files/resources/sr197.pdf).

Medeiros, Evan and M. Taylor Fravel (2003) 'China's New Diplomacy', *Foreign Affairs*, 82(6): 22–35.

——(2009) *China's International Behaviour: Activism, Opportunism and Diversification*, Washington, DC: Rand.

Men Honghua [门洪华] (2001) '*Guoji jizhi yu zhongguo de zhanlüe xuanze*' [国际机制与中国的战略选择] (International Mechanisms and Strategic Choices for China), *Zhongguo shehui kexue* [中国社会科学] (*Social Sciences in China*), (45)2: 178–87.

——(2002) *Heping de weidu: lianheguo jiti anquan jizhi yanjiu* [和平的纬度：联合国集体安全机制研究] (The Latitude of Peace: The Study of UN Collective Security Mechanism), Shanghai: *Shanghai renmin chubanshe*.

Men Honghua [门洪华] and Huang Haili [黄海莉] (2004) '*Yingdui guojia shibai de bujiu cuoshi: jian lun zhongmei anquan hezuo de zhanlüexing*' [应对国家失败的补救措施 ：兼论中美安全合作的战略性] (Responses to Save Failed States: Coupled with a Discussion of the Strategic Dimension of Sino-US Security Cooperation), *Meiguo yanjiu* [美国研究] (*American Studies*), 1: 7–32.

Ministry of Foreign Affairs of the People's Republic of China (2000) 'Some Thoughts on Establishing a New Regional Security Order' (statement by Ambassador Sha Zukang at the East-West Center's Senior Policy Seminar, 7 August, Honolulu (at: www.fmprc.gov.cn/eng/wjdt/zyjh/t24961.htm).

——(2002) 'China's Position Paper on the New Security Concept', 31 July (at: www.mfa.gov.cn/eng/wjb/zzjg/gjs/gjzzyhy/2612/2614/t15319.htm).

——(2005) 'Position Paper of the People's Republic of China on the United Nations Reforms', 7 June (at: www.mfa.gov.cn/eng/wjb/zzjg/gjs/gjsxw/t199318.htm).

——(2009) 'Remarks by Vice Foreign Minister He Yafei at the Opening Ceremony of the International Symposium on Peacekeeping Operations', 19 November (at: www.fmprc.gov.cn/eng/wjdt/zyjh/t631646.htm).

——(2010) 'Hand-Over Ceremony of Anti-Malaria Medicines to Southern Sudan Held in Chinese Consulate General in Juba', 11 August (at: www.fmprc.gov.cn/eng/wjb/zwjg/ zwbd/ t723295.htm).

Morris, Stephen J. (1999) *Why Vietnam Invaded Cambodia: Political Culture and the Causes of War*, Stanford, CA: Stanford University Press.

Morton, Katherine and Jacinta O'Hagan (eds) (2009) *Humanitarianism and Civil-Military Relations in a Post-9/11 World*, Keynotes 10, Canberra: Department of International Relations, Australian National University, March.

Mottram, Linda (2009) 'Praise for China's Expanding Peacekeeping Role', *ABC Radio* (Sydney), 23 November (at: www.radioaustralia.net.au/asiapac/stories/200911/ s2751288.htm).

Mu Yaping [慕亚平] and Chen Xiaohua [陈晓华] (2001) '*Shiji zhi jiaoyi weihe: dui lengzhanhou lianheguo weichi heping xingdong de pingjia yu sikao*' [世纪之交议维和-对冷战后联合国维持和平行动的评价与思考] (Peacekeeping at the Turn of the Century: Evaluation and Thoughts on UN Peacekeeping Operations in the Post-Cold War Period), *Faxue pinglun* [法学评论] (*Law Review*), 110(6): 65–72.

Mulvenon, James (2009) 'Chairman Hu and the PLA's "New Historic Missions"', *China Leadership Monitor*, 27: 1–11.

Nie Jun [聂军] (2005) '*Lianheguo weihe yu jiti anquan bianxi*' [联合国维和与集体安全辨析] (An Analysis on UN Peacekeeping Operations and Collective Security), *Ouzhou yanjiu* [欧洲研究] (*Chinese Journal of European Studies*), 23(3): 28–38.

Nyíri, Pál (2006) 'The Yellow Man's Burden: Chinese Migrants on a Civilizing Mission', *China Journal*, 56: 83–106.

Ong, Russell (2007) *China's Security in the 21st Century*, New York and London: Routledge.

Oster, Shai (2010) 'China Replaces Haiti Peacekeepers', *Wall Street Journal Asia*, 25 January.

Otunnu, Olara A. and Michael W. Doyle (1998) *Peacemaking and Peacemaking in the New Century*, Lanham, MD: Row & Littlefield Publishers.

Pang, Zhongying (2005) 'China's Changing Attitude to UN Peacekeeping', *International Peacekeeping*, 12(1): 87–104.

——(2009) 'China's Non-Intervention Question, *Global Responsibility to Protect*, 1(2): 237–52.

Paris, Roland (2004) *At War's End: Building Peace after Civil Conflict*, Cambridge: Cambridge University Press.

People's Daily (2005) 'Hu Jintao Says China Pursues Peaceful Development', 3 September.

——(2010) 'Chinese Combat Troops "Can be Part of UN Peacekeeping" ', 7 July.

——(2010) 'UN Official Lauds China's Contribution to Peacekeeping Efforts', 30 July.

People's Republic of Cambodia (n.d.) 'Crime of Beijing Chinese Hegemony Enlargement and Servants Pol Pot, Eang Sary, Khieu Samphan During 1975–1978', publisher unknown.

Permanent Mission of the People's Republic of China to the United Nations (2009) 'China's Participation in UN Peacekeeping Operations (1990-2008)', 21 January (at: www.china-un. org/eng/zt/wh/t534321.htm).

——(2009) 'Statement by Ambassador Liu Zhenmin, Deputy Permanent Representative of the Chinese Mission to the United Nations, at the Fourth Committee of the Sixty-Fourth Session of the United Nations General Assembly on Item 33: Comprehensive Review of the Whole Question of Peacekeeping Operations in all their Aspects', 27 October.

Pfaff, William (1995) 'A New Colonialism?: Europe Must Go Back into Africa', *Foreign Affairs*, 74(1): 2–6.

Pottinger, Matt (2000) 'Gusmao Seeks East Timorese Ties with China', Reuters, 28 January.

Pouligny, Béatrice (2006) *Peace Operations Seen from Below: UN Missions and Local People*, London: Hurst.

Pugh, Michael (2010) 'Accountability and Credibility: Assessing Host Population Perceptions and Expectations', in Cedric de Coning, Andreas Stensland and Thierry Tardy (eds), *Beyond the New Horizon*, (Proceedings from the UN Peacekeeping Future Challenges Seminar, Geneva, 23–24 June 2010) Oslo: Norwegian Institute of International Affairs: 56–65.

Purnawanty, Jani (2000) 'Various Perspectives on Understanding the East Timor Crisis', *Temple International and Comparative Law Journal*, 72: 61–74.

Qian, Qichen (2005) *Ten Episodes in Chinese Diplomacy*, New York: Harper Collins.

Ramo, Joshua Cooper (2004) *The Beijing Consensus*, London: Foreign Policy Centre.

Ratner, Steven (1995) *The New UN Peacekeeping: Building Peace in Lands of Conflict after the Cold War*, New York: Macmillan.

Ren, Xiao (2009) 'The International Relations Theoretical Discourse in China: One World, Different Explanations', *Journal of Chinese Political Science*, 15: 99–116.

Reuters (2009) 'Ramos-Horta Calls for APEC Action on Timor', 10 September.

Richardson, Courtney J. (2010) 'China's Growing Involvement in Global Peacekeeping', in Center on International Cooperation (ed.), *Annual Review of Global Peace Operations 2010*, Boulder, CO: Lynne Rienner: 105.

Richardson, Sophie (2010) *China, Cambodia, and the Five Principles of Peaceful Coexistence*, New York: Columbia University Press.

Richardson, Sophie and Brantly Womack (2010) 'China, Cambodia, and the Five Principles of Peaceful Coexistence', Honolulu: East–West Center, 18 June (at: www.eastwestcenter.org/ewc-in-washington/events/previous-events-2010/june-18-dr-sophie-richardson-and-dr-brantly-womack/).

Richmond, Oliver P. (2008) *Peace in International Relations*, London: Routledge.

Roberts, David (1998) 'A Dangerous Game: Managing Consent in the Cambodian UN Peacekeeping Operations', *Studies in Conflict and Terrorism*, 21(1): 29–57.

Robinson, David Alexander (2009) 'Hearts, Minds and Wallets: Lessons from China's Growing Relationship with Africa', *Journal of Alternative Perspectives in the Social Sciences*, 1(3): 861–69.

Rogers, Philippe D. (2007) 'China and UN Peacekeeping Operations in Africa', (US) *Naval War College Review*, 60(2): 73–93.

Rotberg, Robert I. (2002) 'The New Nature of Nation-State Failure', *The Washington Quarterly*, 25(3): 85–96.

Rothchild, Donald, Francis M. Deng, I. William Zartman, Sadikiel Kimaro and Terrence Lyons (1996) *Sovereignty as Responsibility: Conflict Management in Africa*, Washington, DC: Brookings Institution.

Rubinstein, Robert A. (2005) 'Intervention and Culture: An Anthropological Approach to Peace Operations', *Security Dialogue*, 36(4): 527–44.

Ruffert, Matthias (2001) 'The Administration of Kosovo and East Timor by the International Community', *International and Comparative Law Quarterly*, 50(3): 613–31.

Sautman, Barry (1994) 'Anti-Black Racism in Post-Mao China', *China Quarterly*, 138: 413–37.

SaveDarfur (2007) 'Briefing Paper: China in Sudan: Having it Both Ways', 18 October (at: www.savedarfur.org/pages/policy_paper/briefing_paper_china_in_sudan_having_it_both_ways/).

Schulze, Kristen E. (2001) 'The East Timor Referendum Crisis and its Impact on Indonesian Politics', *Studies in Conflict and Terrorism*, 24(1): 77–82.

Security Council Report (2009) 'Cross-Cutting Report: Protection of Civilians No.4', 30 October (at: www.securitycouncilreport.org/atf/cf/{65BFCF9B-6D27-4E9C-8CD3-CF6E4FF96FF9}/XCutting%20PoC%202009.pdf).

——(2009) 'Protection of Civilians Monthly Forecast', January (at: www.securitycouncilreport.org/site/c.glKWLeMTIsG/b.4838015/k.1FFC/January_2009brProtection_of_Civilians.htm).

——(2009) 'Protection of Civilians Monthly Forecast', November (at: www.securitycouncilreport. org/site/c.glKWLeMTIsG/b.5566467/k.B551/November_2009brProtection_of_Civilians. htm).

——(2010) 'Protection of Civilians Monthly Forecast', July (at: www.securitycouncilreport.org/ site/c.glKWLeMTIsG/b.6115659/k.3FB8/July_2010brProtection_of_Civilians.htm).

Segal, Gerald (1994) 'China's Changing Shape', *Foreign Affairs*, 73(3): 43–58.

Seybolt, Taylor (2007) *Humanitarian Military Intervention: The Conditions for Success and Failure*, Oxford: Oxford University Press.

Sheng Hongsheng [盛红生] (2006) *Lianheguo weichi heping xingdong falu wenti yanjiu* [联合国维持和平行动法律问题研究] (*Legal Aspects of United Nations Peacekeeping Operations*), Beijing: *Shishi chubanshe*.

Shi Yinhong [时殷弘] (2000) 'Lun ershi shiji guoji guifan tixi' [论二十世纪国际规范体系] (A Discussion of the System of International Norms in the Twentieth Century), *Guoji luntan* [国际论坛] (*International Forum*), 6: 8–10.

Shih, Chih-Yu (2005) 'Breeding a Reluctant Dragon: Can China Rise into Partnership and away from Antagonism?', *Review of International Studies*, 31(4): 755–74.

Shinn, David (2009) 'Chinese Involvement in African Conflict Zones', *China Brief*, 9(7): 7–10.

Simpson, Gerry (2004) *Great Powers and Outlaw States: Unequal Sovereigns in the International Legal Order*, Cambridge: Cambridge University Press.

Skolgy, Sigrun I. (1993) 'Structural Adjustment and Development: Human Rights – An Agenda for Change', *Human Rights Quarterly*, 15(4): 751–78.

Smith, Michael G. with Maureen Dee (2003) *East Timor's Journey to Freedom*, Boulder, CO, and London: Lynne Rienner.

Song Dexing [宋德星] and Liu Jinqi [刘金奇] (2007) '*Guoji tixi zhong de "shibai guojia" xilun*' [国际体系中的"失败国家"析论] (An Analysis of 'Failed States' in the International System), *Xiandai guoji guanxi* [现代国际关系] (*Contemporary International Relations*), 2: 28–35.

South China Morning Post (2008) 'How Chinese Police in East Timor Won Respect from Locals and Colleagues', 19 December.

Stähle, Stefan (2008) 'China's Shifting Attitude towards United Nations Peacekeeping Operations', *China Quarterly*, 195: 631–55.

Stockholm International Peace Research Institute (2009) *SIPRI Yearbook 2009: Armaments, Disarmaments and International Security*, Stockholm: Stockholm International Peace Research Institute.

Straits Times (2011) 'Chinese General to Head UN Peacekeeping Force', 14 January.

STRATFOR Global Intelligence (2007) 'China: Peacekeeping and the Responsible Stakeholder', 28 August (at: www.stratfor.com).

Sudan Tribune (2008) 'Chinese Oil Workers Kidnapped in Sudan's Kordofan', 19 October (at: www.sudantribune.com/spip.php?article28979)

——(2009) 'China, Kenya Discuss New Corridor for Southern Sudan Oil', 16 October (at: www. sudantribune.com/spip.php?article32803).

——(2010) 'China Should Prepare for Possible South Sudan Independence – Machar', 19 September (at: www.sudantribune.com/spip.php?page= imprimable&id_article= 36295).

Sun Meng [孙萌] (2006) *Lianheguo weihe xingdong weifa zeren yanjiu* [联合国维和行动违法责任研究] (UN's Responsibility in Peacekeeping Operations), Beijing: *Zhishi chanquan chubanshe*.

Sutter, Robert (2008) *Chinese Foreign Relations: Power and Policy Since the Cold War*, Lanham: Rowman & Littlefield.

Suzuki, Shogo (2008) 'Seeking "Legitimate" Great Power Status in Post-Cold War International Society: China's and Japan's Participation in PKOs', *International Relations*, 22(1): 45–63.

——(2009) 'Chinese Soft Power, Insecurity Studies, Myopia and Fantasy', *Third World Quarterly*, 30(4): 779–93.

——(2009) *Civilization and Empire: China and Japan's Encounter with European International Society*, London: Routledge.

Tang Yongsheng [唐永胜] and Xu Qiyu [徐弃郁] (2004) *Xunqiu fuza de pingheng: guoji anquan jizhi yu zhuquan guojia de canyu* [寻求复杂的平衡：国际安全机制与主权国家的参与] (Seeking Complex Balance: International Security System and Sovereign States' Participation to it), Beijing: *Shijie zhishi chubanshe*.

Tang, Anne (2009) 'China Donates $700,000 to UN Peacekeeping Missions', *Xinhua*, 2 December (at: www.reliefweb.int/rw/rwb.nsf/db900sid/JBRN-7YCFEH? OpenDocument).

Taylor, Ian (2009) *China's New Role in Africa*, Boulder, CO: Lynne Rienner.

Teitt, Sarah (2009) 'Assessing Polemics, Principles and Practices: China and the Responsibility to Protect', *Global Responsibility to Protect,* 1(2): 208–36.

Terry, Fiona (2002) *Condemned to Repeat?: The Paradox of Humanitarian Action*, Ithaca, NY: Cornell University Press.

Tipps, Dean C. (1973) 'Modernization Theory and the Comparative Study of Societies: A Critical Perspective', *Comparative Studies in Society and History*, 15(2): 199–226.

Touval, Saadia (2004) 'Why the UN Fails', *Foreign Affairs*, 73(5): 44–57.

United Nations Cartographic Section (2011), 'Timor Leste', Map No. 4111 Rev.11, November.

United Nations Department of Peacekeeping Operations (2008) *United Nations Peacekeeping Operations: Principles and Guidelines*, New York: United Nations.

——(2009) 'A New Partnership Agenda: Charting a New Horizon for UN Peacekeeping', July.

——(2010) 'Ranking of Military and Police Contributions to UN Operations', 30 June (at: www.un.org/en/peacekeeping/contributors/2010/june10_2.pdf).

——(2010) 'UN Missions Summary Detailed by Country' (at: www.un.org/Depts/dpko/ dpko/contributors).

United Nations Department of Public Information (2002), 'East Timor – UNTAET Background', May (at: www.un.org/en/peacekeeping/missions/past/etimor/ UntaetB.htm).

United Nations Document (1992) 'Provisional Verbatim Record of the Three Thousand One Hundred and Forty-third Meeting', S/PV.3143, 30 November.

——(1999) 'On the Situation in East Timor', S/RES/1264, 15 September.

——(1999) 'Protection of Civilians', S/RES/1265, 17 September.

——(2000) 'Protection of Civilians', S/RES/1296, 19 April.

——(2000) 'Security Council Open Debate on Protection of Civilians in Armed Conflict Resolution 1296', S/PV.4130, 19 April.

——(2003) 'The Situation in Liberia', S/RES/1509, 19 September.

——(2004) 'A More Secure World: Our Shared Responsibility', Report of the Secretary-General's High Level Panel on Threats, Challenges and Change, A/59/566, 2 December.

——(2004) 'The Question Concerning Haiti', S/RES/1542, 30 April.

——(2005) 'In Larger Freedom: Towards Development, Security and Human Rights for All', Report of the Secretary-General, A/59/2005, 21 March.

——(2005) 'Reports of the Secretary-General on the Sudan', S/RES/1590, 24 March.

——(2005) '2005 World Summit Outcome Document', A/60/L.1, 15 September.

——(2006) 'Darfur Peacekeeping', S/RES/1706, 31 August.

——(2006) 'Protection of Civilians in Armed Conflict', S/RES/1674, 28 April.

——(2007) 'Draft Resolution on Myanmar', S/PV.5619, 12 January.

——(2007) 'Peace and Security in Africa', S/PV.5749, 25 September.

——(2007) 'Secretary-General Appoints Major General Zhao Jingmin of China as Force Commander for Western Sahara Mission', SG/A1089 BIO/3918, 28 August.

——(2007) 'Security Council Open Debate on Protection of Civilians in Armed Conflict', S/PV.5781, 20 November.

——(2008) 'Peace and Security in Africa', S/PV.5868, 16 April.

——(2008) 'Security Council Open Debate on Protection of Civilians in Armed Conflict', S/PV.5898, 27 May.

——(2009) 'Implementing the Responsibility to Protect', A/63/677, 12 January.

——(2009) 'Protection of Civilians', S/RES/1894, 11 November.

——(2009) 'Security Council Open Debate on Peacekeeping Operations', S/PV.6178, 5 August.

——(2010) 'Report of the Special Committee on Peacekeeping Operations: 2010 Substantive Session (22 February–19 March 2010)', A/64/19, 24 March.

——(2010) 'Reports of the Secretary-General on the Sudan', S/RES/1919, 29 April.

——(2010) 'Security Council Open Debate on Peacekeeping Operations', S/PV.6370, 6 August.

——(2010) 'Security Council Open Debate on Protection of Civilians in Armed Conflict', S/PV.6354, 7 July.

——(2010), 'The Situation Concerning the Democratic Republic of the Congo', S/RES/1925, 28 May.

——(2010) 'The Situation in Côte d'Ivoire', S/RES/1933, 30 June.

——(2010) 'The Situation in Timor Leste', S/RES/1912, 26 February.

——(2010) 'Special Committee Members Commend Performance of United Nations Peacekeepers Faced with Comples Mandates, Lacking Key Capabilities: Delegates Express Views on Early Peacebuilding, Civilian Protection, "Robust peacekeeping" as General Debate Concludes', GA/PK/204, 23 February.

UN News Centre (2010) 'UN Peacekeeping in Consolidation Phase, Says Top Official', 6 August (at: unclef.com/apps/news/story.asp?NewsID=35558&Cr=le+roy&Cr1).

United Nations Office for the Coordination of Humanitarian Affairs, Policy Development and Studies Branch (2009) 'Aide Memoire for the Consideration of Issues Pertaining to the Protection of Civilians in Armed Conflict', May.

United Nations Radio (2004) 'Annan Urges Greater Peacekeeping Role for China', 12 October (at: www.unmultimedia.org/radio/english/detail/45480.html).

UNTAC Spokesman's Office (1992) 'Cambodia's Major Roads', unpublished material.

United States Holocaust Memorial Museum (2011) 'Overview: Sudan' (at: www.ushmm.org/genocide/take_action/atrisk/region/sudan).

Van Ness, Peter (1993) 'China as a Third World State: Foreign Policy and Official National Identity', in Lowell Dittmer and Samuel S. Kim (eds), *China's Quest for National Identity*, Ithaca, NY: Cornell University Press: 194–214.

Vesel, David (2004) 'The Lonely Pragmatist: Humanitarian Intervention in an Imperfect World', *Brigham Young University Journal of Public Law*, 18(1): 1–58.

Wang Jisi [王缉思] (2007) 'Guanyu gouzhu zhongguo guoji zhanlüe de jidian kanfa' [关于构筑中国国际战略的几点看法] (Some Thoughts on Building a Chinese International Strategy), *Guoji zhengzhi yanjiu* [国际政治研究] (*International Political Studies*), 25 November: 1–5.

Wang Yizhou [王逸舟] (ed.) (2003) *Mohe zhong de jiangou: zhongguo yu guoji zuji guanxi de duoshijiao toushi* [磨合中的建构：中国与国际组织关系的多视角透视] (Construction in Contradiction: A Multiple Insight into Relationships between China and International Organizations), Beijing: *Zhongguo fazhan chubanshe.*

Wang, Cong (2008) 'China to Send Navy to Fight Somali Pirates', *Xinhua News*, 18 December (at: news.xinhuanet.com/english/2008-12/18/content_10525310.htm).

Watson, Cynthia (2009) 'The Chinese Armed Forces and Non-Traditional Missions: A Growing Tool of Statecraft', *China Brief,* 9(4): 9–12.

Weiss, Thomas, David P. Forsythe, and Roger A. Coate (2004) *The United Nations and Changing World Politics*, Boulder, CO: Westview Press.

Wheeler, Nicholas J. (2008) 'Operationalising the Responsibility to Protect: The Continuing Debate over where Authority should be Located for the Use of Force', Report No.3, Responsibility to Protect, Oslo: Norwegian Institute of International Affairs.

White, Nigel (1993) *Keeping the Peace: UN and Maintenance of International Peace and Security*, Manchester: White Manchester University Press.

Whitworth, Sandra (1998) 'Gender, Race and the Politics of Peacekeeping', in Edward Moxon-Browne (ed.), *A Future for Peacekeeping?*, London: Macmillan: 176–91.

Wibowo, Ignatius (2009) 'China's Soft Power and Neoliberal Agenda in Southeast Asia', in Mingjiang Li (ed.), *Soft Power: China's Emerging Strategy in International Politics*, Lanham and Boulder, CO: Lexington Books: 207–24.

Wiharta, Sharon (2009) 'The Legitimacy of Peace Operations', in Bates Gill (ed.), *SIPRI Yearbook 2009: Armaments, Disarmament and International Security*, Oxford: Oxford University Press: 95–116.

Woods, Ngaire (2008) 'Whose Aid? Whose Influence? China, Emerging Donors and the Silent Revolution in Development Assistance', *International Affairs*, 84(6): 1205–21.

Wu, Xinbo (2001) 'Four Contradictions Constraining China's Foreign Policy Behavior', *Journal of Contemporary China*, 10(27): 293–301.

Wuthnow, Joel (2010) 'China and the Processes of Cooperation in UN Security Council Deliberations', *Chinese Journal of International Politics*, 3(1): 55–77.

Xinhua News Agency (1999) 'China on Establishing UNTAET in East Timor', 25 October.

——(2000) 'Annan Appoints New Force Commander for UNTAET', 12 July.

——(2002) 'Full Text of China's Defence White Paper in 2002', 9 December.

——(2008) 'Qian Qichen Urges Further Promotion of International Human Rights', 28 October.

——(2009) 'China Actively Participates in UN Peacekeeping Operations', 20 January [trans. by BBC Monitoring Service, International Reports].

——(2009) 'China Donates 700,000 US Dollars to UN Peacekeeping Missions', 2 December [trans. by BBC Monitoring Service, International Reports].

——(2010) 'Chinese Peacekeeping Squad Leaves for East Timor', 11 May.

——(2010) '15,000 Chinese Soldiers Join UN Peacekeeping Missions in Two Decades', 30 July (at: www.chinadaily.com.cn/china/2010-07/30/content_11072464.htm).

Xu Guojin [徐构进] (1992) *'Guojia lüxing guoji renquan yiwu de xiandu'* [国家履行国际人权义务的限度] (The Limits on State Performance of Human Rights Obligations), *Zhongguo faxue* [中国法学] (*Chinese Legal Studies*), 2: 13–20.

Yi Minghai [仪名海] (2004) *Zhongguo yu guoji zuzhi* [中国与国际组织] (China and International Organization), Beijing: *Xinhua chubanshe*.

Ying, A. (1997) 'New Security Mechanism Needed for Asian–Pacific Region', *Beijing Review*, 18–24 August: 6–7.

Yuan, Jing-Dong (1998) 'Multilateral Intervention and State Sovereignty: Chinese Views on UN Peacekeeping Operations', *Political Science*, 49(2): 275–95.

Zartman, I. William and J. Lewis Rasmussen (1997) *Peacemaking in International Conflict: Methods and Techniques*, Washington, DC: United States Institute of Peace Press.

Zeng Lingliang [曾令良] (1998) *'Lun lengzhan hou shidai de guojia zhuquan'* [论冷战后时代的国家主权] (A Discussion of State Sovereignty in the Post-Cold War Era), *Zhongguo faxue* [中国法学] (*Chinese Legal Studies*), 1: 109–20.

Zha, Daojiong (2000) 'China and the May 1998 Riots of Indonesia: Exploring the Issues', *Pacific Review*, 13(4): 557–75.

Zhan Yijia [詹奕嘉] (2006), *'Zhongguo shi ruan shili daguo ma?'* [中国是软实力大国吗] (Is China a Soft Great Power?), *Shijie zhishi* [世界知识] (*World Knowledge*), 20: 5

Zhang Huiyu [张慧玉] (2004) *'Zhongguo dui lianheguo weihe xingdong de gongxian'* [中国对联合国维和行动的贡献] (China's Contributions to UN Peacekeeping Activities), *Wujing xueyuan xuebao* [武警学院学报] (*Journal of the Academy of the Armed Police*), 20(5): 30–32

Zhang Jianjing [张剑荆] (2004) '"*Beijing gongshi*" *yu zhongguo ruan shili de tisheng*' ["北京共识" 与中国软实力的提升] (The 'Beijing Consensus' and the Rise of China's Soft Power), *Dangdai shijie yu shehui zhuyi* [当代世界与社会主义] (*Contemporary World and Socialism*), 5: 10–14.

Zhang, Ping (2007) 'Remarks on the Chinese People's Liberation Army's Participation in UN Peacekeeping Operations', Paper at conference on 'Multidimensional and Integrated Peace Operations: Trends and Challenges', 5 March (at: www.regjeringen.no/upload/UD/ Vedlegg/FN/Multidimensional%20and%20Integrated/Chinese%20Ministry%20of%20 Defence%20%20PLA%20Participation%20in%20UNPO.doc).

Zhang, Yan (2010) 'Military Ties to Help China Develop', *China Daily*, 22 May.

Zhang, Yongjin (1996) 'China and UN Peacekeeping: From Condemnation to Participation', *International Peacekeeping*, 3(3): 1–15.

Zhao, Quansheng (2010) 'Policymaking Processes of Chinese Foreign Policy: The Role of Policy Communities and Think Tanks', in Shaun Breslin (ed.), *A Handbook of Chinese International Relations*, London: Routledge: 22–34.

Zhongguo guoji zhanlüe xuehui junkong yu caijun yanjiu zhongxin [中国国际战略学会军控与裁军 研究中心] (Research Centre for Arms Control and Disarmament of China International Institute for Strategic Society) (2006) *Dangdai guoji weihe xingdong* [当代国际维和行动] (*Contemporary International Peacekeeping Operations*), Beijing: *Junshi yiwen chubanshe*.

Zhongguo Wang (China.org.cn) (2010) '*Zhongguo weihe zhanshi guodu laolei zai sudan xisheng: bei pizhun wei lieshi*' [中国维和战士过度劳累在苏丹牺牲：被批准为烈士] (China's Peacekeeping Soldier Sacrificed His Life Through Excessive Fatigue: Being Canonised as a Martyr), 26 September (at: www1.china.com.cn/military/txt/ 2010-09/26/content_ 21004939.htm).

Zhongguo xiandaihua zhanlüe yanjiu keti zu [中国现代化战略研究课题组] (Committee on the Strategy of China's Modernization), *Zhongguo kexueyuan zhongguo xiandaihua yanjiu zhongxin* [中国科学院中国现代化研究中心] (Centre for China's Modernization, Chinese Academy of Sciences) (2008) *Zhongguo xiandaihua baogao 2008: guoji xiandaihua yanjiu* [中国现代化报 告2008：国际现代化研究] (*China Modernization Report 2008: A Study of International Modernization*), Beijing: *Beijing daxue chubanshe*.

Zhongguo xinwen she [中国新闻社] (China News Service) (2007) 'Chinese Deputy Military Chief on Raising Army's Peacekeeping Role', 22 June.

——(2007) 'Chinese Expert Views Army Counteracting Non-Traditional Security Threats', 20 June.

——(2010) 'China's Military Will Not Pose Threat to Other Nations – Ministry', 31 July [trans. by BBC Monitoring Service, International Reports].

Zweig, David (n.d.) '"Resource Diplomacy" Under Hegemony: The Sources of Sino-American Competition in the 21st Century?', *Working Paper No.18*, Hong Kong: Center on China's Transnational Relations, Hong Kong University of Science and Technology (at: www.cctr. ust.hk/materials/working_papers/WorkingPaper18_ DavidZweig.pdf).

Index

Page numbers in Italics represent tables.
Page numbers in Bold represent figures.

Afghanistan 25, 89
Africa: peace and stability 22
African states 38
African Union (AU) 22
Asia Pacific Economic Cooperation
  (APEC) 78
Asian Financial Crisis 77
Asian security issues 76
authoritative statements (*tifa*) 45

Ban, Ki-Moon 61
Beijing Consensus 2, 39
Bellamy, Alex J. 61
Breau, Susan C. 62

Cambodia policy 87
Cambodian case 11–12, 72; Chinese
  contribution awareness 91, 92; Chinese
  Janus-faced attitude 88; Chinese
  perceptions **93**; Chinese policy 87;
  Chinese relations 90; Chinese support
  90–1; Interdisciplinary perspectives 89;
  Japanese participation 91; Khmer Rouge
  90, 96; military presence 91; National
  Road No.6 88, 92; perceptions shifted
  90, 91–4; political culture 93, 97;
  questionnaires and interviews 88; reasons
  for Chinese contribution 93–4;
  Sihanouk 90, 96; Sihanouk factor 93;
  Tiananmen Square demonstrations
  perceptions 94; UN Transitional
  Administration in Cambodia (UNTAC)
  87, 88
candidate partner states (*zhanlü huoban de
  houxuan guojia*) 37
Caribbean state 3
Carlson, Allen 17
cautions approach 16

charm offensive (*meili gongshi*) 10, 31, 86,
  87, 96
Chen, Xiaomei 37
China International Search and Rescue
  Team (CISAR) 115
China Modernization Report (*Zhongguo
  xiandaihua baogao*) 30–1
China Peacekeeping CIVPOL (Civilian
  Police) Training Centre 4
China-Africa relationship 23; diplomatic
  and business interests 23; medical
  assistance 23; state infrastructure 23
China's National Defense in 2008 (White
  Paper) 51
China's Peaceful Development Road (White
  Paper) 103
China's status 7–9; developing country 8;
  great power 7, 46–7; middle power 7, 9
Chinese leadership 18
Chinese modernization 33–5
Chinese transformation: military
  experience 29; technical skills and
  knowledge 29
civilian deployment capacity 115
Clinton, Bill 78
commercial diplomacy (*shangwu waijiao*) 10
commitment to peacekeeping 3–4
comprehensive national power (*zonghe
  guoli*) 48
conceptual framework **5**
contribution to peacekeeping 4, 21–2
Cook, Robin 78
cooperative behaviour 16
cost-avoiding position 62
counter-piracy involvement 115
country-specific considerations 65
Crum, James 89

Darby, Philip 32

Darfur crisis 24, 86, *see also* Sudan
Democratic Republic of Congo (DRC) 22
democratization in international relations
   (*guoji guanxi minzhuhua*) 83
Deng, Xiaoping 45, 92
developed states (*fada guojia*) 37
Ding, Sheng 40
diplomacy 8, 48
diversified military tasks (*duo yanghua junshi
   renwu*) 7, 51
domestic economy (China) 92

East Timor(Timor-Lester) 72; Chinese
   involvement 77; Chinese mission 73;
   Chinese role 76; Chinese security
   concept 73; Frente Revolucionária de
   Timor-Leste Independente (FRETILIN)
   77; independence 82; International
   Force for East Timor (INTERFET) 78;
   José Ramos-Horta 78; map **72**; May
   Revolution (1998) 80; New Order
   (*Orde Baru*) 80; operational development
   80; orphan conflicts 73–4; Suharto
   regime 80; Taiwanese influence 81;
   territory 76; Taiwan chequebook
   diplomacy practices (*zhipiaobu waijiao*)
   81; UN peacekeeping mission 79; UN
   Transitional Administration in East
   Timor (UNTAET) 72
economic growth model 39, 49
economy: domestic (China) 92
epistemic community 25
ethnocentrism and racism 36

Five Principles of Peaceful Coexistence
   (*heping gongchu wuxiang yuanze*) 30, 76
foreign policy 1–2, 31
Forum on China and Africa Cooperation
   (FOCAC) 22

global peace engagement strategy 102, 103,
   113
Going Abroad strategy (*zouchuqu zhanlue*)
   106
government responsibility **113**
Green, Michael J. 106
Guatemala 3
Gusmao, Xanana 81

Habibie, B.J. 77
Haiti case 105
Haiti operations 3
He, Yafei 65
Hellström, Jerker 106

High Level Panel (HLP) 60
Hirono, Miwa 10, 29, 109, 110
Holmes, John 65
Holslag, Jonathan 96
host government consent 94
Howard, John 78
Hu, Jintao 17, 19, 56, 82, 114
Huang, Chin-hao 11
human rights debates 17
humanitarian intervention 59
humanitarian protection 59

image and global reputation (China's) 18,
   35, 94
inter-state diplomacy 45
interdisciplinary perspectives 89
interests and motivations 104–8
International Commission on Intervention
   and State Sovereignty (ICISS) 57
international community 18
International Force for East Timor
   (INTERFET) 78
international paternalists 30
international peacebuilding operations
   (IPBOs) 102; cautious participation 108–
   12; foreign assistance 115; government-
   centric policy 112; liberal peace 111;
   natural disasters 115; non-intervention
   112; obstacles 110–13; perspectives on
   implications *111*; poverty reduction 111;
   soft power 110; Somali pirates 115; state
   sovereignty 111–12; strategic culture
   shifted 109–10
International Peacekeepers Week 106
International Peacekeeping Day 106
international position 2, 4
International Security Assistance Force
   (ISAF) 88–9
international strategy 19
Iraq case 89

Jiang, Zemin 78
Justice and Equality Movement (JEM) 88

keep a low profile (*tao guang yang hui*) 91
Kofi, Annan 57, 58, 60, 66
Korean War 16

Lanteigne, Marc 11, 29, 109, 110
Latin American case 40
Legitimacy crisis 89
Li, Daoyu 90
liberal triumphalism 30
limitations 24, 51

Liu, Chao 48
Liu, Jianbo 39
Liu, Zhenmin 64
local perspectives 86, 88–9
Long, Daniel 89
long distance manoeuvres (*changtu yanxi*) 76

Macedonia 3
Machar, Riek 95
majority peacekeepers 89
Mao, Zedong 74
Mashatt, Merriam 89
military operations other than war (MOOTW) 19, 114; five forces 115
Ministry of National Defence (MND) 4
Ministry of Public Security: *A Decade of China's Peacekeeping Operations* 104
modernization 33–5
motivations 1, 49
multilateral acceptance 71
multilateral activities 20
multilateral intervention 71

national advantages 10, **109**
national identity 113, **114**
national interests **105**
national security 19, 50
national strength 102
neutral broader policy 97
New Historic Missions (*xin de lishi shiming*) 7, 51, 114
new international order (*xin guoji zhixu*) 75
new paradigm 57
non-consensual force 58
non-consensual intervention 58
non-imperialist developing state 46
non-traditional threats 71
Nyíri, Pál 38

one China policy (*yige Zhongguo zhengce*) 81
Operation *Clean Sweep* (*Operasi Sapu Jagad*) 77

Pang, Zhongying 56, 59
peacebuilding: obstacles 110
peaceful development (*heping jueqi*) 5
peaceful intentions 18
peacekeepers: causes of death **117**
peacekeeping: changing views of 74, 82
Peng, Guangqian 47
People's Armed Police (PAP) 81

People's Liberation Army (PLA) 4, 15, 81, 103
People's Republic of China (PRC) 1
perceptions of peacekeeping 103
peripheral diplomacy (*zhoubian waijiao*) 86
Perry, William 105
policy statements 58
positive force (*zheng shili*) 10
power capabilities 75
practice and principles 15–28

Qian, Qichen 17, 74
Qin, Huasun 79

Ramo, Joshua Cooper 39
regional security issues 23
responsibility 45–6
responsibility to protect (R2P) (*baohu de zeren*) 11; commitment 56
responsible great power (*fuzeren de daguo*) 30, 47, 48, 73
responsible power (*fuzeren de guojia*) 45, 46, 47, 53
Richardson, Courtney J. 11
Richmond, Oliver P. 89
Roy, Alain Le 106

security dilemma (*anquan kunju*) 75
self-professed principles 32
Shared Awareness and Deconfliction (SHADE) 115
Shen, Guofang 111
south-south cooperation (*nannan hezuo*) 6
sovereignty 6
state sovereignty 23–5
state-centric approach 96
Sudan: Chinese Consulate-General 95; Chinese oil investment 95; Chinese peacekeeping implications 94–6; Chinese perceptions 96; Chinese relation 86; Comprehensive Peace Agreement (2005) 95; Darfur conflicts 24, 86; independent implication 95; Janjaweed militia 86–7; local distrust 87; rebel groups 95–6
Sudan People's Liberation Movement (SPLM) 95
Suzuki, Shogo 11

Taiwan status 72
Tang, Jiaxuan 81
Teitt, Sarah 11
Tipps, Dean C. 36
training and exchanges 20–1

troop deployment 15, 45; reasons for 93

UN Peacekeeping Operations (UNPKOs) 29–30, 102; China's views (*lianheguo weichi heping*) 71; Chinese contributions 104; Chinese interests and motivations 104–8; Chinese national safety 106; deployment (best time) **108**; domestic audience 107; expectations 31–2; Hammarskjöld principles 107; mandates and goals 32, 67; military and police contributions **107**; principles (attitudes towards) *108*; safety of peacekeepers **117**
UN Security Council 56; Resolution (783) 90; Resolutions 63–4
United Nations Charter: Chapter VII 8, 79; non-interference principle 58
United Nations (UN): Department of Field Support (DFS) 64; Department of Peacekeeping Operations (DPKO) 20, 64; Mission in Liberia (UNMIL) 114; Mission of Support for East Timor (UNMISET) 82; Office for the Coordination of Humanitarian Affairs (OCHA) 64; Operation in Somalia II (UNOSOMII) 94; principles and guidelines 63; Protection Force (UNPROFOR) 8; Secretary-General's High Level Panel (HLP) 60; Transitional Administration in East Timor (UNTAET) 11

United States of America (USA): post-Cold-War power 75

Van Ness, Peter 36
Vesel, David 61
Vietnam conflict (1955–75) 90

Wang, Guangya 24
Wang, Liao 18
Wang, Min 66
Wen, Jiabao 115
Western states 38, 103
neo-Westphalian views 72
World Summit agreement 61
World Summit Outcome Document (WSOD) 61

Xu, Caihou 105

Yasushi, Akashi 91

Zhang, Yesui 18
Zhang, Yishan 23
Zhang, Yongjin 1
Zhao, Jingmin 21, 48
Zhao, Lei 5, 12
Zhu, Rongji 46
Zoellick, Robert 46

INDEX

Related titles from Routledge

China and East Asian Regionalism
Economic and Security Cooperation and Institution-Building
Edited by Suisheng Zhao

To what extent has China contributed or constrained the development of regionalism in East Asia? What are China's desired roles and objectives in East Asian regional cooperation? What is the level of trust that other regional players have for China in regional cooperation? This book seeks answers to these questions by exploring China's motivations and strategic calculations as well as its policy practices in East Asian economic and security cooperation.

This book was published as a special issue of the *Journal of Contemporary China*.

Suisheng Zhao is Professor and Executive Director of the Center for China-US Cooperation at Josef Korbel School of International Studies, University of Denver. A founding editor of the *Journal of Contemporary China*, he is the author and editor of more than ten books.

February 2012: 246 x 174: 240pp
Hb: 978-0-415-61814-4
£80 / $125

Related titles from Routledge

Maritime Issues in the South China Sea

Troubled Waters or A Sea of Opportunity

Edited by Nien-Tsu Alfred Hu and Ted L. McDorman

The submissions made in 2009 by several Southeast Asian states to the United Nations Commission on the Limits of the Continental Shelf (CLCS) respecting outer limits of extended continental shelves beyond 200 nautical miles in the South China Sea resulted in renewed attention to the maritime disputes over the insular features and the waters of the South China Sea among several claimant States. Questions have resurfaced about the future of cooperation in the region. Furthermore, the improvement of cross-Strait relations between Taiwan and China after 2008 has added a new element to the evolution of South China Sea issues. This book describes these recent developments in depth and provides an examination of possible future developments in the South China Sea.

This book was originally published as a special issue of *Ocean Development & International Law*.

Nien-Tsu Alfred Hu, Professor and Director, The Center for Marine Policy Studies, National Sun Yat-sen University, Taiwan, Republic of China.

Ted L. McDorman, Professor, Faculty of Law, University of Victoria, Canada.

August 2012: 246 x 189: 176pp
Hb: 978-0-415-50636-6
£80 / $125

ROUTLEDGE

Related titles from Routledge

Reconceptualising Arms Control
Controlling the Means of Violence
Edited by Neil Cooper and David Mutimer

This book examines issues surrounding sovereignty, geopolitics, nuclear disarmament, securitization of space, technological developments, human rights, the clearance of landmines, the regulation of small arms and the control of the black market for arms and nuclear secrets. The book discusses terrorism with reference to the case of the suicide attacks in Beirut in 1983 and how the Obama administration is orientating its posture on nuclear arms.

This book was published as a special issue of *Contemporary Security Policy*.

Neil Cooper is Senior Lecturer in International Relations and Security Studies in the Division of Peace Studies, at the University of Bradford.

David Mutimer is Deputy Director of the Centre for International and Security Studies and Associate Professor of Political Science at York University.

November 2011: 234 x 156: 280pp
Hb: 978-0-415-68883-3
£85 / $145

For Product Safety Concerns and Information please contact our EU
representative GPSR@taylorandfrancis.com
Taylor & Francis Verlag GmbH, Kaufingerstraße 24, 80331 München, Germany

www.ingramcontent.com/pod-product-compliance
Lightning Source LLC
Chambersburg PA
CBHW050521280326
41932CB00014B/2410

9 780415 754859